HELL CAMP

A Memoir

by Niki Smart

iMay Productions
Copyright © 2012 by Niki Smart

Cover design: Joni Parenti

To book the author please contact info@nikismart.com

First paperback edition June 2012
ISBN-10: 0985616601
ISBN-13: 978-0-9856166-0-1

ACKNOWLEDGEMENTS

For my lovely, supportive sister, Linda and brave brother, Claude.

I want to extend heartfelt thanks to all my wonderful friends and family, and especially to my fearless mother for giving me the go ahead to expose her vulnerable underbelly. She told me: *tue was du nicht lassen kannst!* - do what you need to do - and I absolutely appreciate her for that.
Further thanks go out to Bronwyn Berry for her fresh perspective, wonderful friendship and inspirational conversation; and to Sheran James for her comprehensive, lightening-speed editing skills. Sheran, you truly wowed me! And a big shout out for the fabulous cover designed by Joni Parenti - thank you so much!
For all the much needed encouragement I received from sooo many people – THANK YOU!
Lastly, much gratitude to the fabulous baristas at several key coffee shops (Koffee Klatch being my fav), who kept me well fueled with coffee and tea and allowed me to sit in peace and type for hours without shooing me away.

People who have read "Hell Camp" frequently thank me for being brave enough to share my story. I believe we all suffer hardships and tough situations, that no one gets a free ride, and that we are all brave in our own way. I truly appreciate the people who trust me enough to share their intimate stories with me. I sense the burden of their secrets, their shame, their unspeakable past. If my story gives you a voice to yours, then I am thrilled to bits. I couldn't ask for anything more healing. So, for all of you that have been hurt, raped, abused, mislead, rejected, abandoned…I offer you my heartfelt empathy. Don't give up on yourself and know that you can move beyond the pain. I promise you, you can. If you were standing in front of me right now, I'd give you a big hug. Sending you love, love, love…

For me writing has been a massive release; a liberating of the awful offal inside. A creative dredging up of the muck to end up smiling, laughing, weeping and cheering; ultimately unloading the emotions of a painful yesteryear to feel better – not bitter. In tracking, stacking, then tacking my thoughts to paper, things churned out in somewhat of a disarray...not unlike the workings of my digestive system.
Welcome to my messy, chaotic vent.

Nobody can unmake the past. The only hope is to digest it, learn from it and move on before it embitters you. Over time (and much bitching) I managed to shift from bitterly bitter, to vaguely bitter, to vaguely miffed, to aw shucks...who gives a flying kanoodle anyway?

Flying kanoodles aside, I don't believe we are truly free of our past until we forgive those that have harmed us. Had you attempted to enlighten me with this fact a few years back, I'd have been happy to spit in your eye (figuratively of course), but now I fully understand the enormous relief forgiveness brings.

And please note: my intention here is not to upset or insult anyone by writing about them...though I can't promise to play nice. That said, I may have flattered or battered you, but whichever it is, I want to sincerely thank you for bringing your uniqueness to my life; good or bad, it helped mold me into who I am today.

Enough already – enjoy!

CHAPTERS:

PART ONE - Hell Camp, South Africa

PART ONE

Hell Camp, South Africa.

Our living room floor

"Please no more therapy
Mother take care of me"
Shawn Colvin

FOREWORD

I was a frightfully fretful child from the get go, chewing my fingernails down to pink bleeding nubs. I think my fear had to do with my mother's repeated warnings that "Black terrorists were coming in the middle of the night to slit our throats. "

Yup. I think that's what did it...because, as you probably know, seven year old girls don't like having their throats slit by black terrorists, or terrorists of any color for that matter. And where is the reassurance in having a parent that insists on dangling a brutal slaughtering over you? It doesn't make for a good night's sleep, I can tell you.

At age seven, I wasn't 100% sure what the word "terrorist" meant, but I grasped the "throat slitting" part fairly vividly, and the images I conjured up in my head left me nailed to my bed at night, stiff as a board, straining to absorb every little sound; monitoring the tiniest movement. Was that a bird rustling in the trees? Was that the wind making those creepy moaning sounds? Was that a car engine purring? Yes it was. It definitively was. Maybe it was the neighbors returning home, or maybe, please God no, maybe it was a truckload of machete wielding, throat slitters pulling up. I'd lie petrified, unwilling to move a muscle for fear of revealing my existence to any potential prowling slayer. This hyper-vigilant scanning and rigid muscle control had me soaking my fear-sweat right through the sheets. Sometimes I'd be so convinced that "tonight was the night" that I'd force myself out of bed and creep to the bathroom where I'd lock myself in. Forsaking my soft mattress for the shower stall, I hoped to trick those nasty black terrorists by curling up on the cold tile floor. Facing the small barred window, I'd wonder what cunning wizardry I could perform if the killers broke down the bathroom door. There'd definitely be no escaping through that window. Sure I was small, but I'd never fit through those burglar bars. Believe me I'd tried, and the most I could squeeze through was a chubby thigh. Perhaps it would be safer to sleep under my bed? No, wait. Surely the terrorists would think of that? They'd search the room, right? I mean, if they'd driven all this way to slit "whitie" throats, they probably wouldn't be satisfied until they'd hacked a good number of us to pieces, yes?

Having successfully whipped myself into a frenzy, I'd dig deep for a last bid at bravery and rush to my mother's room to beg her to allow me to sleep alongside her. And funnily enough, as ill equipped to parent as she was, this was the one comfort I found in her. I could crawl into bed alongside my mother, listen to her steady breathing, and quickly fall fast asleep.

I was too young to understand that this woman sleeping soundly next to me, this woman who offered me comfort in the dark, that *this* woman was the very reason I suffered such discomfort in the first place.

CHAPTER 1 – Inception

Alcohol! Thank God for alcohol. Seriously! How would I have survived without that mood altering, fear squelching, self-esteem boosting, flammable liquid to gulp down as needed? And it was needed. Especially as my mother kept adding to her list of the various ways in which I was sure to die. Not only did she have me in line for a good throat slitting, she further imagined I might be run over, or possibly drown, perhaps fall off the roof, or her definite favorite: starve to death. She fixated on this "death by skinniness" choice of hers, until it became inevitable: I would be succumbing to an early, anorexic death.

"You know you'll never live to see twenty-five," she'd repeatedly tell me.

I found this to be rather bad news, especially since I'd survived a number of years with my throat firmly intact, having successfully managed to evade the black terrorists that lurked in the front yard. Apparently however, this news was far more upsetting for my mother, who, after delivering her doomsday message, would then cling to *me* for comfort while sobbing out her distress.

"Oh Niksi, I don't know if I can survive having to bury a daughter."

Patting my mother's back, I'd ponder the absurdity of having to console her for my own upcoming death, especially when I felt fit as a "fat" fiddle and she seemed to be the one hell bent on inviting the Grim Reaper to step right on in.

Perhaps I would be dead by twenty-five but certainly not for a lack of food. I highly doubted I'd be run over either. Nope. It would be an overabundance of alcohol that would do me in. There'd be no drowning, but the drink might sink me. I could envision me happily chug-a-lugging myself into a premature grave. This would grant my mother the occasion to say "I told you so" to my youthful corpse, and I seriously hated to give her such satisfaction.

Luckily, I was saved from my untimely expiration date by falling pregnant at twenty-three. Granted, I didn't think it so lucky at the time. It wasn't planned and it certainly wasn't welcomed. I was embarking on becoming a Pop Star, for God's sake. A skinny one at that, one that drank a lot, and just so you know, pop stars are absolutely allowed to drink themselves to death. It's practically required: to die young, thin and unwrinkled. This pregnancy nonsense didn't quite fit my picture…bouncing, expectant, pop star. I don't think so.

My "picture" was one of me dominating the South African music scene, me winning over America with my sheer talent, me impacting the world. Yes well, regardless of my lofty, lofty pop star plans, at twenty-three I found myself singing in yet another cover band - which in truth is considered the "arse end" of music. Here I was the front man (or rather woman) of the five-piece outfit *Tokyo Rose*, singing my heart out night after night at *The Glockenberg Hotel,* a crummy hotel in Cape Town. I didn't care how crappy the gig was as this lifestyle respected my needs. That's right, because if you're in a band you can drink on the job. People buy you shots, bartenders slip you freebies, and the management provides you a drink allowance to boot. An avalanche of free drinks showering down - oh happy, happy day!

To further jazz up this "being-in-a-band-dealio" you can sleep with any of your co-workers, or all of them if you like! And if you don't fancy your band members, there is a whole club full of men waiting and hoping to bed you. I got hit on night after night by a variety of gentlemen. This constant adulation was splendid for my ego, but not quite as splendid for our drummer, Melvin, who was also hit upon…physically…by big, hairy fists and misplaced drunken aggression. The problem was, Melvin was black, and in the 1980s in

South Africa, blacks weren't allowed to live in the same areas as whites, and they certainly weren't welcome at the clubs where the whites partied. Music was the one field where it was okay to mix colors...okay...but not necessarily embraced. Testosterone-fueled club-goers itched to "sex me up" and "beat Melvin up", and sometimes, they did precisely that (clearly, uh...baby on board).

One night Melvin was "jumped" in the backroom, by a belligerent, super-drunk Afrikaner (Afrikaners being white South Africans who were staunchly racist in the 1980s). On hearing Melvin's cries, the club owner, Raoul, grabbed his "special" bat from under the bar counter and surged after the drunk with such fury that the drunk landed in hospital with a broken jaw, broken arm, cracked ribs and a surplus of stitches.

The liquor-addled Afrikaner revisited the club while on the mend, trying to determine what had happened. "How come no one helped me?" the drunkard wanted to know. He couldn't remember a thing.

"What do you mean?" Raoul cried. "I beat four guys off you."

"Really? Jeez! Thanks a lot, man. I owe you a beer, man."
(Everyone is "man" in South Africa - be it man, woman or child.)

And so the drunk bought Raoul a beer for beating him to a pulp, which is a perfect example of good old South African logic.

The Glockenberg Hotel assigned each *Tokyo Rose* band member a separate hotel room and further granted us free passage to the colossal kitchen in case any of us saw fit to cook for ourselves during our three month stay. That's how the club circuit worked in the 80's. You played at a club for three months, then moved on - played another club for three months, then moved on - played in yet another club for three months, fell pregnant and...oops - game over!

During my stint at the *Glock* in Cape Town I never once made use of the kitchen. I wanted no part of the kitchen. In fact I thumbed my nose at it and all the little women who learnt to cook in order to secure a husband. Ridiculous rubbish. I had no desire to marry, to lose my identity by becoming Mrs. Bob Bobbiness. Hell no! Domesticity was definitely not an aptitude I cared to develop, so you can understand why pregnancy probably wasn't such a topnotch idea.

Bound by baby - No, thank you.

Besides, I was wild at twenty-three. I mean out-of-control wild. I had a self-destructive streak the size of a small country and was hell bent on pretty much drinking my own body weight in alcohol (Jägermeister being a firm favorite). And worse, in the wee hours of the morning, after copious amounts of imbibing, it appeared that at a certain point I'd seek out sex with whoever was handy. And believe you me, there was always someone handy, some willing young man to take on the task. In fact, they didn't even have to be young. If I drank enough - Shizam! - some regular Joe would suddenly wax handsome. I slept with young, old, thin, fat, short, tall, good-looking, not-so-good-looking, and on occasion even disfigured and vaguely gross individuals.

Sober, I was shy of my own sexuality, pained by my curves, fearful of my pheromones. Seriously! Without liquor, I felt like a straight-laced virgin. It even bothered me that if I tapped my foot to keep time while singing on stage, it resulted in girl-jiggle! I was desperate to render that girl-jiggle motionless, but no matter how tight a bra I wore, my breasts bobbed about to a beat of their own. Mustering attention for themselves with their shameless jostling, they had me longing for a steel bra, some mesh-flesh perhaps? Better yet, why not simply lop those wobbly offenders right off? It caused me naught but trouble being mammiferous.

"Look at her breasts!" Guys ogled.

"No!" I wanted to shout back, "Listen to my voice!"

Or you could simply wait 'til I've consumed a bucketful of booze and then you might see these babies flapping in your face. Indeed, because drunk, I was ready to bed the bedlam brethren. Bring it on chaps. Let's get loose. My bed-partners often mentioned how I "fit" them so well. Great. I was an ergonomic bed partner. A chameleonic, user-friendly fuck!

One morning I awoke to *Tokyo Rose's* bass player in my bed sans recall of how we'd arrived at my room, or as to whether or not we'd done the deed. I leapt from my bed, horrified…whereupon sperm trickled down between my legs. Well, that answered one question.

"What the hell are you doing in my room?" I yelled at him.

"Your room?" he laughed. "This is *my* room. You staggered in here at about 3 a.m."

Damn those hotel rooms. They all looked the same.

I'd done worse. I once woke to a man with only one eye slumbering next to me, an ugly scar slashed through where his other eye had at some point perched. As usual, I'd achieved my effective "black out mode" and couldn't recall anything: his name, how I met him, how we got to this bedroom...etc…etc. It was one of those "I'd like to gnaw through my own arm" moments and, quite possibly, dissolve the rest of my body in acid to boot. As I stared at him in confused revulsion, his good eye blinked open.

"Hi." He smiled.

"So, uh…what happened to your eye?" I asked casually.

That is not to say that I didn't have relationships. I did. However, I cheated on practically every boyfriend I ever had - intentionally. I concluded that sex was a weapon, and it wholly behooved me to wield said weapon first. Sleeping with my partner's buddy was an advantageous trump card to stash in my back pocket.

"I'm sorry, Niki. I have to tell you, I fancy someone else."

"Oh yeah? Well I slept with your cousin last month. How d'you like them shiny apples?"

If I'd already slept with your best friend, your brother, your father, your neighbor (and for my South African readers: *jou oom*), how could you hurt me?

Once, while touring with a band, some "random" came up to me at a nightclub and asked if I'd like to accompany him to his friend's house.

"My friend's a millionaire," he enticed me. "You'll love him. He'll love you."

I'd had a few tequilas. My impregnable coat was on (ha, ha.) I smiled. "Sure, why not?"

Without telling a soul I was leaving, off I zoomed on the back of his scooter, into the night, heading towards mountains, in a completely unfamiliar area. The scooter putted along narrow roads, winding further and further into the dark until city roads crumbled to gravel, me clinging to the stranger's back, and it never even occurred to me that the guy might be fibbing. The only thing occurring to me was: free drinks...hmmmm. Millionaire...hmmmm.

Lucky for me, scooter boy was 100 % telling the truth. We arrived at a glorious mansion set up in the hills, and the friend, a courteous, elderly, bona fide millionaire, poured us each a stiff brandy. Once he'd tipped back a few tots, he bust out in a traditional folk dance, whereupon scooter man and I cheered and applauded, egging him on to kick higher, stamp harder: Go little drunk millionaire...go! When the festivities ended, we remounted the scooter and I was delivered back to my hotel safe and sound.

It's a wonder I didn't fall pregnant sooner. It's a wonder I didn't host a hoard of horrendous STDs. It's a wonder I made it through those frenzied years alive. If I hadn't fallen pregnant when I did, I may well have been right on par with my mother's optimism: dead by twenty-five.

My mother was right about one thing: I didn't need no stinking food. I needed alcohol…barrels of it, and excitement if you please. My temerarious, thrill seeking behaviors steered me towards Dodge E. City. I was reckless to the point of stupidity. I mean, I climbed in cars with strangers, I climbed on the back of motorbikes with strangers …well basically, I climbed *on* strangers. I was drunk and I didn't care. I sought out constant adventure, anything out of the ordinary, anything to occupy my mind. Boredom was equivalent to death. Keep me stimulated, keep me busy, busy, busy, so I don't have to endure the silence, or be alone…in my head...with my ruminating rancor.

Well, you can understand why I harbored reservations about the whole baby business. I wasn't exactly ready to settle down. I wasn't ready to stay home night after night, listening to a baby breathing. I wasn't precisely suitable parenthood material. I simply wasn't!

When a cute unsuspecting drummer from a local Cape Town band wandered into the Glockenberg to appraise *Tokyo Rose's* musical talent, I smiled at him. Little did he realize, I smiled at everyone. This drummer, Leslie, must have appreciated my jiggling form more than most, because he suddenly, and misguidedly, boasted to his friends:

"That is who I'm going to marry."

Yeah, uh…well, don't place all your eggs in that (overfriendly, and apparently fertile) basket.

My partner in pregnancy-crime, my three-week fling, my local drummer boy, did, to his credit offer to marry me. Once we had a firm positive on the pregnancy test, Leslie bought me a ring. The idea of marrying someone I'd only recently met seemed ludicrous. The idea of having a baby from someone I'd only recently met, however, seemed much more plausible. Leslie asked me to move in with him and I figured I might as well experiment with a spot of cohabitation, see how that played out. So when *Tokyo Rose* packed up for their next hotel gig, I stayed behind to torment Leslie.

Within days of moving in with him I was vomiting everywhere and unable to eat anything save vegetable soup and tangerines. It's a wonder I didn't birth a green and orange baby. My new diet, my new surroundings and my new role of pregnant fiancé proved too huge of a modification for me. With no alcohol, no ogling fans and nothing to do other than slowly inflate, life looked bleak.

It was a phone call from my old manager that saved me. He asked if I'd like to move back to Johannesburg and join the newly formed band "*Oh Boy!*"

Oh Boy would I indeed? I leapt at the chance.

So long Leslie…Thanks for the embryo!

4 months pregnant in a midriff outfit with Oh Boy! Oh dear is more like it.

CHAPTER 2 – Abort

Ensuing a few slapdash rehearsals, *Oh Boy!* began performing shows. We were a seven-piece band comprised of four guys and three girls. The guys played the instruments, while we gals sang and pranced about in a sorry attempt at synchronized dancing. *Oh Boy!* wasn't part of the club circuit. We weren't a cover band. We didn't have to play at crap clubs and shoddy hotels. We were a show band, meaning we performed on a much larger scale, playing at impressive stadiums.

Oh Boy! provided me a small income and loads more ego feeding fans, but I still needed a place to rest my weary spinal column. After all, the embryo was on the increase, and couch surfing while pregnant is sooo not proper.

Thank goodness for the *White Horse Inn,* a gloriously bizarre hotel that hosted oodles of noteworthy memories for me. Engulfed in bougainvilleas, the White Horse Inn was a rambling two-storied hotel nestled on the outskirts of Johannesburg. Out front sprawled a dirt car park, and in the back lounged a greenish (verging on swampy) swimming pool.

The owner of the hotel was Basil, a Greek man in his sixties who carried a shock of tousled, grey hair with matching expressive shaggy eyebrows that joggled about on his face while he spoke. You couldn't help but hear when Basil spoke because his deep, raspy voice thundered throughout the hotel. Neither could you could help but notice the interesting saw-toothed scar that zigzagged across his entire neck. I figured the scar and Basil's voice quality were somehow connected, like perhaps he'd had his thyroid tampered with by a shortsighted nurse with a hacksaw. I'd find myself daydreaming about that scar, imagining that the Mafia may have been involved, because if anyone was going to mess with the mob, it would have been Basil. And if anyone was going to survive having their throat slit, it would have been Basil, not me.

Basil was loud, large as life, and again…loud. You could hear him belly laugh from across the lawn or catch his cannon voice booming as he bellowed at his staff. Basil relentlessly assured me that, were he thirty years younger, I'd feast my eyes on him as if he were a magnificent Christmas tree bedecked in sparkling lights! I think it is fairly safe to say that I'd still have viewed him as a raucous (and rather hairy) old Greek.

To match his big voice, Basil had a big heart. On hearing I was pregnant, he offered me one of his nicer rooms for dirt-cheap, and I nabbed the opportunity. I quickly set up camp at the White Horse Inn, grateful that I now had a job, a place to stay, and that my pop star journey had finally hit on the right track. The only snag was that my midriff was bulging…and a lifetime commitment was swelling right along with it.

I contemplated having an abortion. I mean honestly, what was I meant to do with a baby? Where would I keep such a thing? What would I feed it? How would it fit into my schedule of singing, drinking and carousing all night? Drunk rock star is cool. Drunk mommy is not.

Well, this was 1988 and abortions were illegal in South Africa. Sure there were back street abortions going on, but horror stories went right along with them. Knitting needles, steel hangers, infections, jail time. No thanks.

I phoned my older, *wiser*, sister Linda, who had already escaped from the idiotic apartheid society of South Africa to settle peacefully in England. With her typical competence, Linda booked me into a hospital in England, ensuring a legal and hygienic procedure. I thanked her and bought a plane ticket to Heathrow, but right before I skedaddled off to "go scrape baby into a bucket", the bass player from a band called *The Helicopters* phoned me up. He'd heard about my position. Hell the whole music scene knew about my "position" - flat on my back! Being an unwed-pregnant-white girl was not the norm back in 1988 in South Africa. It was verging on scandalous. Seeing as the Dutch Reformed Church played a big part in how the country operated, South Africa had strict rules brought on by religious reasoning. For example: Dancing was prohibited on Sundays.... indeed, that might piss the Lord off big time. Imagine the repercussions of birthing a baby out of wedlock. The Almighty might smite me.

The *Helicopter* musician phoned me out of the blue to extend an invitation for dinner - and no, I hadn't slept with him. He explained how he and his wife had undergone major soul searching in trying to decide whether or not to have their daughter. You see, he was white, but his wife was black, and according to them, they were one of the first interracial couples in South Africa. Only a few years prior, it had been a crime to marry a different color skin. And before you think too badly of South Africa for their racist marital laws, I'd like to point out that miscegenation was only done away with in 1967 in America following the Loving v. Virginia civil rights case. Even later, in 1973, President Richard Nixon went so far as to suggest that the children of an inter-racial couple should be aborted in saying: "There are times when an abortion is necessary. I know that. When you have a black and a white."

Oh Dickie! Meet Barack. We've come a long way people.

Alastair and Adele knew they were facing a whole truckload of "capital T- trouble" by giving birth to a colored child. They fully comprehended that the warped society in which we lived would simultaneously hound them and exile them. Was it fair to bring their unborn child into this prejudiced society, where being colored meant: too black to be white and too white to be black? Double whammy. They had definitely thought about aborting and wanted to share their story with me.

Well, maybe an abortion was also worth contemplating if you were poor, single, had no address other than a lowlife hotel and had spent the past few years prancing about too drunk to think? I packed my bags for London, included some loose, comfy pants for "after", and since I'd accepted Alistair and Adele's invitation, I went for dinner with them. I'd accepted the dinner invitation, more so because a home cooked meal sounded scrum-diddly-umptious, not because I sought their advice. As far as I was concerned they could take their well-meaning advice and shove it.

Good call on the home cooked meal though. It was delicious, and once dinner was over, we retreated to the living room, whereupon Alastair and Adele swiftly excused themselves leaving me alone with their chubby cheeked cherub. I only realized later on how they must have planned the whole affair. *We'll feed Niki, move her into the living room with the baby, and then we'll both scoot.*

So there I was, alone with Samantha, the sweetest baby ever. I'd had limited interaction with any babies of late, so this plump yet delicate foreign entity made me uneasy. I simply sat and stared at her, afraid to handle her. Then Samantha offered me a gummy, heart-stealing smile, and I melted. I couldn't resist. I picked her up and cradled her against my swollen stomach. I adjusted the delightful bonnet on her precious head. The darling curls that stuck out underneath were slightly damp. Baby sweat! Finally! A body fluid that didn't gross me out.

The next day, baby kicked inside my womb. On feeling this first movement of life, my mind sparked crystal clear. Cancel the flights. Cancel the hospital. I am having a baby!

(And I don't mind if it is sweaty.)

CHAPTER 3 – The Inn-habitants

My nesting instincts kicked in. Hard to nidificate in a hotel, but nonetheless, I decorated my room with candles, picture frames, rugs, and cheerful curtains. I liked my hotel room, especially the view onto the sweep of grassy fields and typical South African bushveld. The unkempt fields were dappled with grazing donkeys that sometimes brayed late at night, and if you've ever heard a donkey bray, it's a forlorn sound, as though the creature is crying. I wanted to run out into the field and throw my arms around a scrawny neck, and tell it: "It's okay, everything's fine, don't worry…you're a donkey. Here have a carrot."

I was feasting on carrots myself, along with other veggies and fruits. It felt good to be healthy, plus I wasn't drinking (big thing for me – abstemious behavior). And apart from the occasional hideously disturbing nightmare that baby would be born half animal, half human, things were first-rate. Pregnancy afforded me the opportunity to relax. I didn't need to *do* anything. I was already engaged in something of major value. I was peacefully procreating.

Plus, down the hall in a room not nearly as grand as mine, lived one of my favorite human beings - Rob B. A number of years older than myself, Rob was my forty-something friend, with comb-over hairdo, tanned olive skin and an ample proboscis. He had a sense of calm about him that I envied. A calm that I could only fake (until Xanax hit the scene) and though dogged by bad luck and consistently broke, Rob always enjoyed his day. One look at his derelict car streamlined you to Rob's take on life. With paint peeling off the sides and an interior knee deep in litter, this jalopy usually required a heave-ho around the dirt parking lot to jump-start it. In lieu of a petrol cap, Rob had stuffed a torn T-shirt into the tank opening. Thing is, Rob didn't care one jot. He'd drive that wrecked rattletrap up to the swankiest hotel and tell the valet: "Don't hurt my baby…oh, and you might want to park her on a hill."

Rob and Basil were friends, not good friends; it was more I think that Rob tolerated Basil's eccentric behavior in exchange for cheap lodging. Rob was a food critic. Basil was a life critic. They'd sit and chat for hours, and every now and then, I'd join them; philosophers in a white trash kingdom. Talk - drink tea. Talk - drink tea. Talk - oops got to pee (pregnant, remember?)

Basil was a simple man. He was not educated and he was definitely not refined. He was pretty rough around the edges and his Greek lineage added that continental flair; a flamboyant eloquence evidenced in the way he talked noisily while his hands flew wildly through the air…hell, sometimes Basil talked with his entire body. Like the time he leapt from his chair to karate chop himself on his inner thighs, flanking his proverbial bits and pieces.

"They can suck my cock!" He roared loudly. Chop, chop, chop!

The whole restaurant turned to stare, and for a brief moment I thought Basil looked like a magnificent Christmas tree lit up in sparkling lights! Ah...not!

Rob and I *were* good friends. Friday nights we'd pick up Rob's young daughter (in Rob's peeling, wrecked baby) and go to the movies. Saturday nights, Rob invited me along to critique cuisine at various restaurants. We'd order lamb chops, Kingclip, prawns, spare ribs and feast like royalty. Sundays we spent poolside, eating chicken mango salads and reading the Sunday newspapers, occasionally braving the murky green waters to find relief from the hot summer sun. I adored Rob. I mean, what more could a pregnant girl ask for than a calm, hilarious, generous, gourmet-food supplying friend who never introduce the topic of sex in any way. Thanks Rob.

Peculiar people booked into the White Horse Inn. This being a dilapidated, low-cost place, it lured in all forms of down and outs, and I watched these lonely, broken people wander the hallways, the restaurants and the bars. One couple (who lodged for two nights) spent their entire stay in raincoats although it was hot, dry, sunny weather. They began ordering beers at 10 AM and kept right on ordering until dark. Maybe the raincoats were protection from beer spillage? Or eventual vomit spillage?

Attached to the restaurant was a club that operated nightly, extending its hours to "We Don't Close" on the weekends. In South Africa there was no limit to selling alcohol. "Drink 'til you drop" was pretty much the standard - a standard to which I myself firmly adhered (and planned to recommence the minute the fetus stopped co-digesting with me). No matter the religious beliefs and ridiculous dancing laws, drinking was permissible. Thanks be to God, oh, and the South African Breweries and Wineries.

Ever the enterpriser, Basil hired a male stripper in the hopes of enticing a gaggle of girls to "Ladies Night" at his club. Men were permitted to join after 10 PM, and by this time, the male stripper would be safely long gone.

Upstairs in the hallway, right outside my room, was where the male stripper chose to ready for his act. We chatted a little. Me, fully clothed - him in a leopard g-string. I couldn't help but notice his tanned, smooth skin, his ripped abs, the sinewy muscles in his arms - the angry, ripe boil on his backside.

The stripper asked if I'd be interested in helping him with his act. He performed a fire show during which he needed to persuade a girl from the audience to hold up a tray of candles while he shot a breath of fire from his mouth to ignite the waxy props. The previous helper had flung the tray halfway across the room when the fire belched towards her, and the stripper was worried this might happen again.

"No problem," I told him. "I'm used to being on stage, and I'm used to odd shit. I'll do it. I'll help you"

When the time came for me to be part of the show, the stripper draped a wet towel over my arm and offered me an oven mitt to grip the tray with. He then pulled my hair back and placed part of the wet towel on the side of my face. There I was, arm extended, fully fire retardant, clutching a tray of candles. The stripper circled me a few times, brandished his fire sticks in the air, then deep-throated the burning sticks into his gullet and blew them back to life in a burst of flames. The gathered girls cheered and I started to worry. That hot flame ball was launching my way next. What if he blew a little too far to the left? There goes my hair, or my ear, or possibly the skin on my face. My hands started to tremble. The tray started to tremble. Shit! Why did I agree to do this? I was sober for shits-sake and this was drunk me behavior. This was insanity. One miscalculation and I'd be toast…literally. Crap! I'd forgotten how horribly anxious I got about…about well, everything, and I couldn't use my usual "slam back a drink to take the edge off" tactic.

The angry boil gleamed in the firelight as stripper boy's glistening buttocks sashayed past me. I almost wished I were that boil, safely behind him, instead of exposed out in the open; a fire target. The heat of the fire sticks tingled my face as he re-adjusted my arm. I held the tray as steady as my shaking limbs allowed. Stripper boy then stepped back, pirouetted around and showered me in dragon's breath. WHOOSH.

The heat soaked over me, the candles leapt up in flames and the vapid, giggling girls clapped, mainly for politeness sake. He smiled a thank you at me and I was free to go. As I hurried away from the smoky club, baby kicked me in the ribs as a punishment for stressing us out.

"I know, I know," I whispered. "That was a bad idea. No more consorting with male strippers."

Come breakfast I regaled Rob with my night's adventure. The raincoat couple had moved on, and seated at their favorite table was Rudy, a mediocre musician who lived permanently at the White Horse Inn. Slouched in his seat, virtually sliding under the table, Rudy struggled to eat breakfast. Still hammered from the previous night, Rudy garbled to himself and flopped about (you know, like garbling, flopping, mediocre musicians do). At first his behavior seemed mildly amusing, but then he sneezed...a nasal mucus-explosion that landed right on his eggs! That did it for me. I begged Rob to swap chairs with me in an effort to shield myself from Rudy and his snot-swing-bridge that now threaded his nose to his plate and mingled with his eggs while he happily ate on - oblivious. I had my body fluid issues to think of. I'm not good with phlegm, spit, sweat, drool or sperm...any secretion really. Ironic when I've been slathered in them for a good portion of my life.

Basil shooed Rudy from the restaurant, then sat down to join us at the breakfast table. While we shared coffee, buttered croissants and idle chitchat, a black woman in traditional African costume edged her way towards our table. Within a few feet of us, she unexpectedly dropped to her hands and knees to crawl the remainder of the way. (I, myself, have used this mode, usually to exit venues). Taking position in front of Basil, the African lady flattened herself onto her stomach. Then, with a voice full of despair she implored Basil for a job. She didn't move. She didn't look up. She kept her eyes averted to the ground; a servile, sacrificial lamb for slaughter.

"Please baas. Please baas. I need a job. Me, I am so hungry."

Basil barely looked at her.

"No!" Was all he offered back.

The woman pleaded a while longer, but Basil remained impassionate. Finally she inched back onto hands and knees, crawled away and lumbered to her feet only when she deemed herself far enough away to be respectful. Sniffling quietly, she shuffled away.

I stared after the saddest person in the world, my heart aching for her. With no welfare services in place for poor people, South Africa's underprivileged (predominantly black people) had few options. Without work, they could beg, steal or starve to death.

Basil shook his head.

"Damn Kaffirs. Please baas this, please baas that, always wanting something."

Of course they always wanted something, and that something was primarily food, because they were starving.

"Couldn't you give her some food at least?" I ventured.

"Then soon I'm feeding everybody," he snapped.

"But she's so desperate for..." I began to protest.

"Hey!" Basil cut me off angrily in his loud voice. "I'm helping you."

He was right. He was helping me and I knew when to shut-up.

"Yes. Thank you, Basil. And I appreciate it." I smiled sweetly at him, because if you roiled Basil, the results could be startling.

He nodded his forgiveness, "Let me tell you Niki, if I was thirty years younger, I'd look like a beautiful Christmas tree to you. You'd want a photo of me."

Again, thirty years or not, no radiant Christmas tree came to mind.

Strangely enough, Ladies Night proved to be a huge success for the club, motivating Basil to revamp his beloved White Horse Inn. He roped in another old Greek, Elias, and together they drew up plans.

"We'll take out these three pillars here." Basil pointed to the concrete offenders in the downstairs bar. "That will give this room extra space. Then we'll build a stage and offer live music all week long."

This was only part one of big things to come.

Elias knuckled down to business right away. With a work crew of three, each armed with a sledgehammer, Elias and his men smashed energetically into those pillars. Within a short while, the columns powdered to rubble and soon after, a loud creaking reverberated through the hallways as the upstairs groaned without its extra support. A crack splintered through the ceiling and raced along the corridor all the way from Rob's room past mine to the staircase. Following that, the entire left section of the second floor collapsed by two inches.

You should have heard Basil's lovely voice booming on that day! He raged himself hoarse.

The door to Rob's room sank deep into the carpeted floor, making it impossible to budge.

"I need clothes, Basil." Rob stressed. "I have a meeting."

"Fine!" Basil rasped. He hauled a ladder from the debris on the ground floor and set it up against Rob's hotel window.

"Be my guest," he said...no pun intended.

Rob braved the ladder, then gingerly traversed the stretch to his closet, terrified that at any given moment he might crash through the floor to join the unfortunate and deafened Elias below.

I loved the White Horse Inn. There was never a dull moment at this nutty place, plus it offered just the right amount of human interaction for me. I could mingle anytime day or night and I could retreat whenever I pleased. There was comfort in the knowledge that I was surrounded by people 24/7, yet I could come and go without so much as nodding at them if I chose. These dysfunctional peeps were my peeps and I could keep them at the distance of my choice. Perfect!

Furthermore, the constant populace supplied protection at a time when violence and unrest were mounting. Home security was a growing concern for those living in Johannesburg, especially since the threat of "Kill a white man day" had emerged. (By the way, this threat is still very real – in fact the World Wide Genocide Watch placed South Africa on a level 6 watch in 2011 due to Julius Malema's inciting hate speeches and for encouraging his followers to sing the delightful ditty: "Kill a Boer".)

The White Horse Inn was my safe haven from all this - my substitute family, my sense of belonging - a place to call home while I sat out my pregnancy.

I conscientiously rubbed vitamin E oil over my taut skin in hopes of avoiding stretch marks. I diligently swallowed multivitamins in hopes of staying healthy. I played classical music for my fetus, poking at it every time it kicked me, in hopes of stimulating its brain. I'd read that if you gently probe back when a fetus moves, that this will encourage it to think. Okay…poke…think about that!

I conversed with my future offspring keeping it abreast of the entire goings on in our world, telling it how the upstairs floor had sunk by two inches and what a terrific noise it had made.

"Then creepy crawlies emerged from the crack," I explained to my ballooning belly. "A whooping king-sized Parktown Prawn ran across this very room, and I tell you what baby, you can drop a substantial phone book on a Parktown Prawn and it will just give you a little crooked, cricket smile."

I congratulated my child–in-the-making for being such a plucky little sperm bubble and explained how it had beat out a million other sperm hopefuls to my ovaries. Well done spunky spunk! Well done indeed.

I felt exceptional. I practically beamed with "pregnant glow" until around six months when junior-to-be quit growing. I stopped gaining weight (confirming my mother's anorexic beliefs) and though I was entering my final trimester, I could easily still veil my pregnancy. Twice weekly hospital visits became mandatory with blood drawn each time in order to keep baby closely monitored. I was pronounced anemic and prescribed large iron tablets to swallow, resulting in horrible headaches and nasty constipation. After a few unnerving weeks, junior hit a growth spurt and all was well again. Though I worried for this not-yet-quite-existent thing, I hadn't really absorbed the fact that it was forming into a human. A human being! A human being that would be solely my responsibility!

I kept on performing shows with *Oh Boy!* until I was eight months pregnant, right up until the watermelon belly swinging in front of me finally forced me to quit the band. Thereafter I moped in my room feeling sorry for myself, wishing the pregnancy to be over, wishing to get back on track with my singing career, wishing I'd never set eyes on that drummer-boy Leslie, wishing I wasn't so uncomfortable, wishing I wasn't so lonely, and absolutely wishing that the black hairs forming a path from my pubes to my navel would kindly please go away.

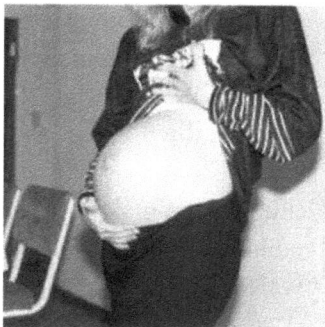

CHAPTER 4 – Birthing the baby

Giving birth hurts. Whatever they tell you, know this: it *will* hurt. Being obtusely naïve, I imagined I would sing on the birthing table. Honestly I did. I told my friends "I'll sing for the nurses while I give birth".

Yeah sure, and the song went something like this:

"I'm fucking dying here. Jesus H. Christ. You guys don't know what the fuck you're doing."

It was not a pretty song.

I never attended Lamaze classes. I thought myself invincible and presumed all that crap was for *other* people. People that didn't know how to sing for example!

I did, however, have enough sense to follow my sister's advice and read a book on giving birth. I remember one part in particular where it said: "When told to hold, pant like a dog and HOLD. If you don't hold, there is a possibility of ripping yourself from your vagina to your anus."

Holy Mother of God! Pant, pant, pant.

I'm happy I read that passage, because I *was* told to hold, and you can bet both your kidneys, I panted like a pack of husky dogs in the Kalahari Desert.

Not having much money as a primigravida, I submitted myself as Ms. Guinea Pig to the Jo'burg Gen. (Johannesburg General Hospital). This meant I had to deliver my offspring surrounded by students. This way, there was no charge for my hospital stay, and in return, all I had to do was endure several nervous looking individuals sticking their fingers inside my vaginal canal to determine if I was dilating. One after another they'd approach and insert, usually apologetic, concurring that I was indeed so-and-so many inches dilated thus far. I really didn't mind the students until in the throes of contractions, baby sought lodging behind my pelvic bone. It was at this point that I realized I was going to die; that these students knew nothing, and that I was about to pay the ultimate price for their stupidity. This is when my language took a nose dive and my maxed out pain scale composition: "I'm fucking dying here" rang out.

When it came time to push, I bore down like Genghis Khan and his entire Tartar army. I was determined to expel that baby from my body A-frikken-SAP. I pushed with such gusto that I ruptured blood vessels in my rectum, which later formed into truly splendid hemorrhoids. I bore down with such gay abandon that I ripped the top of my stomach muscle, which later fashioned into my version of *Alien* - a weird undulating motion under my skin in the abdominal area. And last but not least, my downward thrust saw me practically expel my uterus. It dropped so low that I imagine one day when I sneeze, it will simply plop out onto the sidewalk.

"Oops. Excuse me. Could you pass me my uterus please?"

Near the end of the birthing process came "episiotomy time" which, for those of you lucky enough to have had one know, is a surgical incision cut through the perineum to enlarge the vagina and assist with childbirth. Pure joy really!

In order to administer the slicing of my urogenital area, a nurse rammed an anesthetic shot into my thigh sending an unnatural quiver skittering up my leg, leaving behind a dull ache and an impressive bruise. I had my revenge though. On meeting the same nurse in the hospital elevator three days later, she hoisted her blouse to reveal dark bruises up and down her side. It seems I'd kicked at her during my thrashing childbirth performance. I'd had trouble keeping my feet in the stirrups, and she'd invited me to rest my feet on her side. I'd rested them all right. Like mini jackhammers.

Numb in my lower parts, thighs all-a-quiver, grunting, sweating and swearing, I had yet to eject my papoose payload. Dread mounting, I was thankful when an older nurse appeared at my side. Judging by her age, I surmised she couldn't be a student; she must be a *real* nurse. She must know stuff! This older lady held my hand and instructed me to focus on a clock hanging on the wall.

"7:30 AM your baby will be born," she assured me.

God bless you older, more knowledgeable looking, lady-nurse. I stared that clock down, as if my very life depended on it, and she was darn close. At 7:33 AM baby finally shot out - shot right across the birthing table and landed on her shoulder to stare up at me in surprise. I stared back, equally surprised. Attached to baby was a gnarled, purple, squirming, blood-covered, bad horror movie thing.

"Uugh! What is that?" I shuddered.

I'd always imagined the umbilical cord to be a thin, straight, silver line. Silly me. That's the astral cord, not the umbilical cord. The umbilical cord resembles intestines. This twisted piece of mucous tissue, filled with Wharton's Jelly, protects the one vein and two arteries that carry oxygenated, nutrient-rich blood to and from baby. And there it gleams, in all its slimy gory-glory, slithering out from between your legs and sucking onto baby's stomach like a perverse Alien worm creature.

My obvious revulsion was duly noted.

My chart read: Patient reacted badly to baby.

(By the way, before you toss your unsightly umbilical cord down the disposal, know this – they can now harvest stem cells from umbilical cords, offering the promise of new treatment options for different diseases, spinal cord injuries and multiple sclerosis – *dass ist gut, ja?*)

At the end of the clammy affair, a young man arrived to sew up my perineum! And when I say young, I mean young. I inquired after his age because he didn't look old enough to view my perineum, much less stitch it back together. Unruffled, he disclosed he was 19 and a medic in the army.

"Not to worry," he guaranteed. "I have done this before."
Yeah right! 'Cos those soldiers are dropping babies by the boatload back at base camp.

Too exhausted to care about anything, even a teenager suturing my vagina back together, I mumbled, "just be careful!"

For the first three days of her life, the newcomer's name was Baby. I hadn't picked out a girl's name since I'd been informed I was most definitely having a boy, and Benjamin is pretty gender specific. Friends visited, offering names. Amy, Elizabeth, Kelly, Julia.
Someone said, "How about Samantha?"

I have to be honest here. I had a major crush on that someone, so Samantha sounded first-rate to me. It wasn't until a few months later that I realized I'd ceded my child the same name as the baby that had helped me make my decision. Funny how the universe works isn't it? I now had my own Samantha. And she was more adorable than anything I could ever have hoped for.

CHAPTER 5 – After Birth

The grueling, puerperal stage of my newly found motherhood revolved around a torturous device called a breast pump. Baby couldn't latch onto my nipple (though plenty of others have easily managed), forcing me to pump out milk by means of a (must be a male designed) painful contraption. Was this a sign of things to come? The fact that my daughter couldn't latch onto me? Did it portray a deeper psychological significance? The nightmares started. Sleep itself became a rarity and having it tainted with disturbing imagery tolled unfair to say the least.

My dreams all revolved around baby. Will I lose baby in the park? Will I drown baby in the bath? Where is baby right now? Is she breathing? Why has she grown an extra limb during the night? Why am I punching baby in the face?

I'd wake with my heart thumping staccato in my chest, sharply hammering out my voiceless anxiety, my subconscious terror. My heart beating out the beating I was taking.

"What's that new creature doing in my home?" my churning innards fretted. "Why does it demand sooo much attention?"

I'd rush to check on baby and there she'd be, sleeping serenely, her small fist pressed up against her mouth. The sight of her sent relief flooding through me.

Apparently this stage is quite normal. Baby was a new phenomenon and my poor brain was trying to compute the enormity of what baby's existence implied. Sleeping peacefully through the night was a thing of the past. I could never again go out without making major plans that involved formula, diapers, a change of clothes, feeding schedules, bottles, pacifiers and such like…actually, I could just never go out again. From this day forward any man in my life would have to be versed in baby lingo. Everyone I spoke to would want to know about baby and all my conversations from here on out would be baby related. The extra weight I carried might, or might not, go away. Oh anorexia! Wherefore art thou now?

And, here's the biggie – that little person in the room next door needed ME, from now, until death do us part.

Ahhhhhhhhh that's HUGE. What a gargantuan task. Was I up for the job? Could I be a good parent for Samantha?

Parenting Samantha should have been a cinch because she was a joy, a bundle of bubbly loveliness. I, however, wasn't quite as bubbly. Having to wake up and feed her every few hours throughout the night left me exhausted, and my patience dwindled rapidly at around 3:30 AM. There came a night when Samantha, though satiated with milk and freshly swaddled in a clean nappy, continued to cry nonetheless. Soothing her proved futile and soon the din grated on my worn nerves. Without thinking, I leant forward and poked her on the forehead …fairly hard.

"You stop that noise!" I scowled at her.

Well of course the poke didn't help at all. Samantha's wails scaled to a newfound level. And me? I slumped defeated to the bedroom floor, nipples leaking, ego shot, eyes filling with tears. How was I supposed to manage this?

It wasn't solely Samantha I was struggling with. I'd already moved in with the next boyfriend (bad me) and he was cheating on me (bad him). And although I'd been most excellent at dishing out cheats, it was a totally different story when the tables were turned. It was a bitter pill to swallow. My beau was cheating on me with a hot blonde, a long-legged beauty who carried no residual pregnancy sag around the middle, nor was her vagina malformed by ill placed sutures from a well-meaning 19-year-old army medic. I hated her. I hated him too. More than anything I hated myself. I hated myself for vacillating between wanting Samantha and wishing to be rid of her. I couldn't help it. My life had passed uncomplicated before. Before I could have gone out, drank 'til I stank, and screwed my way back to equilibrium. Now I had to stay home and watch my midriff flop sideways as I curled in a fetal ball, brimming with self-pitying despair.

Samantha's wails gradually subsided as she surrendered to sleep. I stared at her peacefully sleeping face through the side of the lacy crib, feeling torn. I wanted no part of motherhood, but on the other hand, I felt such a tenderness towards my child, I knew I'd hate myself to eternity if I let her down. My first-hand knowledge on what deep seated wounds a bad mother can inflict made me loath to repeat the cycle.

I joined a "New Mother's Group" hoping to find answers, or at least companionship and solidarity. These new mothers, they were consumed by their babies. They could tell you how much their baby ate, slept, coughed, weighed, smiled, hiccupped, spat and shat. Oddly, it was this last activity that seemed to garner the most intrigue.

"My baby filled a diaper with soft, green, foul smelling poop."

"Junior here goes every few hours. A regular nappy can't handle the mass. We double bag him, or else it oozes down the sides of his chunky little legs. Aren't these the cutest legs?"

"Jessica passes pellets. Hard, little brown balls, sort of like rabbit dung. Should I be worried?"

Yes, you should be worried. I was worried. I was forming a scatological obsession. I changed Samantha's diaper with diagnostic purpose. I noted the texture, smell, color and amount…the latter causing me on occasion to exclaim loudly, "Holy shit!" (Once again no pun intended.)

Later on I joined a "Single Mother's Group". This group was no longer obsessed with excrement like the New Mother's Group. This group was no longer fascinated by babies at all. This group was way further down the road. They were hardened, cynical and embittered. Sure babies are cute, but bills are not, and the rent is due, and schoolbooks cost money, as do kids clothes and the kids won't stop growing, or fighting, or whining, or testing your patience. And we all know whose fault it is. Yes sir indeed, the Single Mother's Group, they too harbored an obsession. They were obsessed with their ex-husbands and what absolute losers-bastards-assholes-cocksuckers they were.

This time I couldn't join in the obsessing. I had no ex-husband to rant about. I had Leslie, who impregnated me, nothing more, and I could hardly justify calling him angry names for that. I'm the one who had refused to get married. I'm the one who was careless with her birth control pills. I'm the one who drunkenly spread her legs. I'm the one who would drunkenly spread her legs for just about anyone and that was not Leslie's fault. No, that one I liked to blame on my mother!

CHAPTER 6 – My mother

My mother! My mother had the maternal instincts of a block of cheese. I liked to believe that her lack of mothering led to almost every shortcoming I had, and trust me, I'd amassed an impressive number. Certainly other adults had contributed to my warped-ness; there was my pedophiliac grandfather who molested me when I was nine, my reticent, alcoholic stepfather, René, who occasionally slammed my head into walls while slurring out the reason he married my mother was because I was so diddly-darn cute! There was my biological father who lived seven thousand miles away with his parochial, highly-strung wife, the two of them preferring to hide safely in their "ignorance is bliss" world. Still, regardless of their combined shortcomings, it was my mother who bore the brunt of my resentments.

Although born in "Deutschland, Deutschland über alles", my mother certainly constituted no typical German. The order and efficiency of a true Germanic nature were missing. There were no room inspections to ensure that *alles war in Ordnung.** We weren't forced to polish our shoes or sit pole straight at the dinner table. Instead our household muddled about in a vague and unpredictable disciplinary style. There were no rules until we broke one...not that we'd have any forewarning as to what that might be. For example: hiccupping during a mealtime. Hiccup and...thwack!

Ah, so we're not supposed to hiccup? Make mental note to self: learn to control the involuntary reflex actions of my diaphragm. Sure!

Her parenting style was confusing - an overly lax approach mixed with sudden bursts of irrational strictness; a combo style of "smother-mother" and "no mother at all", a sort of helicopter mom, who every now and then launched torpedoes at us.

*everything was in order

She'd unexpectedly lash out and smack whichever unfortunate kid was nearest, sinking her long talon like fingernails into the closest arm and screeching loudly as she raged about whatever it was that had set her off. Once she calmed down, she'd seek to comfort us, gushing on about how much she loved us and adored us...and needed us. It was this last part, this "needing us" part that somehow always managed to shift from her consoling us, into us consoling her. No, we weren't still mad at her. No, she wasn't terrible. Yes, we still loved her. Yes, a lot!

She projected her feelings and emotions onto us, presuming we were experiencing whatever she was. If she was tired, we were sent to bed. If she was hungry, we were ordered to eat. "Us kids" were merely seen as extensions of herself, not as our own persons. She felt entitled to use any of our possessions without asking us, because in her mind, our belongings were essentially her belongings. If our relatives sent us money, she'd promptly snag it. Gifts, diaries, money, personal items, clothes; these were all hers for the taking. And once we were older, she hogged our boyfriends, manipulated our friends, used our cars, and spent our paychecks...but for some unknown reason, I never fully grasped the extreme to which she would take this taking. *Javol!* I underestimated her.

Having been born in Germany during the locust years of WWII, my mother had an odd fixation with food. It was intolerable for her to waste it. If some odious, unpalatable item remained on our plate, she'd dig right in, be it cold, runny eggs or slimy porridge.

"What?" she'd challenge me and my siblings, noting our disgusted faces. "There's no need to throw this out. It's perfectly good." In her mind, body fat equaled body health – more fat to fight off illnesses with, I guess.

"You're too thin. You don't eat enough." She'd chide me. "Even if you thin down to a rake, your father won't write to you. You do know that, right?"

She must have forgotten that it was her idea for me not to write to my father...*just to see if he noticed*...and she was obviously quite blind to the plumpness of my thighs. I had sufficient "plump" to steer me through a lengthy, bleak winter.

Feeding us was easiest for our mother. Feeding "us kids" *so viel wie möglich.* * No touch, no intimacy, no face to face problem solving; just slap a plate before us and say "Eat, or else!"

Linda and I nicknamed our younger brother, Mister Skeleton, because he was *that* bony. Naturally his scrawny frame fueled my mother's feeding instinct. She'd aggressively force-feed him, ladling food into his mouth, spurring his gag reflex into action. Claude in turn, mustered a show-worthy resistance: kicking, screaming, flinging food and even vomiting on the table if need be. Exasperated, my mother would oft-times give up on Claude and set her attention on me. Now I was not a seriously skinny or underweight child. Regardless, her focus beamed towards me now, and I'd better eat everything on my plate or I'd suffer the "or else" part, meaning the skin rupturing fingernails.

Oh, and did I mention that us kids were frequently covered in boils? No. You'd remember that, right? Well we were, because our force-fed-fare came chiefly from cans. We'd develop these fantastic boils on our skin and our mother would dip thick gauze in boiling water, then clasp it against our pus-filled sores. Suppurated sores or not, the boiling water frikken hurt, and as we hopped about screaming, she'd yell: "Hold still. This is what the doctor ordered to draw the pus out."

*As much as possible

This boiling of the boil procedure had zero effect on one stubborn sore that festered on my left arm. After ample dousings in blistering hot water, this boil distended to the point where I could no longer wear sleeves unless they hung loose. The doctor had to lacerate this bloated baby to drain the rancid gunk out. Nice!

The laceration left me a notable scar on my arm, still, I preferred that boil to the next whopper that ballooned up – a huge, ripe, painful bitch, right between my eyes. It swelled my eyelids shut and when lancing time arrived, the doc told me I was lucky, saying that had this boil been a little higher up, or slightly deeper in, it may well have caused me brain damage.

Oh phhff! Don't worry Doc; I plan on causing my own brain damage later with some zappy alcohol intake.

The feeding wars raged on at every mealtime, occasionally dragging dinner out for hours, with no one allowed to leave the table until we were all finished. As a kid, I chewed up wads of meat, then slyly wedged them into the slats of my chair in hopes of speeding up the escape. Things changed. As a teenager I chewed up my mother, with the kind words of how about she feed me a big, fat plate of "get the fuck away from me".

For Claude, the war ended when he plumped to over 165 pounds by his 10th birthday. The force-feeding combined with an avalanche of chocolate and sweetie bribes had worked too well on Claude. With him nicely overweight, my mother turned her feeding spotlight back on me. Her anorexia modus operandi kicked into high gear and she wouldn't let it drop. She hauled me off to TARA, a unit specifically operated for Adolescent Eating Disorders when I was 14 years old. Her "you'll never live to see twenty five" campaign began in earnest. The once-a-week counseling did zip to improve my appetite, whereas bumping into the skeleton girls in the hallways, their ankles as thin as my thumb joints, *that* encouraged me to race home and guttle down every visible food source in the house.

Nonetheless, even after a report from the treatment center said I was considered "low-risk" for starving to death, my mother's spotlight beamed on, except now the emphasis swung from feeding me to draining me. Not unlike the doc drawing the pus out of my boil, she endeavored to draw out everything inside me: what I was thinking, what I was feeling, what I was experiencing. These withdrawals of my innerness usually ended with "because I love you so very, very much Niksi" and "You know I'll never survive your funeral."

My mother's "love" devotedly enmeshed me into her world. It merged us into a deformed psychological knot, until I didn't quite know where she stopped and I started.

"You are my Golden Child," she honeyed me.

Lying between her legs with my head cradled on her crotch area, she'd stroke my face and murmur: "This is where you came from."

It was her way of bonding; of keeping me close. (The only saving grace here for me is that most everyone arrives on planet mirth through their mother's vagina, still….eew.)

My "golden child" status bequeathed me the privilege of having my mother share intimate details with me, and not only about her sex life. I'd get the run down on her hormonal activity, how her ovaries felt re-awakened, or which of my friends she found sexually attractive. I'd even receive details on the strength of her menstrual flow. It was usually heavy.

"I'm bleeding like a stuck pig."

Fantastic.

"Golden child" was there for her to lean on, no matter what it did to me, and being too young to understand this subtle role reversal, I had no defense against it. She'd snuggle effusively close to me, then spew out her embittered protests over René's lack of sophistication, his boorish behavior, his indiscretions with black women and preoccupation with white men. She'd lament how there was never enough money, and how René referred to Linda and me as leeches (we were his step-children, while Claude was his biological son). She'd complain that she felt alienated in our neighborhood, encircled by such low-class hoi-polloi, especially since she *ought* to be an eminent member of MENSA. She'd gripe over her body aches, her malaise, and how she suffered, and suffered, and suffered.

Listening to her misery pour one afternoon, I became aware of an odd high pitched sound. My mother was glooming over me, complaining bitterly about all the awfulness, only this time, the awfulness happened to be me. Words came spitting from her mouth like: "You're evil...belong in the gutter...filthy whoring child," the usual encouraging mother/daughter stuff.

I could see her lips moving, so I knew it wasn't my mother making that high pitched gride. I was only vaguely listening to her tirade, as my ingenious defense for when she besieged me was I simply floated away. I disembodied myself. Safely distanced from my own being, I watched my mother's mouth move while I concentrated on the odd sound. What the hell was that clamor? It sounded like screaming. Suddenly it hit me that the noise ribboned from my mouth; that it was me, and indeed, I was screaming. The realization brought me crashing back into my body and before I knew it, I was ramming my head into my knees and tearing my hair out. Having lost my dissociative calm, I went ballistic in my attempt to block out my mother's thrum of negativity. Living with mummykins was a torture similar to bastinado (an unsporting beating of the soles of the feet) – it left no visible marks, but it almost incapacitated me.

CHAPTER 7 – A Brief History

My mother was a shapely woman with high cheekbones, blonde hair and big, blue eyes – quite the *zaftig* Arian she was. Men loved her, and she loved them right back. Desperate to leave Germany, she'd married the first non-German she'd come across: a freckly, red-headed Scotsman named Norman…my pops. They moved to Scotland, produced two kids, Linda and me, then called it quits and divorced. Within months, my mother skipped off to once again pledge vows to love, to honor, to cherish and be faithful…conduct she'd already proved herself wholly incapable of maintaining, and returned as Mrs. E., armed with her, this time, Swiss husband, René.

Our new stepfather secured work in Africa and off we ventured, trunks packed, ready to sail on the HMS Windsor Castle. Boarding the huge vessel at South Hampton we were all excited to embark on a new life in a new country. Our destination: Mukanji: a tiny village outside of Freetown in Sierra Leone, North-West Africa.

This itty bitty village was home to about 40 white families, with all the men employed to build, be it roads, pipelines, buildings, sewer lines, electricity pylons, whatever. Africa needed it all. Our scrubby village sprung up in the middle of thick jungle and was prudently encircled by a towering chain-link fence to keep the wild animals at bay. A noisy generator supplied us power, and a quiet African guard (who slept on a mat in the garden at night) supplied us peace of mind.

One of the first things my mother did was cut our hair extremely short. Judging by the outcome, she may have used paper-scissors, or perhaps gardening shears? Ruffling through what was left of our hacked up hair, she explained:

"It's for the heat."

Five year old me did not like my new do.

"But we look like boys," I complained. "Ugly boys!"

"No, you look like two lovely little girls."

"Please can I have long hair, mummy?" I begged.

"No. You'll attract lice and ticks and it will get sweaty and knotted. Be glad you have such a great shaped head and can wear your hair this short." She patted my shoulder.

"I hate my hair and I hate the shape of my head." I sulked.

A haircut of note

My well-shaped head had only one thing to look forward to: Saturday night movies at the clubhouse. The entire social structure of Mukanji revolved around the clubhouse with its large pool, BBQ area, bar and popular dartboard. On Saturday nights, the adults strung a sheet up against the back wall and fired up the projector. Seeing as it was the sole form of entertainment in Mukanji, movie night packed out. There were no cinemas, no restaurants, no TV, pretty much no nothing save jungle, unrelenting heat and bugs galore. Some of these bugs enjoyed movie night too. During flying-ant season, airborne insects swarmed our makeshift screen, giving the film a wavy touch. I didn't mind the undulating film. I minded if someone waved an arm, or lurched past the projector, because then a swirl of black swept the room and if you weren't quick enough to shield your face, those long winged suckers ended up in your hair and mouth.

René had no interest in movie night. He preferred to go hunting with his main bud, Kowzski, a crazy Czechoslovakian. Off they'd zoom in Kowzski's jeep, glugging beers and smoking, bouncing up and down through the jungle at a fervent speed. They returned one evening with a massive gorilla strapped to the hood of the jeep. It was Kowzski's hobby to shoot primates, skin them, then proudly display their skulls in order of size on his desk. This new gorilla would surely be the head of the heads. I felt sorry for the hairy creature prostrate on Kowzski's jeep, much like Jesus on the cross. Stroking its rough paw, the thickness of its palm amazed me.

"I'm sorry they killed you," I whispered into its dead black eyes.

Flying pests and dead gorillas weren't the only thing to adapt to. On arrival in Africa, Linda and I were both instantaneously felled by vicious diarrhea. I guess being born two, white, Scottish lassies, we weren't cut out for the African sun, air and food just yet. In those first few months we suffered chicken pox, mystery pustules, boils in abundance, malaria, fevers, chills and worms, worms, worms.
There's nothing genteel about acclimating to Africa.

Our Mother didn't want us to be sick. It flustered her if we were ill. She needed us to be healthy and cute to ensure that René wouldn't regret his decision. What man wanted to take on a woman with two sick brats? She verged on open hostility with us for our sickliness. Like we discharged mucus and forced pus to stream out of us on purpose; merely to foil her plans. She could have let our freckly father take us. After all, he did want us. So much so, that our dad had come all the way from Scotland to retrieve us as any loving father would do. Drunk, and armed, with a loaded shotgun!

René was away when Norman showed up with his contemporary caveman club, which is probably a good thing. Who knows how it would have ended if they'd had a face off. My mother grabbed Linda and me, and barricaded the three of us in her bedroom. Here we proceeded to scream for help, a vein bulging cry. The kind of scream that contorts your face and pressures it purple whilst spittle flies out your mouth. My young mind struggled to grasp the fact that the bad man on the other side of the door, the bad man with the gun, that *that* was my daddy.

This episode didn't exactly paint the picture of fatherly love a young girl would have hoped for. Instead it managed to instill the beginnings of a deep sense of mistrust in both my sister and me. We understood perfectly. We would never be safe.

CHAPTER 8 – Storms

Arguments flared up between René and my mother. It was my mother's flirty-flirty ways that fired-up René's temper. He recognized she was quite the temptress and it tormented him - tormented him to the point that he decided she was having another man's baby when she fell pregnant with Claude. Nice and sizzled, he staggered home one night, yelling at the top of his voice: "That *worm* in your stomach is not mine! I'll have nothing to do with it."

Our highly pregnant mother responded by shoving René down a flight of stairs, ripping his shirt buttons clear off as she let him fly. Having an inebriated "floppy-body" advantage, René flumped uninjured down the narrow staircase, then picked himself up and charged back up to strike his pregnant wife's shrieking face. Meanwhile Linda and I cowered in our bedroom. Was he going to kill her? Like he killed the gorilla? It was the first of many physical fights. When the *worm* wiggled out as Claude - a beautiful, bouncing, baby boy - René never again mentioned that it might not be his. Instead he settled into his fatherly duties and bought us a spiffy house in Johannesburg, South Africa. So long Mukanji, hello Johannesburg.

Full of optimism, I waltzed into my new, civilized school with my well-shaped head, freckled face, sun burnt body and super short, ratty, jungle-hair.

"Are you a boy or a girl?" A playground prefect immediately teased me.

"I'm a girl," I answered confidently. "I'm wearing a dress."

"You could be a boy wearing a dress. How do you know you're a girl?" She spiked a pitiless finger into my chest.

"I'm a girl." My voice wavered, my assurance waning.

"Prove it." She sneered.

I bit my lip and stammered something unintelligible.

"Stupid boy!" the older girl spat and moved off, snickering.
I stared unhappily after her. God I wanted to grow my hair long.

"Please, please, please, Mummy, can I grow my hair? PLEASE!"
She wouldn't budge, "Maybe when you're older."

When I'm older? But I need golden tresses now dammit!

I hated my stupid, ugly hair. I'd sit in class staring at the other girls, coveting their flowing locks. They arrived at school with braids and ponytails, clips and headbands. They flicked their manes, curled ringlets between their fingers and chewed on the ends of their lengthy, shiny hair. They all looked like girls. Damn them!

I noticed another disparity between my female classmates and myself. They had nice legs, thin and shapely with delicate knees. I had my stocky legs with bulky, square knees. Damn them some more.

The biggest difference, however, the one that truly bothered me was, all my classmates had a mother *and* a father. No one in my class had stepparents. Damn them good and plenty.

Feeling ungainly, un-girlie and unloved, the next impediment to trounce was Afrikaans. This derivative of the Dutch language is a guttural, throaty, phlegmy dialect, spoken solely in South Africa. In every school, learning Afrikaans was compulsory. It was an all important part of the school curriculum from day one to day done. In fact, if you failed Afrikaans, you failed the entire year, therefore, subsequent to much resistance: *ek kan dit praat* – (*I can speak it.*)

So I stressed about the length of my chopped hair, the width of my fubsy legs, and my inability to death rattle from the back of my throat in order to form guttural words like *gooi,* (the "g" sound simulating the hocking up of a lugie). My wimpy worries were ridiculous compared to the major unrest that was brewing a few miles away where the famous Soweto Uprising was taking place. I guess black students were also stressed about the gurgly-grating throat language, and they outright refused to learn Afrikaans. They saw Afrikaans as the language of the oppressor. The language of those who enforced apartheid. Basically they saw it as *groet kuck* * so they boycotted their schools and gathered in the streets of Soweto instead, to sing and chant their protests to the recently installed Afrikaans Medium Decree. Children singing and chanting in the streets? Good heavens! You do understand how petrifying that can be, right? The government (comprised mainly of Afrikaners) handled the situation with Draconian flare. They open fired on the marching schoolchildren, killing a number of them and inspiring the rest to rush out and learn some choice Afrikaans sayings like: *"Nee wat - fok jou. Fok jou dood!"* *

Dead school children did not factor into my world. It would be years before I even registered these things had occurred. For the time being I was preoccupied with submerging myself in the glorious swimming pool that we now owned. Swimming underwater was the one place where I felt completely at ease. No one could see me, touch me, or yell at me. No screaming parents existed at the bottom of my sanctuary pool. So I swam: first thing in the morning, with birds singing and fresh day smells tingling in the air. I swam in the afternoons accompanied by the neighborhood kids, dive bombing for hours then warming up on the slasto between swims, drowning ants with water that dripped off our hair (well, some of our hair).

Night swims were my favorite. There was something magical about a hot night in Africa: crickets chirping, heat blasting, stars twinkling and the pool lights dancing shadows underwater.

The other thing I loved about Johannesburg were the afternoon thunderstorms. On hot days, I'd perch myself on the veranda for a sizzling summer afternoon display. As the air grew increasingly muggy, the clouds would gather dark and ominous, and you could

*great shit

* No way - Fuck you. Fuck you dead.

hear electricity crackle in the sky. Then KABOOM: the heavens would burst open as engorged raindrops showered the earth with a rush of relief. An afternoon thundershower was a spectacular cleansing of the day that left the world steaming in its wake.

Ah Africa!

I could virtually hear electricity crackle through our family life, too. If only a thundershower could have cleansed us. I sensed a strangeness in my mother's behavior, but I had no voice for my misgivings. It began with little incidents, like when I invited some friends over and my mother lit several candles, placed them on the floor, and instructed us to dance around the candles. We did, and it was fun, right up until she hoisted her shirt and knelt over the candles to extinguish them with her bare belly. When my friends looked at me, I shrugged my shoulders. I was eight. "Self-destructive behavior" was not an explanation housed in my vocabulary. Neither was "uncontrollable mood swings" when my mother punished me for some minor offense. All I knew was that when she shoved me to the ground and kicked me in the ribs, I had to clamp my eyes firmly shut, because the expression on her face terrified me.

Thankfully it was usually René she was mad at, so I'd simply offer them a wide berth when their arguing fired up. If it amplified to unbearable, then into the pool I'd plunge. Things weren't great, but they were manageable; we were almost happy for a year or two. Then, out of nowhere, my mother decided she wanted to sell our lovely pool home, and she wanted to do so without René noticing.

"Don't let René know that people are coming to view the house," she instructed us.

What about the *For Sale* sign in the front yard? That might be a bit of a give away.

Prospective buyers arrived to assay the house with my mother scrambling to schedule the showings to coincide with René's work hours. Of course he arrived home early one day to encounter an eager couple screening our house. It didn't take him long to figure out this lopsided equation.

Slipping into my bedroom he sat down on my bed and asked me quietly, "Does your mother love me?"

I shook my head slowly...No. I was old enough to know that she didn't love him.

Rene sucked his breath in. "Do you love me?" he asked.

I nodded this time.

"Yes, I love you," I automatically assured him, then stared awkwardly at my blankets.

Rene's bottom lip quivered and suddenly his ever-absent emotions swelled up and broke him into a flood of tears. I clumsily placed an arm around his shoulders, quashing a sense of panic. I'd never witnessed a grown man cry and it flustered me no end.

I suffered guilt too. I wasn't altogether convinced that I did love him. I mean, he never hugged me. He never showed me any affection. He never said the words, "I love you" to me.

I sincerely wished my mother would love him, so I could be free of the obligation. Instead, my mother reminded me daily that *all* men were absolute bastards, and René ranked considerably high on that list. She badmouthed him steadily around the clock, citing every possible shortcoming known to mankind.

The house soon sold (René noticed) and after another long screaming match, it was decided. They were done! Finished! This marriage was over. Over, you hear me! Oh, if only.

CHAPTER 9 - The Isle of Man... man!

With the extra house-cash in her pocket, my mother decided it was time to split up the family, disband the household, collapse the clan. She shipped Linda and me off to spend a year with our dad (in the Isle of Man of all places), while Claude was neatly packed off to a military-style boarding school at the tender age of five. This dispersing of her children was meant to free my mother up to sort out her life and finally escape the evil clutches of René.

This fabulous plan of hers didn't work too well for us kids. I hated the Isle of Man and I hated Linda. Linda hated the Isle of Man and she hated me. Claude hated being alone, so he wet his bed with resolute regularity and expeditiously failed his first year of school.

And what about our mother? Did she sort out her life? Not quite. She simply moved in with some guy named John H. and about the only thing she sorted out was where her belongings should situate in that man's house. I was a bit bitter, I must say.

The Isle of Man was a difficult adjustment for me. I missed my friends, my pool, my little brother and the warmth of Africa. I was acutely homesick and cried everyday until I couldn't stand myself.

"I'm done with crying," I affirmed one day. "I will never cry again."

Not much success there. I was boohooing again within a few hours. I cried because I was homesick, I cried because I was lonely, I cried because try as I might, I couldn't fit in. My accent was different, my clothing was different, my outlook was different, even my sense of humor no longer worked: Did you hear about Little Lotta? She was gang raped, but she didn't care 'cos Little Lotta kept her money in her sock...what? Why are you all staring at me? That's hilarious where I come from.

And who the hell was I meant to flirt with at the private all-girl school that my father insisted on sending us to? I missed having boys in my class.

My knowledge also proved different. I knew nothing about British history having only learnt arduously about the Boer war, the Voortrekkers and Wolraad Woltemade year after year in the patriotic South African schooling system. I knew zip about the Isle of Man - as you probably don't, either.

Please permit me to fill you in:

The Isle of Man lies in the North Irish Sea, between England and Ireland. It is approximately 32 miles long and 15 miles wide and homes roughly 80,000 people plus a few fairies according to folklore. Apart from being a tax haven, the Isle of Man's main claim to fame is the renowned annual Tourist Trophy motorbike race - the TT races. This event used to be one of the most prestigious motorcycle races in the world, attracting everyone with a machine between their legs onto the island. Inundated with motorbikes, the usual sleepy streets now showboated steel hogs and leather-clad bike enthusiasts. Life narrowed to a single lens that focused solely on the races. Even the expensive (very expensive and we can barely afford it, so you better be damn grateful) school shut down for race-week, because the noise level stole any prospect of studying.

Our street beset by bikes

The second claim to fame for the Isle of Man is the Manx cat: a cat without a tail – a kitty with a spinal mutation that shortens its tail to a stub. And the word "Manx" is not only a stubby-tailed feline, but furthermore, it is the language that the die-hard locals speak. Derived from North Germanic, Gaelic and Old Norse (Viking-speak), it rivals Afrikaans with its guttural gruntings.

Cha nel mee toiggal – I don't understand.

Abbyr shen areesht, my sailliu – please say that again…uh…and again…because it sounds remarkably like you're strangling yourself with an astral-traveling-umbilical-cord. Maybe Manx people suffer some strange sesquipedalian sickness tied to a tongue-twisting titillation? *Ooilley kiart Dy liooar.* All right, enough.

Not only could I not fit in, I didn't exactly relish living with my dad or my stepmother. I wasn't precisely comfortable with *daddio* whom I hadn't seen in years and had only had a vague relationship with up until now. I wasn't that sure about this daddy fellow, although he did once buy me a birthday present that mightily impressed me. He phoned me in South Africa to ask what I'd like for my 8th birthday. Racking my brain, I decided a canoe would do nicely. Imagine my surprise when he actually sent me one.

I didn't much savor my stepmother Lisa, either. She was certainly not happy peachy fun to live with. She was an overwrought neurotic who chastised my dad from morning to night, complaining endlessly that he was useless (which by and large he was) and she let it loudly be known how she felt about having his two daughters thrust upon *her* household.

Linda and I had hardly settled in, when, wouldn't you know it; I started my first period. How embarrassing. I'd had no clue that this privilege was in store for me. No one had enlightened me to this joy.

At the sight of brown, clotted blood leaking from my V, I deduced death must be imminent and I rushed to my sister's room.

"You're such an idiot." Linda sneered.

"But what is it?" I whimpered feeling completely lost.

"It's your period," she snapped and slammed the door on me.

I had no choice but to confide this shamefulness to my father. He stammered and blushed, and finally recommended I telephone my mother in South Africa. My mother kindly filled me in on what feminine hygiene products were and informed me I would be leaking blood every 28 days for the next 40 odd years. How unfair is that?

Next up on my pre-teen joy-list came the necessity for a bra. Oddly enough, I'd been picked for the swim team at my super-costly private all girl school. Although I love swimming, I'm an atrocious swimmer. By British standards, however, it appeared that I was a goddamn dolphin. Showering off after the pool, I noticed all the other girls my age were deftly strapping on bras. I had nothing to strap over my faintly plumped up areolas. Oh Lord! I needed a bra. I needed one yesterday!

After the menses fiasco, I was reluctant to ask my dad or my sister for advice. Lisa was the only one left and I sure as hell wasn't going anywhere near her.

"I have to phone my mother again," I stipulated to my dad.

"These calls are expensive you know." My stepmother scowled at me, her glower conveying more than the phone expense. It listed the school, the food, the uniforms, the travel expenses, the everything. I got the message: Linda and I were an unwanted outlay.

"I need to phone my mother," I repeated stubbornly.

My dad dialed the numbers and soon my mother's voice sounded on the other end of the line.

"I need money," I barked at her the minute my dad handed me the phone.

She asked to know what for.

"To buy a bra," I mumbled into the receiver, embarrassed to voice such things out loud.

Naturally, she couldn't hear me and commanded I speak up. With Lisa and my dad hovering close by, curious as to my behavior, I hit frustration overload.

"To buy a bra!" I yelled into the phone, slammed it down and elbowed Lisa out of my way to flee the room crying.

My elbow in the ribs maneuver prompted much castigation and several tears, after which, Lisa agreed to take me shopping. As we inspected training bras of all shapes, colors and materials, a passing lady shopper smiled at us and stooped towards me saying:

"Sweetie, you look just like your mum," (meaning Lisa).

"That's not my mother!" I virtually spat at the poor woman.

I held a strong sense of loyalty towards my mother. Her photograph nestled in my jacket pocket wherever I went, allowing me to whip it out and proudly confirm her to all. I clung to my belief that my mother was amazing. I wanted nothing to do with Lisa, as if accepting her would somehow eradicate my mother's existence. I didn't listen to Lisa. I didn't respect her. I made it quite clear that she was of no lasting consequence to me whatsoever.

Linda disliked the Isle of Mundane as much as I did. There wasn't much to like. We were a grueling three hour seasick ferry ride from the mainland, trapped on a boring, freezing land mass with a beach overrun by worms, and worse: residing with our nitpicking stepmother and unimpressive dad, who grunted, coughed, and hummed tunelessly while scratching and picking at his various scabs. Watching Lisa buttering our helpless father's toast for him, Linda and I ached for our mother.

Linda wrote in her diary:

The Isle of Man is a dump. I miss mother playing her records, her Tchaikovsky and Beethoven, and Hitler's speeches. I miss being her friend and having her tell me who her latest boyfriend is.

(Neither Linda nor I can remember our mother playing us Hitler's speeches, but I guess she must have...*himmel*.)

I hung the end of the year in my sight, like a fat, dangling carrot of encouragement. I counted down the days to my release from the Isle of Bile. But come the end of the year, my mother suddenly reneged on her promise to let us go back to South Africa, and out of the blue moved us to Scotland. Scotland? What? Why? Noooooooooooooooooo!

CHAPTER 10 - Tantrums and Meltdowns

We schlepped our way up to Scotland where my mother rented a cheap mobile home to help us settle into the subzero temperatures. Oh, the misery. I refused to shower. It was too f-ing cold to get wet. I refused to budge from the mobile home. It was too f-ing cold to step outside. Seriously, if your mission was to fetch the post from the mailbox at the end of the driveway, you had to factor in – am I going to die? On opening the front door, cold air slapped you in the face like a steel spade. What torturous ploy was this? I wanted none of it. I stationed myself resolutely between the heater and a small black and white TV, sequestering myself firmly in old Elvis movies. "Fun in Acapulco"…yeah, whatever, Elvis.

This couldn't be happening. Hadn't my mother promised that a year of banishment from my beloved South Africa would guarantee me a ticket home? HOME! Not some freezing cold mobile home park near the town of Aberdeen. What the hell were we doing here?

I couldn't stand it. I felt totally betrayed. I'd done my prison time only to have a worse sentence slapped on me. This lack of control over my own destiny cornered me into an out-of-control meltdown. Time to issue a thunderous oral attack - let the fulmination begin! I let it all out, no holds barred. I ranted and raved, practically frothing at the mouth, demanding that my mother take me back to South Africa "this bloody instant!"

My demands were quickly shot down.

"We can't go back to South Africa. René is there, and he'll hurt me."

So? The idea of someone hurting her didn't seem too bad. Plus, I had no beef with René. I tried my hand at hysterical begging.

"Let me live with René. Send me to boarding school. I'll live with the old neighbors. I'll live in a tent. I don't care. I'll do anything. Please! PLEASE, mummy, please! Let me go home."

The begging was futile. It was *ixnay* on my *ogay omehay lanpay*.

"You know I can't live without you, Niksi."

Those words infuriated me. What utter horseshit. Hadn't she just managed a whole year without me quite splendidly? My childlike conviction that "my mother could do no wrong" shifted to a pre-teen bitterness that "my mother was a big, stinky liar".

My longing for home raged unabated. I couldn't bear Scotland. The ice-cold inclement weather, the incomprehensible accents and the depressingly inadequate hours of daylight made it, unbelievably, worse than the Isle of Man. I struggled to exist in the cold weather – extremophile I am not…oenophile: now *that* I am. It was in Scotland that I discovered alcohol: twelve years old and drinking to stay warm. Drinking to stay sane. Drinking to feel something other than dead inside. When Hell freezes over, it will undoubtedly resemble a mobile home park in Scotland.

The positive outcome of my mother dragging us to Scotland was that Claude was hauled right along with us. I'd missed him enormously during my Isle of Crap year, and it was wonderful to reunite with my little brother. Sure, he'd failed his first year of school, and wet his bed nightly, but at least he'd learnt some impeccable manners from his time at boarding school.

"Pardon me madam for urinating in my bedding."

This new, well-mannered Claude stood up if a woman entered the room. He asked permission to leave the table after meals, and went so far as to give a little bow when saying, "thank you".

The cold didn't bother Claude. He ventured out into the snow to play, and one afternoon he "politely" unhanded a hefty slab of concrete onto his left foot, crushing his baby-toe clear off. Man, ice sure can be a slippery business.

A short hospital stopover and plentiful stitches later, Claude returned on crutches with a fleshy stub that he dubbed "Bob".

"Please come and watch Bob exercising," he'd invite me, as he'd flex and flop his freshly formed nub.

Claude crutched into his new Scottish school, snappily failed more classes, and rapidly lost his good manners altogether. Instead of bowing courteously, he now exploded in impressive, uncontainable tantrums. Whatever it was he was protesting, he sure invested heart and soul into the rebellion.

"I will not brush my teeth," he'd unyieldingly inform our mother.

"Oh yes you will!" she'd shoot back.

"Never madam!" Claude would tell her. "Never, never, never." (Okay, so he was still somewhat polite.)

"We'll see about that," she'd fume, and soon it was "game on", time for full-scale, physical combat. Claude would rage until his neck veins distended to a pulsating purple, leaving him with a swollen, dark red face that looked fit to burst, while my mother lugged him kicking and swelling down the hall towards the bathroom to have his teeth forcibly brushed.

I certainly didn't mind Claude raging at our mother. I was in full support of his yelling in her face, especially since I couldn't muster up the energy to do so myself. What was much more disturbing was when Claude unleashed his purple rage against himself and his own belongings. Toys were torn apart and shattered to pieces. Posters of his beloved heroes: the A-Team and ABBA, were ripped from his bedroom walls. Knitting needles were plunged through his favorite bongo drums. Books were shredded to confetti. Sadly, Claude usually destroyed the very things that he liked the best, once even battering his brand-new, prized plastic machine gun against the garden wall. He loved that gun. It was life size and made gratifying "rat-a-tat-tat" sounds when you squeezed the trigger. Claude wept bitterly as he smashed his precious gun against the bricks, but he couldn't, or wouldn't, stop until it was well beyond repair. There was no becalming Claude once he let loose, and afterwards, there was no comforting him either. He'd be inconsolable and exhausted.

Four, freezing cold, Northern Hemisphere months later (that felt like an eternity), my mother finally conceded that perhaps Scotland wasn't the best fit for us. Conceivably Claude's mulish tantrums and my unwashed, sulky carcass cemented before the TV, finally wore our mother out?

"We're moving to London," she abruptly announced.

London? What? Why?

Off we trooped to enroll in yet another school, and settle in with one of my father's friends, Mike G. At least here the temperatures were bearable and the neighbors were somewhat interesting. I was almost beginning to enjoy London when, out of nowhere, my mother decided she was dying. Dying of what we'll never know, but like one of Hollywood's top drama divas, she extemporized a magnificent meltdown in Mike G's kitchen, outperforming any of mine or Claude's wobblies.

"Please don't bury me in Germany," she wailed hysterically. "I can't be buried in Europe."

She flung herself about Mike G.'s kitchen, slapping the counters with her hands and bashing her head into the cupboards.

"I can't. I won't be buried in Europe. Oh my God, I have to get back to Africa."

And snip-snap, we were comfortably seated on the next plane home.

CHAPTER 11 – The useless Ping Pong table

I was ready to kiss the scorching runway when we touched down in Johannesburg. Woo-hoo! I was so happy to be home. What glee to suck in a lungful of hot, dry, high-altitude African air. Oh, yes please!

Our first few weeks back saw us crowding in on one of René's friends - quite handy that my mother's husbands had all these friends who tolerated us living with them. We moved in with Cornelius, a bearded Dutchman who smelled not unlike a sewer, quite possibly because he worked on the sewage pipelines.

My mother, Linda, Claude and I lay "cheek by jowl" on a stained mattress on the floor in the dingy guest-bedroom; all four of us packed tightly together in sleep. We'd arm ourselves with shoes (my wooden clogs worked well) ensuring we were fully equipped to kill the cockroaches that scampered about us in the dark. WHACK! Squash those nasty buggers into the floor.

My mother soon moved into the smelly Dutchman's bedroom, leaving Linda, Claude and I to fend off the night crawlers by ourselves.

I didn't care. I was back in my homeland, back in my beloved Africa. Back in the sweltering sun surrounded by familiar accents, fashions, foods, friends, space and wilderness…and tanned faces, with no pasty-white Brits in sight. And that's not to say that I prefer cockroaches to British people.

Within a few weeks, things fell apart in the kingdom of Cornelius, and my mother, fresh out of men to shack up with, rented a modest house in a suburb called Randburg. And in we filed: my mother, Linda, Claude and me, carrying our suitcases. That's all we had…our clothes. The unsuccessful yearlong jaunt around the United Kingdom trying to shed René had proved successful only in shedding everything else we'd ever owned. I arranged my clothes in the closet, then lay on the bare floor listening to the house throb its stark emptiness. This was our sixth move in four months, with each move serving to tilt me further off balance.

My mother bought lawn-chair cushions to function as mattresses. You had to draw several together to form a full bed, but the cushions invariably slid apart during the night and left you with tender spots from whichever bone bore down on the slatted wood floor. And with no curtains to shield us, the African sun soaked in to heat you awake by 6 am. Sore boned and sweaty I'd awaken, dubious about the future.

Not that adept at acquiring employment, my mother opted for a new boyfriend instead. A few nights with an unsuspecting sucker produced a couch, along with curtains and bedding, even a kettle to make tea. Thanks, misters, whoever you were.

Permitted to choose my own curtains, I selected ones of bright, orange, bamboo decorated fabric. The flowing drapes cheered up my bedroom and proved useful in the middle of the night when I awoke crying. I'd lean over and elegantly blow my nose on the back of them. A tad unhygienic, I agree, especially when the bamboo pattern ultimately stiffened from its green crusty backing; still, it didn't bother me in the slightest. It is other people's body fluids I take offense to, not my own. I was far more bothered to climb out of bed in the middle of the night to locate a tissue. No way José. I was terrified of the dark, and those pesky throat-slitting terrorists might detect me.

It didn't take long for René to show up, and he and my mother performed the fandango, moaning away in the front yard, taking refuge behind René's *bakkie* (truck). Two days later René moved in and everything careened back to square one. So much for sorting things out! The whole Isle of Man/boarding school/Scotland/London/smelly Dutchman experience had been an utter waste of time.

My mother kindly explained her decision for letting René move back in, illuminating the fact that she and he were hot stuff together in the sack (oh quick…ear muffs!) Well, how splendid for them. Still, whether or not their makeup sex rocked the Casbah, it by no means meant that their relationship had improved, or that our lives had stabilized. I guess they thought differently, and to prove how "normal" they were, they installed a full-size Ping Pong table smack dab in the center of our living room when, honestly, a throw rug or coffee table would have sufficed. Perhaps my parents envisioned us staying home and playing Ping Pong together, rather than me sneaking out to steal/drink/cause havoc and shag the neighborhood. Alas and alack, that timber babysitter did diddly-diddley-doo to keep me out of trouble. I imagine a million Ping Pong tables would have been hard pressed to supervise our family.

Hence, with the Ping Pong table blissfully unaware, I lost my virginity at 13, or rather, I handed it willingly to C.H. a nice enough 17 year old. Dressed in a svelte, black silk dress, I felt feminine and sexy. Not so much at 4 am, when C.H told me I should lick on his penis.

"Just like an ice cream," he coerced me.

Ice cream? That gross purple thing, smelling of smegma, oozing slimy, salty stuff into my mouth was nothing like ice cream. My abhorrence of body fluids was acutely exacerbated, and ice cream hopped onto the blech-list right along with liver, tongue, bone marrow and all the other weird meats that René enjoyed cooking.

C.H and I lasted a whole month as boyfriend/girlfriend. Then he smooched on his ex-girlfriend at a party, leaving me to weep under a tree. This added to my personal edification on sex and love. It appeared that sex and love were two very different beasts. I could lose in love, but gain in sex. Love was guaranteed to hurt, but sex only occasionally hurt. I had sex for several reasons, and none of them were because I was suffering an overactive libido. I had sex to *acquire* things, to *solidify* my power, and, on an unconscious level, to *punish* myself.

Punish myself for what? Well, here's the cracker. I believed I was somehow responsible for other people's actions by way of my own…for example: my grandfather's diddling. I believed *I* had somehow caused that, somehow allowed it. What happened to my fight or flight syndrome? I hadn't done either of those. No, I'd opted for the third choice "submission". And to make things worse - I had giggled. Who giggles mid-molestation? I hated the fact that I'd giggled. Like my tittering had somehow condoned his actions. Like it somehow said, "Hey that's okay, gramps. Go ahead. Stick your dirty, old fingers in me. Pump me full of sperm while you're at it, why don't you."

I giggled while my grandfather had his fingers deep in my hoohoo, and across the room I could see my brother and sister preparing breakfast. It was pretty damn awkward. It was pretty damn surreal. I didn't know what to do, or how to behave. I didn't know what was expected, because I was nine…so I giggled. Eventually, I hauled the covers over my head, hoping that no one would witness my shame.

My grandparents had paid for Linda and me to fly from South Africa to Nice, France to vacation with them. They'd rented a chic beach apartment right on the sand and when my dad got wind of our 6-week vacation, he jumped in his camper van and hauled ass out to Nice to spring a surprise visit (since England is a lot closer to France than it is to South Africa).

Upstairs in the beach apartment, the intercom crackled to life when my dad buzzed from the car park below.

"Hello? This is Norman."

My German grandparents spoke very little English.

"Wer ist da? Was wollen Sie?" *(Who is it. What do you want?)*

My father spoke very little German.

"Ich bin Norman. Herein kommen bitte?" *(May I come in?)*

It required a bit of back and forth before my grandparents grasped the situation. Once they understood that Norman was here in their parking structure, they adamantly refused him entry to their holiday home. Their logic was: since he hadn't contributed to the cost of flying Linda and me to Europe, why should he reap the benefit of seeing us?

Hearing my father's voice coming through the wall, I assumed the intercom to be a type of telephone. I figured my dad was calling us from his home in the Isle of Man. When I realized that he was actually standing several flights below my feet and that my grandparents were *not* going to allow my sister and me to see him, I plain ruptured.

"I want to see my daddy!" I screamed.

Smacking at my grandparents' age-spotted hands, I rushed the front door, fervently focused on escaping the apartment, preparing to bolt downstairs for a glimpse of my father whom I hadn't seen in years. While my grandfather restrained my kicking, squirming body, I keenly howled my distress.

"I want to see my daddy! I want to see my daddy!" I yowled.

"Nein, das kommt nicht ins Frage." *(No, no question about it)*

"I hate you both!" I shouted at them so loudly that my throat hurt.

Despite the language barrier, my grandparents understood this perfectly. They relented, judging it preferable for me see my father, rather than have me "kablooey" right there in their vacation apartment. My grandfather released his grip and I tore out the door, flew towards the staircase, sailed down 15 flights of stairs and launched myself breathlessly into my father's arms. I loved him more than anything in world at that moment…daddy, daddy, daddy!

You see, it was at this chic beach apartment in Nice that grandpa started his diddling, and nine-year-old me desperately wanted... needed...to be saved. Here was my father, a knight in shining armor, come to do exactly that - save me. Sadly though, my father didn't know about grandpa and I could find no language with which to tell him. In my young mind, I hoped he would somehow intrinsically identify my plight, somehow sense that his daughter was in peril. But he hardly knew me, or Linda, so instead he argued about money with my grandparents in his broken German for a good few hours, then whisked us off to a park and shortly after, went on his merry way.

Leukemia claimed my grandfather in his 62nd year, but long after he was dead and buried, the damage he inflicted lived on. My shame, which I could effortlessly hide from others, I couldn't hide from myself. That shame silently adhered itself to my innermost being, saying, "Niki, you are good for one thing only. A fuck!"

Ah, there's the rub! With molestation, first the perpetrator harms you, but once you get the hang of it, you take over from them and you harm yourself. "Don't bother sticking it to me, buddy. I'm sticking it to myself big time."

And stick it to myself, I did. By age 12, I was smoking and drinking up a storm and by age 13, I was having sex indiscriminately. It was my punishment for being desirable; my punishment for having a vagina; my punishment for being alive. Take that, you tortured trollop. Swallow that, you stricken strumpet.

CHAPTER 12 – Teen spirits

Diary Entry - 28th August 1978 (age 13)
Mummy says she hopes I leave home soon…that she hates me 'cos I'm "full of fucking shit". I feel soooo lonely.

To guarantee myself an unflappable assurance, I chugged down Cinzano Spumantes, Old Brown Sherry, beer, Southern Comfort, wine coolers, Tequila. The list goes on…and on. And to enhance my sophistication, I sucked on Chesterfields, Benson & Hedges, Camels or whatever brand I could mooch. Enveloped in my comfortable cocoon of mixed cocktails and cigarette haze, I felt nothing. So what if my mother said she hated me? So what if I was failing school? So what if I felt dirty and disgusting? So what if I was "full of fucking shit"? In my numb state, none of this bothered me. I liked who I was when I was drunk. I was happier, sexier, funnier, everythinger. Drinking was my drug of choice. If I were sad, I'd drink. If I were happy, I'd drink. If I were angry, I'd drink. Any emotion, feeling, occasion, celebration, event - drink, drink, drink…yeehoo!

Sober I was ugly, vulnerable, nervous and clumsy - a walking raw, open wound. A mere glance cut me to the deep. I imagined that adults could x-ray through my outer layer of skin to see inside of me, right down to my rotten inner core. Their odium was tangible to me. I knew I was bad deep down inside…and I knew they knew it too. It's another wonderful side effect of sexual abuse – you believe you are dirty, dirty, dirty.

Yes, sober I was definitely unprotected, rendered defenseless, and for that reason, I detested going to school. High school required that I attend not only sober but furthermore wearing an unflattering short grey tunic uniform. Since I suffered from a severe *fat leg* complex, having my stumps dangle out of a short frock caused me "exposure agony". A kid once asked: "Do you kick-start jumbo jets with those legs?" and that was it. Imagining my legs to be gargantuan and my core to be putrid, school was no happy picnic for me. Teeming with teenage angst, I skulked and sulked, gloomed and glowered; a regular wretched scowling scholar.

At times I'd reward myself for going to "that stupid f-ing" and "I certainly don't need it" school by concealing a bottle of Malibu rum in my schoolbag. I'd drop a straw inside the bottle for some sly-sipping access and sneak it onto campus. The rum smelled similar to the suntan lotion that the girls liked to smooth on their (well proportioned) legs, so no one found the potent coconut smell suspicious. Sitting cross-legged on the school hall floor for morning assembly, the purpose of my schoolbag straddled across my lap was twofold. First, it camouflaged my thunder thighs and knobbly knees, and second, if I slipped the straw in my mouth, it merely looked like I was resting my head on my schoolbag. Without attracting attention, I'd suck on my straw during assembly, sucking the headmaster's drone into bearable. I'd suck on my straw during class, sucking those bitches around me into tolerable. I'd suck on my straw throughout the day, sucking the whole sucky system into oblivion.

I functioned fairly well loaded. I wrote my final English paper for Standard Eight while agreeably pickled. The teacher was impressed enough to read my essay aloud to the class a week later, which was nice for me, too. It was like hearing the story for the first time. I wrote that? Bully for me.

Three sheets (or possibly four or five) to the wind, I sailed triumphant. *Drunk me* trumped *sober me* in every arena – the most important factor emerging as: drunk, I held no fear. Having adults probe my insides (in more ways than one), I was constantly worried. What if people found out I was bad? What if they thought me disagreeable? What if they deemed me worthless? Adding to my anxiety were my mother's constant warnings of my imminent death.

"You do know black terrorists are coming in the middle of the night to slit our throats," she would calmly remind me.

Seriously? Do you have to keep telling me that?

I don't think she meant to scare me or my siblings with her doomsday premonitions; it's just that death was a thing of hers. Her world loomed dark and dangerous, a volatile place where nothing good ever happened. And I? I was the nervous outcome of my mother's doom and gloom...and womb (apologies - I simply had to add that).

Overflowing with unplumbed fears and blighted with the occasional full-blown panic attack, I suffered from fear of elevators, crossing streets, heights, flying, roller coasters, airplanes, darkness, big dogs, sheep (all cattle really – it's the unblinking eyes) and general anesthetic. I envy people who can sky dive and horse ride, hang glide and parasail. Luckies.

I trust you can understand how the drinking helped to mollify my nerves. Indeed it filled my tank with eye-blistering Dutch courage. I could face anything drunk. Give me enough wine and I braved to invincible. Give me enough vodka and I bolstered to unbeatable. Give me enough Jägermeister and I blanked to unemotional, give me enough alcohol and my throat beefed up to solidly un-slit-able.

Clutching my bottle of rum-support for school. And look at those legs dingle-dangling out!

CHAPTER 13 – From A family to B family

When I was 15, two men in army uniforms raped my mother. She was "bleeding like a stuck pig" at the time. She went so far as to show them, but apparently they didn't care. They went ahead and raped her anyway.

She arrived home crying hysterically, her chiffon dress torn and bloody. René had abandoned her at a party leaving her to find her own way home, and my mother, free bird that she was, decided to hitchhike home. You know what they say about hitching: you can get raped. Well folks it's true. Ask my mother.

Linda and I were outraged. We marched into René's bedroom and shook him awake to scream in his face:

"Mummy was raped because of you!"

His eyes opened, but never quite focused. He was drunk, kaput, blotto, sozzled, finito, schnocker-rooed! Bleary-eyed, he lay limply as Linda and I hurled obscenities at him.

"You bastard, you drunken asshole…look what you let happen. Look what you did."

Once satisfied that we'd screamed sufficiently, Linda and I hoity-toity-ed out of the room. Hah! We'd showed him…ah not. René came charging after us, clad solely in a pair of faded beige underpants with a blank, psychopathic stare in his eyes. (These beige underpants made several appearances over the years - none of them good).

Things escalated rapidly as he lunged at my sister first, ripping her dress up over her head. Why? I have no idea. Next he walloped my head into the living-room wall (told you) and I bounced off feeling like a cartoon character, complete with the flashing stars and a flesh egg welling up on the side of my noggin.

That set my mother off, and here's where I have to praise her – I mean imagine you've just been raped and now your husband is attacking your children. Well, she didn't hesitate. She lustily joined in the fray. Un-strapping her shoes she hurled a high-heel at René and her perfect aim saw the stiletto slice neatly into his throat. Jumping Jesus! Nothing like a bit of jugulation to get the party started.

This was way out of control. We needed help. I raced towards the neighbors house shrieking: "Help!" Yup - just like that.

At the same time, my mother and Linda had managed to shove René's semi-clad body out of the house, but as they slammed the front door on him, they realized that I was out there too. Yelling for me to get back inside, they reopened the door slightly, willing me to slip back in. And slip in I did. But René managed a slip too...only a partial slip though. His body was now inserted half in and half out of the doorway. Oh what to do? Hit him of course. And so all three of us: my mother, my sister and I, we pounded on René. We thumped and thumped, with closed fists, hitting wherever and whatever we could on his stout frame. Screaming and thumping, we wailed on him until his body shuddered and gave in. Flesh that had felt firm beneath my fists slackened as René quivered into jelly and crumpled to the ground. Watching my stepfather writhe and groan on the floor almost made me throw up. Not with disgust at him, but with disgust at myself, for pounding on him so hard.

My mother decided that she'd had enough. That she deserved better. That we were moving in with the B. family down the street. That she was leaving René...for good...again.

Linda and I, still incensed from the rape event, scuttled sanctimoniously along with my mother, while Claude being only 9, based his decision on the size of the television. He chose to remain with René seeing as the B. family only owned a crap, little, black and white TV.

The B. family consisted of Mrs. B, (who bore a gumma looking mole on her forehead) and her three strapping, acerebral sons. Mrs. B was a highly committed alcoholic, guzzling neat gin from sun up to sun down, or until she keeled over. Her sons periodically poured the gin down the sink, but Mrs. B had reserves stashed throughout the house. Their house was big enough for stashing gin, but it certainly wasn't big enough to stash all of us. A dusty tent was hastily thrown up in the backyard and I can tell you, Linda and I weren't too impressed with our new domicile.

Linda spent her days either reading or snogging with the middle son. He was a good-looking kid with a pleasant enough nature.

"You should marry him!" my mother encouraged her, never mind that my sister was only 16 at the time, or that her erudite brain spun and whirled whilst the middle B. boy's brain merely sort of blobbed about.

I spent most of my time up on the roof, preferring to hide out up there, or I'd steal a bottle of Mrs. B's gin, traipse down to the veld at the bottom of the street, and get blitzed out of my belfry. One time I staggered back to the tent and passed out only to have Mrs. B carry me to her room and - big yuck here - I awoke in her bed. Apparently she'd passed quite a bit of time with me in her bed?
How was I, Mrs. B? Did I "fit" you?

My mother spent her day spying on René. Who knows what she was hoping to accomplish, but she'd stride half way up the street then drop to all fours and crawl the remainder of the way…so that René couldn't see her. The rest of the neighborhood however, they *could* see her.

I walked along beside her once, just to piss her off.

"Get down, he'll see you!" She hissed at me.

"So what? He knows where we are."

"I don't want him to know we're watching him." She waved, frantically beckoning me to drop down.

"You look ridiculous, you know," I scoffed.

"Fuck off then, why don't you?" she gracefully retorted.

She was a mystery to me, swearing at me the one minute and hugging me tight the next, confusing me with her rollercoaster emotions.

Then there was her peculiar one-upmanship.

"How do you feel about what so and so did?" she'd ask.

"It upset me quite a bit," I'd answer, grateful for her concern.

"Phhf, that's nothing compared to what René did to me. The one time he beat me; cheated on me; embarrassed me; tried to kill me ...etcetera, etcetera."

She persistently trumped any feeling, thought, idea, or hurt that I expressed. Her experiences were always bigger, more painful, more meaningful and more dramatic, reducing my world to insignificant.

René and my mother soon smoothed things over, and hey presto…we were back in our own beds…not some old troll's. Shudder.

Claude greeted us at the front door. He'd recently watched a cheesy war movie, chock-full of violent torture entitled "Hell Camp." He smiled as he fed us the movie's tag line, "Where civilization ends and survival starts - welcome to Hell Camp…high five, sisters!"

Mrs. B didn't fair too well. She underwent brain surgery to have a bloody big tumor removed (okay, so it wasn't a gumma), and on her release from hospital, she downed a bottle of gin instantly. That pretty much did her in. I'm betting her boys were relieved to bury her.

CHAPTER 14 - Religion and Sex – oh no!

Craving validation in any format, I entered a local beauty contest, mailing in a photo and bio that read: "I love to water ski, horse ride and play badminton" like I'd actually done those things. Still, I was chosen to compete in the finals. High excitement except … it called for a dress. I had to wear a dress! I didn't own a dress and certainly nothing my sister wore could win me a beauty contest. My mother (not all bad) gave me R20 (twenty Rand) to purchase a new outfit. Unfortunately R20 didn't quite crack it. I brooded with a girlfriend from my high school, NV, who skillfully solved my predicament.

"Which dress do you like?" she asked, after I'd tried several on in a cramped cubicle of a popular clothing store.

I pointed to a plain, but well-fitting, lavender dress and NV promptly stuffed it in her school bag.

"Right. Let's go."

It was that easy.

Our crime induced "high" turned to shame and guilt as we ordered burgers, fries and cokes at the local Wimpy bar with my R20 dress money. Munching our way through greasy burgers, the idea struck us that we should go to church. Of course! God would forgive us and we could rest easy. We planned to attend the following Sunday, but NV lived far away and never made it to church. I however, was determined to go, especially now that I'd appropriated myself a whole new wardrobe, and these pilfered garments were intensifying the irksome compulsion to seek forgiveness.

Sunday arrived and I beelined to the nearest church, ready for arms to embrace me as if I were the prodigal son returning. Being a truly repentant sinner, I felt I was a worthy cause and imagined the church might want to slaughter a goat for me, or at least celebrate my inaugural visit. To my surprise and indignation, when I arrived at the church, smiling religion-imbued folk blocked me at the door.

"You must wear a hat to come inside," an overweight lady with a smug sense of self-righteousness (and a lovely hat) instructed me.

"I'm sure God won't mind if I don't wear a hat," I reasoned with her. "He'll be happy to know I'm here. I never come to church. This is a big step for me." (...and where exactly do you keep the goats?)

"You can't come in without a hat on. That's the rule." The lady crossed her arms, preparing to do battle for God's bonnet decree.

Anger welled in my chest. Had she not just heard me say this was a big step for me? Rome wasn't built in a day. Maybe if I liked the program, I'd come back the next week, and if I felt so inclined, maybe the following week, too. Perhaps I'd even steal a hat for myself the week after that.

The whole religion thing annoyed the heck out of me. Who seriously believes that God thinks you should wear a hat to church? (Or that you should lop off your foreskin for that matter, if you're Jewish?)

I wanted to scream at her jelly neck-fat, "God doesn't give a baboon's ass what you wear on your head. He cares about what's in your heart!"

God must have loved me a little, because I won that beauty contest. And my prize? A twenty Rand gift voucher to Papillion: the very same clothing store that had unwittingly supplied me my well-fitting, lavender dress.

With a look of amazed disbelief on my now "proven pretty" face, I was crowned Miss Teenager of Randburg. Accepting my award I sure didn't feel like a beauty queen. Would they take back my prize if they knew I was wearing a stolen dress? Would they decorate me with handcuffs instead of a sash and tiara? In retrospect, I should have been crowned: Miss Promiscuous, Alcoholic, Shop-lifting, Brimming with

Rage, Mighty Miserable Teenager of Randburg...but I guess that would've been a tad wordy.

So what do you do if you're a promiscuous, alcoholic, shoplifting, brimming with rage, mighty-miserable teenager? What do you do if your mother is unable to nurture, protect or love you? Well, in my case I decided to "na-na-na-na na-na...get my jiggy with it."

Sex granted me a semblance of affection. Sex awarded me, dinners, attention, flowers, compliments, dances, cards, chocolates, trinkets, a ride in a car, a night at the movies, a night in someone's bed! That was the prized one - my mini escape. For me alighting to a stranger's house and sleeping in their bed anticipated a night away from my own world. Fine by me! I'd go out, get drunk, hook up with some guy, stagger back to his place, screw and pass out. Drink, drink, drink...and now, adding on...fuck, fuck, fuck.

Interestingly enough, even though obliterated during these sex "mini-vacations", I could always recall where the bedroom door situated and which direction the stranger's bed faced. I guess a part of me remained instinctively on high alert just in case I needed to make a quick getaway. The names of these one-nighters elude me, and I can't picture their faces, but I can remember the layout of each and every bedroom I've ever slept in. Nifty huh?

Call me a slut. I'd have to agree. I was a drunken slut-whore-harlot and it helped me function...sure, and it also pained and stained my very core.

Diary Entry August 1979 (age 14)
Last night I had sex and blow jobs. Even writing this makes me feel sick to my stomach. I wish someone would say to me: "you're better than the rest - they do worse things than you". But no, Mummy says I'm a whore and I think I am too. I'll go with just about anybody. Still I don't care.

There came a week when I slept with a different hombre every night. Seven nights equaled seven men. That was a tad intense even for me. Quite frankly, being only fifteen at the time, it scared me. I realized my behavior wasn't *ganz normal* and I hastily set an appointment with a psychologist.

I'd already visited a number of "shrinks" for different reasons. There was the anorexia, a brief stint of family therapy (where we all ganged up on the unsuspecting therapist and reduced her to tears), and I'd been called upon by therapists who were treating my mother.

"She's bat-shit crazy!" I'd assure them.

"Would you care for a mint?" they'd smile at me.

My mother adored psychology. She lapped up the lingo and flung enough psychobabble about to manipulate her therapy sessions any which way she chose. Her enjoyment of psychoanalysis made me a hard sell on the idea. Still, my wildness had rattled me enough to surrender myself for an hour-long couch session.

The psychologist inquired after my sexual history.

"When did you first have sex?" He probed.

"If you count my granddad sticking his fingers in me, 9. If not, then 13."

"Where is your granddad now?"

"He's dead."

"Did you tell anyone about this abuse when you were 9?"

"Yes. I told my mother."

"What did she do about it?"

"She laughed."

He paused.

"It's not funny though, is it?" His tone softened.

"No it's not."

I didn't tell the psychologist the half of it. My mother had slept with the entire neighborhood herself. Like mother like daughter -

young, old, short, fat (even the eldest B. boy down the road who was utterly underage at the time…maybe that was my mother's payback to Mrs. B for dragging me to her bedroom). Adding to my mother's sexual conquests were her twelve car crashes, one attempted suicide, three rapes (one with a four year old watching - according to mama) and the capacity to cheat on her husband with such zest that she procured an apartment for her extra marital curriculum. Naturally she found it amusing that her father had molested me.

"He tried to rape me, too" she shared, laughing loudly.

Her world was like that.

One morning, when I entered my mother's bedroom to wake her in time to take Linda and me to school, I found her already awake. She was awake and sobbing, swaying back and forth on her hands and knees …buck-naked.

"I have a condom stuck inside me," she squalled, "I can't get it out and I don't remember who it's from. Help me get it out will you, Niksi?"

WHOA NELLY!

Did I help her? This is where I suffer the ultimate sensory overload…I can't recall a thing. That part I've blocked out - blocked out for good. To this day I have no memory of how that scenario played out. After all, who wants to remember wading their fingers about in their mother's vagina?

I do remember going to school, though, and surveying my classmates, wondering if they too had to retrieve used condoms from their mother's genetalia? Did they also have to beat their step-fathers into quivering Jell-o? Had they seen their mothers arrive home smeared in blood, crying that they had been raped? Had their grandfathers stuck fingers in their private parts? I thought it highly unlikely, and it made me hate them. Fuck them for living such happy lives. Fuck them for their unspoiled childhoods. Fuck them for having parents who could actually parent. Fuck!

I cancelled my next appointment with that psychologist. I felt it a downright waste of time. How was he going to help me fill the enormous void in my chest? No talking on a couch for an hour a week could do that. Not all the sex and alcohol in the world could do that. Nothing could do that.

The psychologist did assist me with one thing. I confided in him my fear of the dark. I told him how I lay awake at night, sweating and panicking, imagining people breathing outside my windows. I explained how I could actually hear them breathing and *knew* they were coming to get me. The breathing stretched on for hours, like these people had nothing better to do than linger outside my windows inhaling and exhaling. Oh, and these weren't the throat slitters, these were simply large-lunged-loiterers drawn to my window.

"Try leaving a light on," the psychologist recommended.

Well bugger me backwards with a big, blunt object! I'd honestly never thought of that. Talk about shedding light on a problem. From that day forward, I slept with a small nightlight on to ward off all the heavy-breathers.

CHAPTER 15 – Neighborly love

9 June Ave, Bordeaux, Randburg, Johannesburg, and yes, I can freely publicize that address because the place no longer exists. *Hell Camp* was buried – as true as Bob! Towards the end of our ten years there, a work crew excavated a huge hole in the ground, razed our house flat, bulldozed it in and smartly covered it with dirt. I found it an appropriate ending to that miserable place. Bury that woe-begotten bastard…bury it good and proper. The house burial echoed my own teen-hood which I myself aspired to bury deep, hoping that all the ugliness that occurred there, would somehow simply vanish!

It was at *Hell Camp* that my mother had her encounter with the raping army guys, and I had my encounter with C.H's purple ice cream. It was at Hell Camp that my mother asked me to "Go Fish" in her vagina, and I started drowning myself in bottles of Fire Water (lethal hooch deceivingly presented in shampoo bottles). It was at *Hell Camp* that I developed my uncivilized coping skills of drinking, smoking, screwing, stealing, bunking, lying…you get the picture. *Hell Camp* was hell.

The boy next door became my savior, my escape, my entire world. Mike R. I loved him with the unmatched intensity reserved for youth. We were inseparable.

At 17, Mike already carried a three-year suspended sentence for stealing six cars and two motorbikes. He smoked Camels and zol (pot), drank quite splendidly, stole car radios on a weekly basis (usually siphoning the gas tank dry for good measure) and found himself endlessly in trouble with the law. I adored him!

Much to my mother's disgust, and my pleasure, the police escorted Mike and me home on several occasions. We were persistently in deep dwang, together emulating a mini "Bonnie and Clyde" team. We broke into a cinema, happily ransacking their candy supply. We broke into a bank, even more happily ransacking their booze supply (they must have recently thrown an office party). I nabbed various rubber bank stamps to emboss my forehead: Barclays Bank -Thank you.

Mike taught me to bunk school. Once I got the hang of it, I bunked school whenever humanly possible, because as you know, school sucked big, stinky ass. I ditched school, choosing to spend the mornings in downtown Jo'burg instead, shooting pool with my shoplifting gal-pal N.V. Thereafter we'd catch the bus home, in our uniforms, acting the sweet high school innocents. One afternoon, having vanquished my bus fare at the pool tables, I decided to hitch a ride home (having learnt nothing from my mother's hitchhiking lessons), and - oh rotten luck - the vice headmaster of my school stopped to offer me a ride. He recognized straight away that I was a student from his school and asked why I hadn't attended school that day. I lied (no - say it isn't so) and told him I'd been at a doctor's appointment in the city.

The vice head, not a complete ignoramus, demanded that I bring a doctor's note with me to school the following day. Arriving home, I rushed next door to Mike to sob out my dilemma. I was already in trouble at school for wearing the wrong school shoes (no - say it isn't so again) and for repeatedly missing school. Mike solved my problem with his usual unruly aplomb. That night he broke into a doctor's office, stole the doc's prescription pad and wrote me a very legitimate looking note, politely excusing my absence from school for the previous day. My hero.

My hero further suggested I learn my mother's signature in order to withdraw money from her bank account. I studied her scrawled signature, scribbled a few practice shots, then signed a check, and abracadabra, the forgery worked like a charm. While withdrawing R30 from her account, my conscience turned on me.

"Hang on. Don't steal from her - she has nothing to steal."

My conscience was right. Her signature proved far handier in writing notes to excuse myself from whichever horrific school event I wished to avoid, be it physical training, religious instruction, youth preparedness or the whole bunch of them.

With no money and no car (not even a stolen one), Mike and I defaulted to hitchhiking, sometimes traveling as far as Durban (600 km away) purely for a weekend. All types of freaks stopped to pick us up, but we were young, dumb and presumed ourselves to be unassailable. Plus, we'd devised a crafty precaution. Mike customarily slid into the backseat and positioned himself behind the driver, then twisted a cord of wire around his fingers - all set to garrote the freakoid if any funny business happened.

We were uncontrollable teens: stealing, drinking, smoking, running away, playing truant, lying and cheating, feeding off each other. US against the world.

Then schooling ended for Mike. At seventeen, he found himself drafted directly into the SADF, the South African Defense Force. Here, he had to complete two years of compulsory military service. In South Africa, all white males were forced into the army, and during the 80's, the majority of them were sent to join "the Border War". Sure, you could object and spend up to six years in military prison if you preferred. It was shrewd of the SADF to grab these young boys (not men) straight out of high school so they could pummel their heads full of propaganda against the "Swaart Gevaar" (the black danger). The danger being that these Blacks were Reds...as in Communists.

Loads of stories seeped through the apartheid government's "non-information" system (no freedom of press here, people). Stories of unwarranted violence, stories of conscripts going completely *bos befok* (bush berserk). One guy relayed how when six puppies wandered into their camp, they'd cut off their ears and tails as a joke. Possibly little bleeding dogs do provide comic relief when you have to witness your friends being blown to bits on a daily basis?

The Border War – the border between sanity and insanity.

How was Mike going to deal with this military madness? With his rebellious character, how was he going to knuckle under and follow orders? Orders to load up his R4 assault rifle, pull the trigger, and send bullets ripping through a supposed black-red? Hmmm?

And, after two years of spending almost every second together, it was unbearable for us to be apart. Stationed in Potchefstroom, Mike was now a three-hour drive from our homes. Way too far.

I missed him badly, sadly and madly…but in my usual style, life moved on. My 16th birthday rolled around and my mother invited me to a steak dinner at Mike's Kitchen, not to remind me of Mike, but because Mike's Kitchen (a chain of family steakhouses), was walking distance from our house. She ordered filet mignon and champagne for the both of us. Under age drinking wasn't a big deal in SA, thus no one voiced concern that I was pounding champagne at my 16th birthday celebration.

A table of guys plunked down next to us, and my mother quickly engaged them in conversation.

"Have some champagne," she offered.

They accepted, and before long, they purchased another bottle of champers…and then another, until we raucously reached the end of our welcome at Mike's Kitchen.

"Come back to our house and we'll open more wine!" My mother smiled invitingly at the three guys. Again they accepted. By this time I was way loaded. My head grew heavy and my sight grew dim, I had to stop for the night (yes – thank you, Mr. Henley.) I struggled to focus and walk upright.

Arriving back at *Hell Camp*, I headed straight (well, probably not that straight) for my bed. With the world spinning, I was done. No more happy juice for me.

I lay in bed, gripped by nausea, wondering what Mike was doing, and praying I wouldn't throw up. Without warning, someone clambered into bed with me; one of the guys from the restaurant, and he promptly began to feel me up and down. With my back towards him, I found it impossible to move without the universe whirling.

"I'm going to be sick," I warned him. "Leave me alone."
Noli me tangere – dude!

"Ah, come on baby," he crooned, sliding his hand under my top to grope at my breasts.

I swear I didn't do it on purpose. I couldn't help myself. I rolled over to graciously implore him to get the "F" out of my bed and the rotating movement must have churned up my alcohol soaked organs. Vomit flew from my mouth, spraying that guy. He hopped out my bed primo-pronto.

So there I sprawled in my own upchuck, unable to muster the will to move, and missing Mike desperately. Within minutes another guy from the restaurant emerged in my room.

"Sweet Jesus," I thought. "Here we go again."

This guy was older than the last one, which meant he was probably all of 23. He searched my closet for fresh pajamas then helped me to the shower. He stripped me, showered me, towel dried me, and kindly redressed me in clean clothes. Finally, he ushered me to my mother's bed, tucked me in, and switched the light off.

"You'll be okay," he promised.

Grateful for his help, I thanked him profusely, over and over... although my appreciation probably sounded more like a congested warthog, my communication skills having dwindled to grunting.

Queasy and uneasy, I lay wondering what the hell my mother was doing? Why hadn't *she* come to help me? Why hadn't she tucked me into a fresh bed and reassured me that I was going to be okay? What the hell was she doing? Was she performing the "fandango" with one of those guys right now? In our living room? Presented with this thought, my stomach lurched anew and I retched again, miserably fouling my mother's bed with spew as well. Happy birthday to me.

CHAPTER 16 – Through the Smashing Glass

On his end, Mike wasn't fairing much better. He'd survived his basic training; a training aimed at physically breaking you down to the extent that you'd do and believe anything told to you. This didn't work to well on Mike, who didn't believe anything any of them told him. Instead he offered the SADF his middle finger and went AWOL.

When the Military police arrived to question me about Mike, I stared at them defiantly, refusing to answer any questions. To demonstrate my displeasure with their ridiculous military operations, I threw a Rubik's cube at them, which proved highly ineffective. It merely smashed to pieces on the ground. I hated the South African Army for taking my *Morkel* away from me. I was lost without him.

Mike hid out in the veld at the bottom of our street, the same place where I'd steeped myself in Mrs. B's gin. I joyfully pilfered food and blankets for him. Hooray! Mike was back. Everything was going to be okay. And everything *was* okay, for roughly five days. Then it became painfully clear that this was no solution. Mike needed to shower, to shave, to have a bed…to have a life! Living in the grass just wasn't enough. Who'd have thunk it?

Mike solved his problems the same way I solved mine. He drank! When he staggered to my bedroom window late one night, reeking of alcohol, demanding that I open the front door for him, I knew better than to grant him access to me. I stayed safely in my bed and endeavored to talk him down through my side window. There were security bars on the window (as were on most windows in South Africa), but the window was slightly ajar, wide enough for us to converse through the slit.

"Go sleep it off in the veld," I recommended. "I'll come and talk to you tomorrow morning."

"You're not going to let me in?" he slurred.

"I don't think it's a good idea."

"If you don't let me in, I'll smash all your windows." He swayed slightly as he belched out his warning.

Yeah, whatever. I didn't believe him.

"I'm not opening the door for you, Mike. Be my guest...smash away."

Mike stepped back, paced to and fro, then turned away. I relaxed. Thank God he was leaving. Ah...wait, no, he wasn't leaving. Instead he suddenly rocketed forward and punched his fist WHAMO through the center of my window; straight into my incredulous face. As the glass shattered around me, I instinctively yanked the blankets up over my head for protection. I heard him yell something incomprehensible as he lobbed a stray wooden crate clear through the largest of my windows. Glass exploded in all directions, jolting me to action. I leapt from my bed and crunched my way over a sea of shrapnel, oblivious to the shards sinking into my feet. My focus was on getting the hell out of that room. I fumbled to my room door but my hands trembled so hard I couldn't unlock it. I swung around in time to see a savage look of hatred twisted on Mike's face as he prepared to punch out the last, remaining window.

CRASH!

Glass showered towards me, splaying into slow motion. I stood transfixed as the glass glittered into a fairytale of splinters and sparkles, cascading beautifully through the air. Then, as shards of glass sliced into my skin, I dove headlong into my closet to bury myself deep beneath my dirty laundry.

The shattering glass roused the neighborhood, and as lights flicked on, Mike ran off. Shivering in my closet, I heard a timid knocking on my door.

"Niksi? Are you okay?" my mother whispered through the keyhole.

Never have I been quite so glad to hear my mother's voice. I scrambled out from under my whiffy washing heap, unbolted the door and toppled into the hallway. My mother, not the best in a crisis, took one look at my blood-soaked nightie, said, "I feel woozy" and fainted.

"Get up, mother, I need you….oh hell, on second thoughts, don't bother."

I didn't need her. I went through to the living room to eek out comfort elsewhere. A young guy was staying with us at the time, Gary. L.

Needless to say I'd already slept with him, cheating on Michael in order to secure the trump card…my tramp-trump card.

Tweezers in hand, Gary cautiously dislodged glass slivers from my back, and assured me that he'd unleash a comprehensive ass whooping on Mike at their next meeting. Freshly released from prison, Gary had had nowhere to stay and René had kindly offered him a job…and our living room couch. After picking me clean, Gary lifted his own shirt to reveal several unsightly holes in his chest where *crabs* had eaten into him.

"From the prison blankets," he enlightened me.

René phoned the police, and soon the house was a flurry of activity. The police requested a photo of Mike, which I grudgingly surrendered to them. They didn't need a photo to capture Mike. A dithering idiot could have deciphered which way Mike had fled since his blood trailed over the garden wall and up the street. The police apprehended him a few hours later with a soggy, blood-soaked T-shirt wrapped around his virtually severed arm. One hundred and thirty three surgical stitches later, Mike was handed over to the military police, who promptly locked him in the detention barracks. At first Mike was cocky, loudly telling the MPs in no uncertain terms, where they could "shove their shorn heads".

They responded by chaining his arms above his own shorn head to leave him hanging for several hours. This pendulous punishment swung Mike's "*cocky*" to "*meek*", and at length, buckled him all the way to a complete nervous breakdown. Within three months, his constant crying and inability to function procured him a dishonorable discharge from the South African Army. His parents furtively bundled him off to a destination unknown to me. And they kept it that way. No matter how much I begged and pleaded to know where he was, no matter how much I begged and pleaded permission to contact him, his parents stayed stumm.

Yes, those are *the* windows behind Mike.

CHAPTER 17 – Sisterly love squelches a vial of ills

Not long after Mike's banishment, came my mother's suicide attempt. I should have guessed something was up given that she'd scribbled several suicide notes a few days previously…that's really a total giveaway isn't it? Linda and Claude each received a half page of sentimental ramblings whereas I prompted four pages. Golden child remember? Four pages expressing how much she revered us, loved us, doted on us, *lived* for us…hang on…I call oxymoron.

Due to a shortage of toilet paper in my bathroom, I'd drifted through to my mother's bedroom in hopes of scavenging spare loo paper from her bathroom en suite. Her bedroom was in disarray, clothes strewn everywhere and she, face down on the bed amidst the explosion. It wasn't unusual to find her sleeping midday, but the room was torn apart.

"Is this you packing?" I sneered, knowing full well that she was leaving for Germany to attend her father's funeral - the old bastard having finally succumbed to leukemia…yes-aah!

My mother stared in confusion.

"I swallowed these," she finally rasped in a wooly voice, pointing at an empty pill bottle.

I had a friend over at *Hell Camp* that day. Darryl A. We were rehearsing for our newly formed duo - "The Whizz Kids". We'd received some piddling news coverage and were playing at various Civic theatres. Undeniably whizzy stuff. Fortunately, Darryl was also studying to be a doctor.

I handed him the empty vial. "What do you think?" I asked.

"I think we need an ambulance," he determined.

The ambulance arrived within minutes. Paramedics rushed in, hauling a gurney with them on which they tried unsuccessfully to make my mother lie. There was no way my mother would agree to lie down on *that thing or any other thing*. She was quite happy, thank you very much, and they could all bugger off. On second thoughts, would they care to hear her sing a German folk song? She blabbered away, stoned as Keith Richards.

The paramedics ended up ushering my unsteady mother on foot to the ambulance and as they loaded her in, they asked if I wished to ride along with them.

"I have to pick my brother up from school." I haughtily proclaimed, which was true. Who would fetch Claude if I rode with my "can't even kill herself properly" mother?

"And besides...I'm rehearsing. I'm part of the Whizz Kids."

Somehow I don't think the paramedics fully appreciated the importance of my rehearsal.

The death of her tyrannical father was impacting my mother. His funeral loomed as a grim obligation wherein she was duty bound to console her mother, who was devastated over the death of her beloved *Hans*. My mother foresaw it to be just another slap in the face. She knew what she could expect from her mother:

I preferred my husband to you – slap.

Always did – slap.

He was my everything – slap

Hans, Hans, Hans! – slap, slap, slap.

I don't care if he did molest you – oh ssss-lap.

Or your daughter – slappity-slap.

As an adult, I can grasp the lengths that my mother was prepared to go to in order to avoid his funeral, but since I was yet a teen, I wanted a mother who wouldn't scoff down pills to avoid unpleasant situations. I needed a mother who thought me, and my siblings, were possibly worth staying alive for. I needed a mother to provide at least a vague level-headedness and a smidgeon of maternal instinct. Yes sir that would have been real nice. But I'd been born to a woman who dispensed enough melodrama to fill a channel of daytime soap operas; a woman who whipped up such fabulous attention seeking behaviors that she made Courtney Love appear well-adjusted…wait that's an exaggeration. No one can make Courtney look well adjusted. (Francis Bean, you have my full sympathy.)

Fainting was one of my mother's favorite attention grabbers. At length I steeled immune to her pale-faced passing out. Past the millionth swooning, my patience rubbed thin. Hearing her timid knock-knock on my door, I knew if I ignored her and refused to open my door…THUD…she'd collapse right outside. I wouldn't even bother to poke my head out.

René once retuned from the bush sporting two black eyes and a swollen nose. He'd done a spot of drunk driving, and run two guys off the road. They, in turn, threw away his keys and beat him senseless. At the same point in time, as if their faces were synchronized for-a-battering, my mother had one of her fainting spells and nosedived into the refrigerator. She connected with the massive fridge handle and, two black eyes and a swollen nose later, what a gosh-darn cute couple they made.

Fainting wasn't my mother's only ploy to secure the spotlight. If being sick got her that attention, fine! Her doctor consultations ran into the hundreds. If sleeping with the neighborhood got her that attention, terrific! Her sex partners strew the pathway. If crashing her car got her that attention, no problem! Twelve cars wrecked and counting! Anything and everything was fair game…but sadly, it was never enough. Try as she might, my mother could not placate the vast need inside her, the hungry hole that demanded constant feeding. That saying, "give a finger, they want a hand; give a hand, they want an arm; give an arm, they want all your limbs; and then eventually your first born", well, that saying was dead on for my mother. Like Bill Murray's character in "What about Bob?" my mother was pure, "Give me, give me. I need. I need."

Linda and I visited her in hospital on the eve of her suicide attempt. With a freshly pumped stomach, and for some odd reason, her toe tagged, she motioned us to draw near. "I'm in the fourth stage of death," she whispered, "but it is okay. I'm relaxed. See? They've already tagged my toe...for when I die."

And the odd thing is: a wave of panic hit me. Yeah sure, I'd wished her dead, but hearing her sluggish voice, inhaling her fetid breath, clasping her puffy hands; it proved a touch too real for me. I mean how many young girls really want their mother's to die?

I bolted into the hallway and accosted the first doctor I came upon, grabbing fistfuls of his white jacket front.

"Tell me the truth," I shouted at him, yanking on his medical mantle. "Is she going to die?"

"The patient in room 24?" He squinted at me, gently prying himself loose.

I nodded, swallowing hard, expecting to hear she'd be dead by morning.

"She's going to be fine. Luckily she got here just in time."

Hmm...I guess my toilet paper requirements may have saved my mother's life.

Turns out, my mother wasn't in the fourth stage of death, she was merely in the continuing stage of zonked. Once I returned to her bedside, she geared up with her death chat again.

"Shut up!" Linda snapped at her. "Can't you see you're scaring Nicola!"

Huh? Wait - what was that? An unfamiliar sensation clenched my chest. Someone was protecting *me*; someone was worrying about *my* welfare. I stared at my sister, mouth hanging open, feeling a weighty sense of gratitude.

CHAPTER 18 - Boemsie

Linda and I did **not** get along as children. In primary school, I was "little miss popular" while Linda was the nerdy bookworm. I was invited to all kinds of parties, while she was to none. My mother even tried to coax me into trailing my sister along to my shindigs.

"I'd rather stick razors blades up my nose, thank you!" I'd boldly inform her.

Not that Linda had any desire to attend any of my *stupid parties* anyway. She preferred to stay in her room, with the door firmly locked, reading and reading; reading her way into saner households for a start. Even on New Year's Eve, whilst we enjoyed a celebratory soirée out on our patio, Linda refused to leave her room, spurning our *pathetic* count down to midnight, opting instead for a satisfying blubbering session with George Eliot's "Mill on the Floss".
It pissed my mother off something fierce.

As kids, Linda and I fought incessantly. I hurled my clogs in her face; she shoved my head inside the washing machine. We slapped each other, pinched each other, punched each other, pulled each other's hair, stole each other's clothes, and broke each other's belongings. We niggled at each other relentlessly and without mercy.

Lying on my back one night, I kicked against her locked door with both my stubby legs, begging her to let me in. I was scared (as usual) because our parents were out (as usual), and I created such a screaming fuss that she finally flung the door open to drag me down the hallway by my hair.

Her screeching: "Shut up! SHUT UP!"

Me screeching: "I won't! I WON'T!"

In high school, Linda ratted me out every time I ditched school – in retaliation, I open mouth kissed her boyfriends. We reminded each other with heartfelt regularity: "I HATE YOU!"

Still, it was my sister who, at age 12, advised me not to climb in bed with my grandfather anymore. It was my sister who scaled a sheer rock-face to rescue me when I lay trapped on the ledge of a waterfall. It was my sister who patiently taught me mathematics so I wouldn't fail the year. It was my sister and I who dressed up in funny clothes, painted our faces and staged plays; my sister and I who lay in the dark listening to "Scary Tales" on the radio; my sister and I who crept under the table when a Scotsman came to dinner, curious to see if he wore skivvies under his Kilt.

It was my sister who woke me at 5 AM and spread a blanket outside for us to laze on and watch the sunrise while eating plutchs (a hybrid of plums and peaches that ripened on a tree in our garden).

It was my sister I found crying in the school bathroom after some girls had teased her for having dandruff and fat legs, and though she was my archenemy at the time, I longed to kill those bitches.

It was my sister who later gave me a place to stay in England; my sister who helped me through my various meltdowns; my sister to whom I placed late night phone calls for advice. It was, and is, my wonderful sister, who has remained staunchly at my side and has never, ever let me down.

I wasn't quite as supportive. I remember one afternoon, Linda and I noticed a rumpus out in the street. Two black guys were manhandling a third, and as they jostled their victim past *Hell Camp*, he broke free and flung himself towards our patterned garden wall. Gripping his dark hands around the palm leaf mold, he clung on desperately. Undeterred, his captures kicked furiously at his hands. Blood splayed from his knuckles as he shrieked in pain, while Linda and I stood rooted to the spot, staring in horror through our glass sliding door. The man must have sensed us staring at him because suddenly he looked up, and stared right back at us.

Oh Shit!

Releasing his death grip, the prisoner somehow managed to elude his captures and rushed to our sliding door, and tugged violently on the handle.

"Let me in!" he begged

Linda and I were terror-stricken. We certainly didn't want the bleeding man in our house, or the incredibly threatening, geared-to-kill men racing up behind him. Slamming our full body weight against the sliding door, to keep it securely shut, we screamed loudly. He was screaming loudly too. Then silly me let go the door to race out back to enlist our maid's help. My panic was such that I didn't realize I was deserting my sister, leaving her to single-handedly prevent the sliding door from skimming open; leaving her utterly defenseless.

The maid's *kaya* (the maid's quarters) was deserted and I flew back to Linda's side in time to see the two men haul our bleeding man away. He was crying and begging for mercy...which we all knew he wasn't going to find.

Within a few minutes a neighbor scuttled over to peer at us through the sliding door.

"If you girls ever need anything," he shouted through the glass, "just scream."

Well, either that neighbor was totally deaf, or he enjoyed a warped sense of humor.

Linda flopped down on the couch, quiet and pale.

"You're such a chicken shit." She reproached me. "How could you run away and leave me?"

I started sobbing. I don't think she believed me when I explained I was attempting to recruit reinforcements. Sorry, Linny. If there was any way to have a do-over, I'd stay firmly put at your side.

And a quick side note: for some baffling reason, my sister and I nicknamed each other "Boemsie". Boemsie was the polite word we substituted for "fart" when we were kids. Why we chose this word to name each other is a mystery.

"Did you boemsie, Boemsie?"

A complete mystery indeed.

Consequently we are: Boemsie and Boemsie, but only to each other. No one else calls us by this name…no, don't you try it.

Boemsie and Boemsie with René's infamous beige undies on our heads!

CHAPTER 19 – Christina

Our mother was relegated to the mental ward of J.G Strydom hospital for the next two months. Initially, her doctor (who, according to Boemsie, our mother was having an affair with) had recommended Sterkfontein Mental Home, a total nuthouse for the criminally insane. My mother was somewhat half-baked, imagining her body to be riddled with tumors, and suspecting everyone of lying to her and poking fun at her impending death...okay, so not sane, but not whack job, psychotic-break crazy like a Jeffrey Dahmer.

René stayed clear of the whole messy business, working in his cherished "escape-clause" bush, leaving Linda, Claude and me to pretty much fend for ourselves. It turned out that Claude, though only 10 at the time, was a fine cook. He prepared us pancakes and omelets, happily placing himself in charge of the kitchen. Our maid, Christina, who had been employed with us for several years, began spending more time with us. Her usual job of cleaning up after us widened to include befriending us. We were motherless and fatherless; Christina stepped in to comfort us.

I'd never given much consideration to the person who retrieved my carelessly discarded, dirty clothes from the floor and made them miraculously reappear back in my closet - washed, ironed and neatly folded. The person, who silently dusted, swept, mopped, polished, wiped and washed, keeping the house spotless. The person who forfeited being with her own children in order to earn enough money to support them. The person who hid her hair under a *doekie,* and wore a maid's uniform day in and day out. Until now, I'd been as oblivious to Christina as I'd been to all our previous maids. Most every white household in Johannesburg employed a black maid. And we were poor, so I can only imagine what small pittance Christina earned. We continuously had maids and I continuously took them for granted. I further took for granted the freedom I enjoyed, a freedom that neither Christina, nor any of our previous maids were able to enjoy. Every black person in South Africa had to carry a *Pass*: a form of identity that specified their racial group…Black, Indian, or Colored. They had to carry it at all times, because failure to produce said pass could result in immediate detainment...and detainment could last a few months, no questions asked. Imagine, I'm popping into the corner café and whoopsie, I'm in prison for 6 months, wrong jacket pocket, dammit.

None of this impacted me. I was a shiny white teenager, and besides, *Hell Camp* consumed my entire brain capacity. Political affairs meant nothing to me, nor did Christina's hardships. I was oblivious to anything, save my own survival.

Christina had lived with us for three years before I ever stepped foot in her room. I realized I had no idea what it looked like inside her *Kaya* as I knocked on her corrugated iron door.

"Christina? May I come in?" I pleaded. I was sixteen and those nightmares of having my throat hacked open had inundated me.

Christina opened the door and invited me in.

Bare walls flickered in the paraffin lamplight. Her tiny room was sparser than a jail cell. And hoisted about 4 feet in the air, was a single bed, balancing precariously on cement blocks.

"Why do you have your bed up so high?" I was curious.

"You don't know the Tokoloshi man?" she frowned at me.

"Nope. Never met him."

"Oh no. You don't want to meet him. He is evil and hairy, and he will come in the night to nookie with you because he has a very big one."

I had to think about that for a moment. Clearly I'd had hairy, big ones come to nookie with me at night a number of times. Maybe I did know this Tokoloshi fellow?

"And he can't get you if your bed is up high?" I deduced.

"Yes. He is also very short, like a monkey…Come!" She patted the bed next to her. "Come sit".

Not only was Christina scared of the Tokoloshi man (who happily nookied you, then caused you illness and death), she was furthermore petrified of chameleons, believing that chameleons were Satan in disguise (a little, leathery, lizard Satan who was capable of changing his appearance to bamboozle mankind). While cleaning windows, rubbing at the panes atop a small stepladder, Christina spied a chameleon on the ledge next to her…and simply fainted. (What's with the fainting people?) She crashed backwards off the stepladder and thudded to the cement ground in our courtyard. Funny how what you believe affects you isn't it? In Christina's culture, witchdoctors were called on to cure aliments and to root out those who were lying, stealing or cheating. And if the witchdoctor put a death curse on someone, chances are they'd be dead in a few weeks, simply because they believed it to be so. Such is the power of the mind.

Over the orphaned weeks, a closeness developed between Christina and me. I camped out on the counter tops, while she mopped the kitchen floor. The window granted us a view of the street, allowing us to appraise the passersby as they came and went. Christina filled me in on "who was who" in the barrio.

"That one is a black bitch." Christina nodded towards a pretty African woman.

"Why?" I laughed.

"Look how beautiful she is. I have to call her that."

The pretty lady came closer, then waved happily at us. Christina yelled joyfully out to her:

"Evie, you black bitch. Come in here!" And the two women broke out in peals of laughter.

I got a kick out of hanging with Evie and Christina. They were gossipmongers, guffawing and giggling as they tittle-tattled tidbits of juicy information. They had the low down on "the hood". And most importantly, since I was too young, they were happy to oblige me and buy *Old Brown Sherry* from the bottle store, as long as I paid for a bottle of beer for them too.

Christina began to feel at home in our house. Soon Evie and she were relaxing on the couches during the week, feet up, watching TV, sharing their laughter, stories and companionship with me.

On the weekends, René, Linda and I visited my mother in the loony bin. Claude stayed home with Christina as he still didn't know exactly what had transpired. He knew our mother wasn't well, but that was nothing new in our household. On our first visit, Linda bought our mother a slab of Swiss chocolate complete with liquor-filled centers, while René bought her, her favorite Juvena skincare lotions. I bought her nothing...*nichts*. I felt no urge to reward her for trying to off herself. One bite into her expensive Swiss chocolate, my mother spat it out.

"Uugh!" I believe were her exact words.

I saw a look of hurt flash over Linda's face. I was glad that I had brought her nothing. Maybe I'd bring her some razor blades next visit, help her get the job done properly.

There were several beds in the room and a young, twenty-something girl occupied the one alongside my mother's.

"You and Linda should take her ice-skating," my mother suggested, thumbing her neighbor's sleeping form. "She's a lovely girl."

Linda and I exchanged dubious looks.

"Why is she in here then?" I asked.

My mother lowered her voice.

"She pitches fits every now and then. It's quite disturbing really. She shoves her head under that steel bar at the bottom of her bed and then bangs up against it, again and again. I had to call for help last time she did that."

"Wow, I can hardly wait to take her skating." I smiled sardonically at my mother. "I could always bash her over the head with a pair of skates a few times, if she starts feeling out of sorts."

It irked me that my mother was so keen to unleash crazy onto Linda and me, be it her own or someone else's. And it really, really bugged me that she thought this girl next to her was so lovely. Linda and I were lovely, and we didn't need to clobber our own heads to prove it. Why didn't she recommend that someone take us ice-skating? She had a flair for complimenting other people...but never us. We were each assigned a compliment early on in our lives, where after we had to hear them ad infinitum. Linda was the clever one, Niki was the pretty one, and Claude had the best bottom in the family. I can't tell you how many times I heard that growing up. It sunk in, too. My school reports were atrocious, because first, I hardly ever attended school and second, I reckoned that, that was my clever sister's department. My job was to smile at every boy in sight, which I managed to do quite well and then some. I guess Claude faired the worst. Who wants the best bottom? That's not even a compliment really. It's more of an insult, especially if you're moderately overweight and don't want any attention aimed at your rear end.

Two months later, they released my mother from the hospital and she returned home to find a new lady of the house. There was Christina laughing and joking with *her* children, sitting with them at *her* dinner table, patting them on the shoulders, rubbing their backs. Jealousy flooded my mother (further fueled by rumors of René having slept with Christina. True or false, we'll never know.) Whatever the case, Mommykins picked up a tennis racket and chased Christina out into the front yard, managing to get close enough to whack her over the head with it, which knocked Christina's *doekie* clear of her head.

What a palaver! The neighbors gaped as the screaming white woman chased her equally screaming black maid about the lawn. I wondered what they thought of *Hell Camp* with its relentless domiciliary disturbances. Let them gape, I figured. They had their own dirty laundry hanging high. The kid next door received beatings with religious regularity. Poor guy wasn't allowed to do jack-shit. The woman down the road dragooned her daughters, forcing them to kneel in the front yard while she administered a beating with a solid wood plank. She had caught her daughters shoplifting (hone your skills, girls) and their desolate screams carried eight houses over. Then there was Mrs. B. who, when fully loaded, trotted about in a flimsy negligee, screeching about fishing poles and penguins. Maybe the entire neighborhood was insane?

The racket brandishing to-do was the last I saw of Christina. She vacated the premises the same day and I never even got a chance to say goodbye to her. This only served to quadruple the level of loathing I directed at my mother.

CHAPTER 20 – Cancer Scares

With the suicide fresh in our minds, we tiptoed on eggshells, whilst our mother brandished her newly discovered weapon. We sat silently as she eagerly threatened her next death attempt. Even her popular fainting technique took a back seat to these calculated suicide threats. And sensing she'd come close to losing us to Christina, she renewed her efforts to reel us in tight. It was simple:

"I love you so much. If you don't love me, I'll kill myself. Hey! Wanna play some Ping Pong?"

Claude escaped to his best friend's home, scarcely stepping foot in *Hell Camp*. In fact, within a few months, his best friend's family showed up on our doorstep to ask René if they might adopt Claude …bit of a shocker for René who had managed to remain delightfully oblivious to our plight. This adoption request saw René sticking closer to home for a spell.

Swell! Now both my mother and René were back in the home fulltime, kicking up their heels. The *sturm und drang* amplified until I could no longer stand it. I'd had enough. I was fed up. (Again for my South African peeps – *gat vol*)

I was 16, and it was high time to move out. I was done with school, too, not that I attended very often, and then when I did, they'd suspend me for not attending and threaten me with reform school. Plus, I was pretty much failing all my classes. Geography, history and math were of little help in my world - no, I don't know when Napoleon was born, but I can placate a drunk stepfather and rouse a depressed mother. I knew how to survive *Hell Camp* and that should've earned me an A+.

I told my mother I'd be leaving home, and in her customary dramatic style, she flipped out.

"Who needs pots and pans?" she bellowed as she hurled crockery about the kitchen, smashing plates to the floor. "I have no family left to cook for."

Well, there's still Linda, Claude and René.

Her theatrical response to my intention to move out hindered me *nichts*. I moved out anyway. I moved all the way from Johannesburg to Cape Town. I didn't need a family. I didn't need anyone.

I imagined this would be awesome. I could drink on the beaches, I could drink in the mountains, I could drink in the forests. Hell yeah! I was ready to triumph over the whole goddamn miserable world - without mumsy. I rented a room in a boarding house in Muizenberg, right on the beach, yet somehow Cape Town wasn't far enough away to offer me relief from my mother. I noticed a relentless, nagging guilt frothing away inside. Beneath my bravado, I was yet hooked to my floundering founder.

My clogs came in handy again - this time to wedge an upside-down iron in place so I could use it as a stovetop to warm up a can of spaghetti. And note the potty under the bed - living the high life in Cape Town, I tell ya.

Three months in, my mother phoned to report she was dying of cancer. Crying heavily, she said she had only a few months left to live.

"Please, Niksi darling, please come home right now."

And naturally, stupid sucker me, I did.

On finding me back home, my mother stared at me in confusion.

"What are *you* doing here?" she asked, apparently unaware of her hysterical phone call.

I was at a loss. Did she or did she not have bloody cancer? I should have been used to her fishy ailment alerts by now. According to my mother, she'd had a smattering of nearly every disease known to mankind. Years ago, she'd pulled Claude aside to say, "Look, I don't like to tell my children this, but…your mother is dying."

I don't think Claude was too worried.

I phoned her doctor who assured me that my mother was completely cancer free. Fit enough, in fact, to go out and find a job. Now bear in mind that this was the same doctor she was sleeping with, and the same doctor who prescribed her Valium and Obex as if they were jelly tots. The Valium helped her sleep and the Obex (an amphetamine prescribed for weight loss) revved her up. What escaped the attention of this fine physician was that my mother's thyroid gland wasn't functioning at normal levels, and it may well have been his fault because an overuse of Obex can lead to hyperthyroidism. It required a plethora of doctors to figure that out, and by the time they did, my mother's mal-operating thyroid and undiagnosed mental state had reigned supreme for a good many years, making life miserable for all of us.

At nineteen, I had my own mini adventure with cancer. Following a routine pap test at a campus clinic, my results incited a flap. Rushing to find me, the campus staff offered to drive me to the hospital immediately to have my abnormal cervical cells taken care off. Their urgency (although appreciated) scared the crap out of me. A nice lady drove me to the Johannesburg General hospital and within minutes I was in a chair with my feet hooked in stirrups. The doctor explained how he was going to burn away several inches of my cervix where cancer cells had begun to cultivate. As he spoke, he fastened a pair of plastic goggles over my eyes to offer protection from the laser.

"How big is this beam going to be?" I wondered.
Judging by the size of the injection the doc whipped out - ginormous! The needle measured roughly the length of my forearm.

Owwww! Come on.

"You won't feel a thing," he assured me, noting my eyes widen in fear.

After administering the monster syringe, he began burning away parts of my innards. As promised, I didn't feel a thing, but the smell was another story.

"That's my flesh burning," I realized with nausea rising.

Once the procedure was over I stood up to leave, and lo and behold, the fainting fad claimed me. I flopped neatly to the floor. Later, the words: "I sink to my knee in syncope" - played tunelessly through my mind. (Syncope, pronounced - sing kuh pee)

Cups of sugary tea were forced on me before I was permitted to leave the office and then, unsteady and bleeding nicely, I caught the number 80 bus home.

At *Hell Camp*, René was shouting into the phone, arguing with my mother who had run away from home (as she did on occasion). They yammered back and forth when suddenly, to supply her an extra special little jolt, René blurted out:

"Great mother you are. Do you even know your daughter has cancer?"

I heard her screams from where I stood.

René handed me the receiver. "She wants to talk to you."

Cringing I placed the phone to my ear.

"Is it true?" she screeched.

"Well, I've had a treatment for cancer but …"

Sobbing loudly, she blubbered on without giving me a chance to finish my sentence.

"I can take anything, but I can't take this. I can't bear this. No, no this is too much. My beautiful daughter with cancer, my special darling with…THUD!

"Hello?"

I knew she'd fainted on the other end of the line.

"She falls to her knee in syncope," I hummed to myself.

So, had her one-upmanship kicked in? Or was it merely, my daughter needs me…time to check out? And why was she fainting? Wasn't she the one who had forecast my early death with zeal?

Dragging my dejected self over to her run-away, hideout-hotel room, I picked her up of the ground. Comforting her was perplexing. I seriously hated her, yet simultaneously felt sorry for her.

"Don't worry, I'm not dying." I patted her arm while she moaned and sobbed.

Once I'd calmed her down, I returned to *Hell Camp* where Claude took one look at me.

"Alright cancer bag, how about I make you some hot tea?" He smiled.

Thank you, Claudie. Man, I wish you had been my mother.

CHAPTER 21 - BPD

My mother wasn't well...wasn't well in the body...wasn't well in the head. Her life started off poorly, what with her being born amidst plummeting bombs, raging fires, brutal poverty and efficient mass executions. There was little time to bond with her overly anxious mother (who was rendered a lot jumpier by the exploding mortars and grenades) as children were whisked from the German cities to live in the countryside where it was judged safer. Subsequently, my mother lived with her grandmother, miles from her parents, for the first three years of her life. On reuniting with her parents, she unhappily discovered that her grandmother was a hell of a lot kinder than her parents. Her father (the lecherous, limaceous, low-life) beat her, berated her and bid to bed her; while her mother, having kowtowed to this megalomaniac husband of hers for years, pooh-poohed any complaints against her precious *Hans*, thereby neatly refuting all my mother's traumatic experiences. That's crazy-making shit right there. This injurious childhood slapped together with that sloth of a thyroid established in my mother a considerably cockamamie outlook. It accorded her that exasperating flawed thinking...I really, really love you; give me everything you have...yes, even the baby you're hiding behind your back. I'm not kidding, hand over the baby!

I'm no shrink, but I'm placing my mother's diagnosis at "Borderline Personality Disorder". And you're probably thinking: Ah yes, the blind labeling the blind.

"You're curvy! Men like that," my mother grinned at me. "They like it when you strip for them." She proceeded to show me how to strip. "You cup your breasts like this," she crooned sensuously, sliding her hands under her breasts to fondle them.

Sadly, I had no breasts to cup. I was eight.

"I have mushrooms." She blinked up at me, her eyes brimming.

"I don't understand." I blinked back, my eyes dry.

"Down there. I have mushrooms down there. René's been sleeping with black women, God knows where, and now he's given me mushrooms."

(Good old René - the fun guy.)

I shuddered as she reached towards me for a hug. I was twelve.

"Where have you been whoring about all afternoon?" She ranted in front of theater patrons at the cinema where she worked selling popcorn and candy. "You're evil and dark. You should live in a gutter. You'll never amount to anything."

People looked away uncomfortably. I stared at the floor. I was thirteen. I hadn't whored around…yet.

"I'm so scared of dying," she said, clasping my hand tight. "I think something is wrong and I'm going to die."

She pulled my hand between her legs, pressing it against her parts, crying all the while.

It was disconcerting. I was sixteen. I had no clue how to comfort this woman. This woman who was so lost, so alone, so fubar.

I was in high school when she started "running away" from home - disappearing without a word for weeks at a time. She ran off so many times I couldn't keep up and lost track of her whereabouts. It didn't worry me, though. I had a sixth sense when it came to my mother.

"Mum is going to pick us up from school today," I confidently announced at breakfast one morning, even though our mama had been out of the country for over two months sans communiqué.

"How do you know?" Linda asked. "Did you hear from her?"

"Nope. I just know. Call it a hunch before lunch."

And there she stood after school on the pavement, arms wide, waiting for us like all the other loving mothers.

The definition for Borderline Personality Disorder is: a pervasive pattern of instability of interpersonal relationships, self-image and emotions. Furthermore, many individuals with BPD report having had a history of abuse, neglect or separation as young children. Oh Bingo! Here's a list of BPD symptoms:

- Frantic efforts to avoid real or imagined abandonment. Fear of being alone.
- Unstable and intense interpersonal relationships, alternating between extremes of idealization and devaluation.
- Identity disturbance: persistent unstable self-image or sense of self. Chronic feelings of emptiness.
- Impulsivity in areas that are potentially self-damaging: promiscuous sex, reckless driving, gambling sprees or drug use.
- Recurrent suicidal behavior and threats or self-injuring behavior such as cutting, or picking at oneself.
- Strong emotions that wax and wane frequently
- Intense episodes of anxiety or depression

- Difficulty controlling emotions or impulses, inappropriate anger, frequent displays of temper, sometimes escalating into physical confrontations

And my mother owned a good number of these. Oh joy of joys!
The "*frantic effort to avoid abandonment*" resulted in my mother clinging desperately to us kids, readily using us as floatation devices, telling us we were magnificent...or revolting, depending on which part of the "*extremes of idealization and devaluation*" was in play. She'd sink her nails into my flesh, screaming at me not to touch her wardrobe, when a previous dress up in the identical clothes had

prompted a photo shoot and "you're so adorable" veneration. It was not easy to gage her mood. Labile could have been her middle name.

The "*persistent unstable self-image*" meant she was unable to hold down a job. Not that she thought herself unworthy of the job, quite the opposite. She deemed every task beneath her and of no noetic value. But the persistent, pesky problem that usually cost her, her job, was that the boss always wanted to boff her. Her unstable self-image needed bolstering through men. If they slept with her, it proved she was of value. They literally humped her to worthwhile, and then fired her!

Boffing was part of our upbringing: "*self-damaging promiscuous sex*" -oh hell yeah! I remember coming home to find a man's clothes sprinkled down our corridor. I pictured this man flouncing down our hallway, yanking off his gear in anticipation of a good old romping session with my mother. I wiped my feet on that man's linen trousers. That's right, horny dude. Your pants - my mud! Mind you, who was I to get high and mighty? I'd certainly done my fair share of reckless-writhing.

Reckless writhing, and hot on its heels, reckless driving. My mother drove with the forbearance of a crack addict. She ran red lights, honking at the rabble, mounting pavements to avoid traffic; and once even went so far as to bumper up to the car ahead and forcibly shove it through an intersection. Winding down her window, she then let rip with some rhyming German, much to the stupefaction of the woman driver:

Fahr doch zu, du Blöde Kuh (Drive on you stupid cow)

She clipped the lollipop man at the school crossing, causing him to spin like a toy top. When he yelled, "bitch" after her, she slammed on the brakes, flung the car into reverse, and threatened to run him over again. We loved driving with her as kids. It provided high excitement, until the day she asked me to light a cigarette for her as she tore through the neighborhood. There's twelve year old me, sucking on a Pall Mall, willing it to fire up. The minute it sparked, I panicked and dropped the flaming fag onto the floor of the van (which wasn't our car, but on loan from a friend). My mother abandoned the steering wheel in order to retrieve the smoldering ciggie, and in a split second, we ramped bumpingly up onto the pavement and crash-bang into a tree.

"Don't tell anyone," she said. "And next time, don't be so fucking clumsy."

Surfing waves of extreme ups and downs made life pretty chaotic. Past due bills piled up on our hallway table, the loud red envelopes announcing their urgency. Although it stressed my sister out to watch this ever-mounting stack, it didn't trouble our mother one bit. A broad sweeping gesture of her arm rounded those puppies into a trashcan. House keeping? Done!

Forming adult friendships was another area my mother struggled with. Soon the neighborhood teens, whom my sister and I had befriended, became my mother's buddies as well. She partied with us, drinking, smoking, experimenting with pot, and playing her favorite game: "Earn the burn".

In this game, you placed your arm alongside someone else's, dropped a lit cigarette between the two, then waited to see who'd pull away first. My mother won practically every time, laughing victoriously, her arms covered in blisters and oozing purple scabs. Ah, the *"self injurious behavior"*.

On the plus side, she taught the neighborhood kids to waltz and to knit. Each visitor was required to learn the obligatory *one-two-three, one-two-three* and to knit a square. The waltzing never quite stuck, but in the end, we stitched all our respective squares together and formed a collective blanket that was marvelously hideous.

This unsightly, woolen aberration was what my mother chose to cover herself with when she retreated to her couch, curtains closed, TV continuously on, crippled by her depressions. As the *"chronic feelings of emptiness"* and *"intense episodic dysphoria"* claimed her, she'd refuse to get dressed and would spend weeks in her dressing gown, shuffling from the couch to her bedroom, unable to function. These were the times when she'd tirelessly talk about illness and death. For her, everything fell dark with no light in sight.

Of all her disturbances, the depressions hurt me the most. I'd find myself drowning right alongside her in her sea of misery. Since my young self had taken on the responsibility of her well being, the depression placed a ton of bricks directly atop my shoulders. I tried everything I could think of to help her, but as one idea after another failed, I began longing for freedom from the heavy load. Hey, I ain't no Atlas. I wanted relief from the "mother burden". When my teenage years hit, I rebelled with gusto. I thought myself to be a rebel with a fucking splendid cause.

CHAPTER 22 – René

I guess René wanted relief too. Fresh out of ideas on how to handle his wife, he decided to kill her. His cunning plan was to run her over with his new Mercedes, and this may have been because my mother had reversed his brand new car out of the garage and "accidentally" scraped the entire length of the vehicle as she backed out.

"I fainted," was her ingenious defense.

René yanked her from the car and floored his wounded Mercedes towards her now "fully conscious" body. It was young Claude that leapt in front of the car and begged him not to. René's next effort involved getting my mother drunk and dragging her to Emmerentia Dam where he planned to drown her. This time, passersby thwarted his scheme. Foiled again.

Unable to rid himself of this blasted wife problem, René sought refuge in the bottle. Wherever we went, he'd speedily drink himself jolly, jolly; and once he was jolly, jolly, his filter would quit working and he'd blurt out whatever he bloody-well pleased.

"Listen here," he once bellowed in a Greek restaurant. "I hate Jews."

Naturally, the owner hastily propelled over to ask René to please vacate the premises.

"Listen here," René bellowed once more in an attempt to cajole him. "I hate Arabs too."

The Greek restaurant owner, Theo, was a short, squat, no-neck with plenty facial hair and a hirsute potbelly to boot. Not exactly an Adonis. His restaurant was one of the few that existed in our neck of the woods that stayed open past 9 pm, so Theo was familiar with our family. More than familiar. I'd seen Theo at our house, late at night, while René was away working in the bush. Little, paunchy Theo, relaxing in our living room with a whisky sour balanced on his belly, his fleshy lips sucking on a Benson and Hedges. I wondered if he was the mystery condom man?

The night René voiced his anti-Semitic feelings so succinctly, my mother, embarrassed by his plebeian behavior (cough) deserted him at Theo's restaurant. I, on the other hand, stayed behind to ensure that René didn't attempt to drive home, and more precisely, I hadn't quite finished my glass of wine yet. We lived close by, so I lumbered René home on foot then heaved him atop the living room settee. Unlacing his mud-crudded work boots, I swung his farmer-tan legs up onto the couch. René stared cock-eyed at me.

"I'd like to rape you" he slurred out, his breath reeking of alcohol.

"Uh…okay…sleep well." I said, switching off the light and quietly shutting the door.

Back in my own room, I sat staring at the wall. I'd always had a weird uneasiness when it came to Rene. I knew Rene would never touch me, but I'd always sensed that he wanted to. And now he'd voiced it. This attraction to me made him as uncomfortable as it made me, hence the scornful put-downs and nasty criticisms he constantly aimed at me, and hence the unattractive clothes I chose to wear about the house. I had a distinct bag-lady appearance at home.

Yes, I was super wary of René. Our relationship had always had a hint of what-the-hell-is-this? I mean, we bathed together until I was roughly 6 or 7 years old. He'd fill the tub with soap bubbles and in we'd climb, submerging in the soapy suds. Then I'd play the game "invert stepfather's penis," a fun game in which I liked to fold René's penis back in on itself, thereby converting him to female. At least I can rest easy in the comforting knowledge that René did not have a hard on. How could I have played this game if he had? Nope, he definitely had a soft on, although that doesn't explain why he was in the tub with me pushing and squeezing on his junk? Where was the rest of the family? Shouldn't we all be in the bathtub prodding and poking on each other's privates? No?

Don't get me wrong, I'm fine with adults being open about nudity with their kids. The catch here was that Rene never touched me when he *was* wearing clothes. This sort of sent the message that naked we could grab each other any old way, but with clothes on – no, no...no touching!

I was wary of René for good reason.

"Where's your mother?" he'd once screamed into my nine-year-old sleep addled face as he hoisted me clear out the bed by my nightie and shook me like a rag doll.

Dangling mid-air, my teeth clattering together, I knew exactly where my mother was. Furthermore I knew she'd be in *grosse scheiss* if I told René. But I was so frightened that I blabbed out the truth before I could edit myself.

"She's with Ned Pell at their house."

The Pells were friends of friends. We'd all gathered for swimming parties, movies and the occasional braaivleis (South African's version of a BBQ). I guess Ned and my mother orchestrated a little Hokey Pokey together. It was as if my mother couldn't help herself. If there was a man, she had to win him over to prove her worth, no matter if he was married, or if she was married, or if he was a friend of René's, or a friend of the family's. Consequences be damned.

Well, René careened over to the Pell's house to salvage my mother's worth for himself. He boxed Ned several times in the face, busting his nose and jaw, then dragged my mother out of there while she screamed in protest at the top of her lungs, filling René in on what an uncouth animal he was, what an embarrassment he was...*und so weiter, und so weiter.*

Arriving home, she screeched at me too, for spilling the big, squishy beans on her. Back in my own bed, I cried myself to sleep. Everything was my fault. I was stupid, stupid, stupid.

A few nights later, as René and I sat at the kitchen table working on a drawing together, an odd aroma wafted out of the oven. René cracked the door to check on the dinner that simmered away in there: a chicken roasting on a baking tray surrounded by potatoes and onions. A quick inspection located the problem. Cursing, René removed a plastic bag containing giblets that had been inserted into the chicken's rectum for safekeeping.

"Dumb bitch left the bag in," he swore under his breath.

I shook my head at the mess of melted plastic and stinking ruined dinner.

"Dumb bitch," I agreed, to mollify René.

To my astonishment, René's left foot shot out, connected with my ass, and hitched me right up off the floor. This swift-foot maneuver left a bruise the size of Jakarta on my backside.

"Listen here," he railed at me." Don't you talk about your mother like that."

You simply couldn't win in that household.

So? Did I feel love for René? Yes...No? I felt confusion and trepidation. I was fearful of his temper; that unpredictable alcoholic storm that could flare up when you were smiling and laughing, and knock you off your feet.

Good thing was, René loved to cook and his meals were definitely a welcome change to my mother's cooking which could be slightly suspicious. She'd sometimes cook meals that she herself couldn't quite identify.

"That meat was on sale at the butchers," she'd explain, pointing to the curled bits of gristle on our plates.

Oh goody! Cheap meat! I've always longed to try sheep entrails, though these bits of meat more closely resembled sheep hemorrhoids.

If René was home, he'd take over the kitchen, blissfully messing up the entire area, soiling every pot in sight (oh please, don't worry, we had a maid remember?) Magnificent meals graced our table, but on occasion, like my mother, he'd concoct somewhat out-of-the-ordinary dishes. He may have patronized the same butcher as my mother, because every now and then, undesirable meats like cow's tongue or bone marrow ended up on our plates. One night, a batch of René's weird meat sought revenge after dinner, causing all five of us to regurgitate during the night. By the time I dashed to the bathroom, our toilet was already clogged solid with upchuck, and someone had resorted to puking in the bathtub. Entering a space fermented with vomit stench and a tub brimming with recycled "weird meat dish", well, that grants license for instant emesis. Which I did, heartily heaving my portion into the bathtub. The family that sprays together stays together. Really? No, not really.

Continuing on the topic of disgorging: though he liked to drink, René never missed a day of work. I'd hear him vomit at 4 AM, but by 6 AM he'd be up and at it, ready to conquer the world. René worked mainly in the bush and wasn't home very often. His job landed him in underdeveloped spots like Lesotho, or Lebowa, far off remote places that were in dire need of roads and pipelines. Being a land surveyor, René was never short of work. He'd set off into the bush for weeks at a time and arrive home covered in layers of grime, having not set foot in a bubble bath (and most probably not having had his penis inverted either) for the entire time.

René taught me to do the calculations for his angle readings. It was simple. There were certain formulas to follow. I'd punch in numbers and symbols on a Hewlett Packard calculator (a hefty machine back in the 70's), then neatly write the results on graph paper, in pencil. Both Linda and I did calculations for René whenever we could, because he'd pay us generously.

Though René never earned huge money, he liked to dream up elaborate schemes, convinced that his next plan would bring in the "millionies." From exporting African artifacts to constructing pianos, he had an assortment of harebrained ideas. He further had this grand plan to build us a house, well, not so much a house as a compound, where we would each have our own living quarters in a circle of thatched rondavels. He drew designs for our complex sketching out five cottages around a swimming pool with outdoor showers and a BBQ area. Scanning the drawings with him, the thought of this fabulous living situation really excited me. This utopia was going to be damn dandy. I could even handle their fighting if I had my own little cottage and a pool. But as time went by, I realized that Rene's dream house was just pie in the sky - pastry in the clouds, man.

Propelled to endless activity, René was busy, busy, busy and always in a hurry. He walked fast, drove fast, ate fast and this haste left him scant time for details. An erratic, slap-dash approach claimed the order of his day. For example, he once scribbled his important end-calculations (about three months worth of work), on the back of an expired calendar that hung on our kitchen wall. Eating breakfast one morning, I'd viewed said otiose calendar, and decided to toss it in the trash. I thought nothing of my actions until I heard yelling a few days later. Yelling was commonplace in our household, except this time, René was shouting loudly at Christina. I heard Christina crying hysterically, followed by a door slam. I walked into the kitchen to find René weeping at the table, his head down on his arms, his brawny shoulders heaving.

"What's wrong?" I stared at him in horror. This was the second time I'd seen René cry and it made me fiercely uncomfortable.

"Christina threw away my calculations." His gloomy eyes turned up at me. "I'll have to re-measure everything. Three months of work…three months!" He thumped his fists passionately on the table.

I highly doubted that Christina had done such a thing. She never interfered with his paperwork. No way.

"She never touches your stuff. Are you sure?" I asked hopefully. "Maybe your papers are somewhere in the house?"

He shook his head. "I wrote all the end co-ordinates on the back of the old calendar, and it's gone. Christina said she must have thrown it away. I could kill that dumb *kaffir*." He sobbed and seethed.

My stomach dropped to my feet. My palms converted to sweat pads. Should I keep quiet? Let Christina take the blame? René would want to kill *dumb me* now.

"Oh God, René" I spluttered. "I threw it away. It was two years out of date. I figured it was okay…I'm sorry."

I braced for impact, readying for a head slam.

René simply stared at me, his face empty. Then he dropped his head back down, defeated.

Every now and then René hauled us kids along on a surveying job. All three of us joined him in Lesotho for a month-long job in a far-flung village. How far-flung? Far-flung enough that we had to fly in on a four-seater plane because there were no roads to speak of. Poor Claude turned a light shade of green, groaning in the cramped back seat, passionately clutching his barf bag.

A sparsely furnished house situated right next to the village school was our home for a few weeks. With only a smattering of white people in this area, most of the black school children had never set eyes on a white child before. Sure, they'd seen white men, but not white children. Claude fascinated them. At 7 years old, he had a head of soft curls, big blue eyes, and was super–duper cute. When the school bell rang to announce lunch break, the pupils would rush out and pack themselves tightly against the fence, calling for Claude, eager for a glimpse of the strange looking white child.

"Cloud! Cloud!" They chanted.

Poor Claude. He hid behind the kitchen door saying: "I'm not going out there. Please don't make me."

"Don't worry Cloud, we won't."

During the day, we'd tag along with René into the field. Up and down we'd bounce in the back of his *bakkie,* navigating dirt roads. At times there were no roads at all and we'd simply reel off and tear into the bush. I loved the open back. Standing up tall, I'd grab onto the cab top and enjoy the wind tangling through my now shoulder length hair (score one for me). I'd pretend I was flying. I'd sing loudly. I could practice primal screams if I wanted (which I did when a passing thorn bush punctured my scalp), but nothing could be heard above the straining engine noise.

René's truck was an old, yellow hunk-of-junk with "The Mighty Rattler" spray-painted in bright orange letters on the side of it. And rattle it would. Mightily! It would also break down on a regular basis, forcing René under its hood to swear up a storm.

"Yessas, Yessas. These fuckers!" He'd lament at whichever engine parts were "giving him grief".

Yessas is a common saying in South Africa. It took me forever to realize it was simply "Jesus" in Afrikaans. I wish I could pronounce it for you. I wish you could hear it in René's voice. Yessas, Yessas! When René worked on the Mighty Rattler, we kept quiet, because he could whip himself into quite a frenzy over that vehicle, and we sure as hell didn't want him to mistake us for one of "those fuckers".

Land surveying with René bordered on unsafe. He'd set us up with his level (to gain a horizontal line of sight), then off he'd hike into the distance, commanding us to hold the level straight. Within minutes he'd dwindle to a tiny figure on the horizon, focusing in on us through his Theodolite, flapping his arms frantically if we slackened our grasp on the level. One time, he left me and Claude perched in a tree holding that damn level pole for what felt like hours. As time wore on, I became increasingly aware how vulnerable Claude and I were up in that lone tree. Here we were, just me and my soft, curly-haired brother, up a tree, in the middle of savanna-bush teeming with snakes and lions and hyenas and leopards and rhinos and elephants. Holy Moly, René. Come back already!

I doubt it occurred to René that we might be in danger. He felt completely comfortable in the bush. I mean, he lived in it 80% of the time and was a diehard bush-warrior. He loved Africa, and had long since vowed never to return to Switzerland where his nine older siblings and parents still lived.

Even when all hell broke loose in South Africa, René stayed put. When all the "white" rats left the sinking ship, he bought a bed and breakfast in Warmbad (about two hours from Johannesburg), completely revamped the place and hunkered down. He developed a website for his B&B, "The Gallery Inn", which years later, while sitting in my mobile home in America, I viewed with a sense of longing. The Gallery Inn consisted of a circle of thatched *rondavels* that surrounded a swimming pool, complete with outdoor showers, an immense fire pit, abundant views and sunsets that fed the soul. René had built his utopia after all. There was one photo in particular on the website that delighted me. It was of René with a dog resting its head in his lap. With one hand, René pets the dog, while his other hand hoists a glass of red wine. Dusk is settling behind him, and the sky boasts a typical African sunset extravaganza. René wears khaki shorts, a rumpled shirt and flip-flops; while reading glasses slip down his nose. His thin hair is wind-blown as he lounges by his enormous fire pit with various friends. He comes across so completely content that it makes me want to cry. Not a sad cry, a cry of relief. Relief that one of us actually made it. That after all those years of torment, of vicious arguing, of dysfunction and deceit, of lies and bitterness, that one of us had finally found their bliss.

René lived happily in his slice of heaven for eight years until one morning he drove over a beehive on his tractor. The tractor slit the beehive open, agitating the bees, and Yessas, Yessas! those fuckers stung him with such a vengeance, that René was dead within three minutes.

The school kids calling for my soft curly haired brother

My soft curly haired brother

Me and Claudie boy

CHAPTER 23 - Claude and Celebrations

After failing his first two successive years of school, a teacher finally recognized Claude as severely dyslexic. One of the symptoms of dyslexia is an incredibly low threshold for frustration, which accounted for Claude's terrific tantrums. Claude wasn't a stroppy kid, his tolerance level simply overloaded when his brain confused letters, numbers, sounds and meanings. Once his dyslexia was brought to attention, Claude was placed accordingly in special classes where his condition quickly righted itself. No more failing (or flailing). The tantrums quietly tapered off and Claude morphed into a calm, steady, hilarious and exceptionally brave human being.

I harbored a maternal propensity towards my younger brother. Not that I'd always done so. When Claude was two, I pretty much hated him since he had usurped my position of "cutest in the family". I had the urge to tell him exactly how much I despised him one day in the kitchen.

"I hate you! I hate you!" I screamed at my toddler brother, backing him up against the kitchen cabinets. "I really, really hate you!" I spun around to make sure no "adult" was watching my abusive tirade and when I turned back to continue yelling, Claude had disappeared. How had he run out so fast on those skinny little legs? A soft whimpering emanating from a cupboard clued me in. Poor Claude. To escape my hate, he had somehow managed to squeeze himself into the cupboard amongst the pots and pans. Finding my brother scrunched behind the dishes, crying in the dark, I suddenly felt sick with guilt. I reached in and pulled him out.

"I'm so sorry," I said over and over, as I hugged him. And I truly was sorry. I didn't hate him. I hated how messed up everything was around us. Claude was just a little boy, scared and alone like me.

It became my mission to protect him. I wanted to look after him, I needed to shield him. He was 6 years younger than me after all, and I could save him. Save him like I wished someone had saved me. Claude, however, must have realized I wasn't exactly competent savior material and found his own way to cope. He mastered the fine-art of sublimating his anger and hurt into humor, and was damn funny as a result (he still is). And he had the capacity to remain positively unruffled through all sorts of deranged shit. While René and my mother dug ferociously into one another, Claude (age 8) would saunter through the living-room-war-zone to ask: "Could you keep it down please? I'm trying to do my homework. And between yelling if one of you would like to make dinner that would be tops, man."

He further invented his own language, devising words like: "*doo doo dief*" which meant - something was good, and "*map*" which indicated - go away.

"How's it going, Claude?"

"I'm doo doo dief...now map."

No matter how deep my maternal instinct ran for my younger sibling, it didn't stop me corrupting him, or damaging his little liver. My protective intention was to elucidate for Claude how to escape all pain, meaning I basically dragged him along to parties and plied him with booze. One bash in particular sticks out in my memory, when Claude was freshly 14. I'd driven us to the shindig (with no driver's license and only one headlight) and on arrival, I downed a cauldron of cocktails and was soon unable to walk, never mind drive. I "hands-and-knees-ed" it out into the garden, where, flopping onto my back, I gazed slack-jawed and slack-brained at the numerous spinning moons and quickly passed out. Luckily, I was wearing a heavy coat that night which protected me from the cold winter temperatures. Claude didn't fair quite as well. Although a novice drinker, he'd chosen to suck down Harvey Wall Bangers – hey, you might as well start big! – but now those Bangers were threatening to spurt right back up. After trying in vain to wake me, Claude finally gave up and burrowed under a corner of my coat. Those spinning moons spun Claude mercilessly until he barfed all over himself and part of me, obliging him to spend the rest of the night shivering in a wet, vomit soaked shirt, purging every few hours.

Claude vomited 12 times in all, but – like brother like sister - this regurgitation session did nothing to deter him. We partied again a few weeks later. Only this time, we stayed securely home, drinking cheap wine coolers and emulating the Solid Gold Dancers on TV by boogie-wooging atop the coffee tables. We gyrated about the living room, shoving the Ping Pong table aside to create extra dance space. Claude figured that his hamster could benefit from a dance class, too, and soon poor Hammy flew about the living room, alighting on couches, landing on chintz curtains, even scoring a touch down on my back. Sweating from our dance performances, Claude and I decided it would be "chill" to drag our mattresses outside and sleep in the front yard. We lugged our bedding out into the cold night, collapsed onto our makeshift beds, siphoned down more bubbly dance-potion and blacked out. Yoohoo, throat slitters - over here!

At some point during the night, René came staggering home and lurched past us to mutter: "Yessas, yessas. Crazy bastards!"

There were Claude and I, fully clothed in our beds, empty bottles strewn across the front lawn, sleeping with Tuesday, our boxer dog (whom we got on a Tuesday), and Venus, an annoying Alsatian, plus our black cat, Ninja, curled up on top of us. A motley crew indeed.

Claude told me years later, that there'd been times when he'd vented his anger on those dogs at *Hell Camp*. He related how he'd punched Tuesday over and over on the snout.

"The more he howled, the harder I punched him." Claude confessed, tears streaming down his face. It was not an easy thing for Claude to share.

I completely understood that little boy pounding his dog in the face. I understood the utter sadness, the frustration, the desolation and the staggering ugliness of the situation. We lived that family cliché: dad hits mom, mom hits kid, kid hits dog, except our margins were somewhat blurry, and we all kind of thumped on each other.

My mother and René set a high standard. These home-loving pugilists threw hot coffee at each other; extinguished cigarettes on one another; hit, slapped, screamed, kicked and punched each other, supplying plenty of household entertainment for seventeen years! And all the while the Ping Pong table did squit-squat to stop things running amok. It merely watched woodenly as we ramped out of control. Our family life verged on ludicrous, with celebrations serving to bring out the worst of our behaviors.

At Claude's 7th birthday, René's alcoholic stupor was disturbed by the home movies Claude and his young friends were watching. Clad solomente in his notorious beige underpants (let's hope he owned several pairs), René charged into the living room and, ranting in Swiss, cut the speaker wires. Claude's little buddies looked shocked, but Linda and I managed to sooth the youngsters and reconnect the speakers. Then we continued with the movie. It didn't take long for René to storm back into the living room for round two of combat with the speakers. This time, René ripped the speakers clear off the wall and hurled them across the room. Claude's young chums sobbed and begged to go home. Happy birthday, Claude!

At my 15th birthday party, René attacked the speakers once again and finding no joy in this assault, he then pounced upon one of my guests. I (unwisely) yelled at René for striking my friend and he in turn backhanded me with such force that I stumbled back several steps before falling over. Happy birthday, Niki.

Hell Camp saw plenty of parties and impromptu get-togethers over the years, many ending in extreme drunkenness, occasional violence and those "so-not-sexy" beige underpants putting in an appearance. Claude didn't attempt another party until he turned 16. At this birthday celebration, it was our mother who misbehaved quite fabulously. It was her turn to be blotto, and in her drunken logic she imagined it a tremendous idea to hurl baked potatoes at Claude's guests. (It is quite a magnificent idea if you think about it). And with that, she let rip! Ah, the sheer joyous delight of family get-togethers. There she was in all her glory, flinging foil-wrapped spuds about the room, her face lit up with glee. Hot potatoes exploded on people's chests and foreheads, bringing the partygoers to a dazed standstill.

Once her vegetable ammunition dwindled, my mother stumbled outside to weep drunkenly over a remark that René had made earlier in the evening. He had stated loudly that in his opinion Spanish women definitely have the shapeliest breasts. Olé, man!

Then the parties came to an abrupt end. All of a sudden René and my mother got divorced. Seventeen years of miserable torture and suddenly they decided this wasn't working? I wonder what clued them in? Whatever the reason, they finally, finally, finally - thankfully - got a divorce. Well done, guys! This calls for a real celebration. Why don't we throw a party? We'll drink, and drink, and drink, and burn each other's arms with cigarettes, strip to our underwear, and lob speakers and potatoes about the room - Yippeee!

PART TWO

The Pop Star Plan!

My first guitar

"And if I reach for stars, I know that I will soar
I am invincible for sure"

Invincible.....Pieces of Me, CD

CHAPTER 24 – Musical Interlude

Right! Let's get back to the Pop-Star stuff now that you know the story of my childhood. I always desperately really, really, really, really, really wanted to be a famous singer. I painted a bright green statement on my closet door for the entire world to see:

My name is Niki Smart and I am going to be a famous singer.

Unfortunately that closet door was buried right along with the rest of *Hell Camp*...hmmm.

At age 10, I noticed a guitar lying about at a girlfriend's house. I picked it up, and curiously couldn't put it down again. The urge to play that guitar was so strong that I barricaded myself, and the instrument, into my girlfriend's family caravan (much to her dissatisfaction). Then I played that guitar until my fingers bled - yes siree - just like Bryan Adams "got my first real six string - played it 'til my fingers bled - t'was the summer of '74 (more or less)…la-di-la-di-la."

And so my first love was born, note upon beautiful note. Chords ringing out to feed my starving soul! I rushed home begging for a guitar, which thank you, not-entirely-awful-parents, I received for Xmas. I practiced and practiced, driving the whole household batty, bashing out "House of the Rising Sun", not the most melodious song ever written, singing along at top volume. I took a few guitar lessons but was forced to quit when we ran out of money for extra frivolities.

On explaining to my guitar teacher that I couldn't afford the lessons, he told me not to worry, that he would continue to teach me for free. And bless his (rather sexy) soul he did. He'd pick me up in his VW combi, drive us to a river and, seated on prickly grass, he'd teach me to play Joni Mitchell, Arlo Guthrie, Bob Dylan and Jim Croce, opening a door to a world where at last I felt I belonged. I could sing out my pain. I could craft my sorrow into a song to express it harmoniously and lyrically, like this:

I find myself inside a hole
As deep as hell and black as coal
With no way in and no way out
A hole made up of my self doubt
I know that I am truly caught
This enemy cannot be fought
To free myself I must untie
I from me and me from I

I could aim poetic arrows at my mother in the hopes of piercing her.

Your unending need sucks me in with a touch
As you siphon my childhood to use as your crutch

My musical/lyrical brilliance would have people weeping in the streets. Their crying for me would diffuse my own need to cry. Let the world shed my tears for me, and let them pay me handsomely for the honor. What a tremendous plan.

I craved fame. I demanded fame. Fame was my road out of *Hell Camp*, my sensational escape route. By the time I was 14, I played guitar pretty damn nicely (thank you, oh generous guitar teacher, John Van Nierop) and by 15, I was out performing gigs, singing and accompanying myself on guitar in various restaurants. I composed my own songs, entered them into song contests and even won a couple of awards. My first big win came at age 16 in the "Inter High School Battle of the Bands". I won "Best Vocalist" and "Best Original Song" for my song entitled "Empty Stage."

Revisiting my *Empty Stage* song now, I can't help but think what a load of hoo-ha my lyrics were. Nonetheless, at the time, it was a big dealio for me. I hoped it might help me gain access to the "in crowd" at my high school. However, when my momentous moment was mentioned at the next school assembly, I was announced as Nina Swart…who the hell is that? I want my damn kudos, man! (Thank God, I had my rum-straw for comfort.)

On leaving school, I won the South African National Hymn Writing Competition. That earned me two thousand Rand plus an appearance on the SABC's (South African Broadcasting Company) Six o'clock news. What's more, a religious program filmed an interview with me.

"What moved you to write this Hymn?" they wanted to know.

I cheesed out some hogwash about the Lord vibrating His will through my music, keeping my motivation for the cash prize and my contempt for their foolish religion securely veiled. I am soooooo not religious. On the contrary, for me religion is a load of hoo-ha, too. (In case you hadn't gathered that already.)

I joined numerous bands in different capacities. Not that these names will mean much to most of you, but those that partied-hearty in South Africa during the 80's, may possibly remember (and get a kick out of) these names. That said, I played keyboards with Robbie Rob and Angie Peach in a short-lived band called "The Affections". I quit that band when their drummer, Bruce, bit my leg on stage one night. It left an angry, purple bruise and an uneasy feeling. Bruce later cut off a section of my hair when I bumped into him at a nightclub a few years later. He had a pair of scissors on him, because, as you know, scissors come in mighty handy when out frolicking and rollicking. Bruce whipped scissors from his pocket and cut a chunk out of my hair before I even realized what he was doing. Odd dude!

Next I played bass guitar in a crazy Indy band called "The Sanity Inspectors." How crazy? Crazy enough that the lead guitarist tuned all his strings to E and played an entire set before noticing. Not crazy enough though, to bite my legs or cut hunks of my hair off.

Following the Sanity Inspectors, I played with Chattabac, Tokyo Rose, *Oh Boy!* Chess, Outland and Steve Hofmeyer. There, now you know. Hopefully you are agog with the wonder of it all.

While playing bass for the Sanity Inspectors, I embarked on a college tour along with "The Cherry Faced Lurches", and those Cherry Faced bastards kept sleeping in my sleeping bag, leaving behind a stench so strong, I couldn't bear to sleep in it myself. The head Lurcher, James Philips, made it to the front page of the Billboard music magazine when he died in a car crash at age 36. James had penned an album in Afrikaans, making him the first musician to point a mocking (rocking) musical finger at the dictatorial Afrikaner culture. For his efforts, the SABC swiftly banned his album. Despite the ban, his song "Hou my vas Korporaal" (*hold me tightly Corporal*) played as an anthem for the anti-conscription campaign during the 80's, when South Africa still had that silly, compulsory balderdash about every white male having to donate two years of service to the South African army. Boo! Hiss!

James himself became a conscientious objector and I realize he means nothing to most of you, and only a few in South Africa remember him, but he was an inspiration to me. Before James, the Afrikaans charts were clogged with insipid, saccharine songs like "Waterblommetjies" (*Little water flowers*) and "Trein na Maatjies Fontein" (*Train to little friends' village*) seriously cheesy drivel. Yeah, why don't you white-staunchies pick your little water flowers, jump on that choo-choo train to your little friends' village, and quit whipping/torturing/killing the black man?

James watched me perform a fairly complicated original song on my 12-string guitar at the Witwatersrand University. Following this nerve wracking, clumsy performance, I thought for sure I'd bungled the entire song, and fled the building in shame. James stopped me.

"Your song gave me goosies," he said. "Look at this!" he held up a thin goose-fleshed arm. "I know you struggled with that song, but you shouldn't give up. You definitely have potential."

Now, just so you know, inducing goose bumps in someone is a huge compliment for a musician. It is proof that your music has truly touched someone, has resonated within them. So thank you James, your praise sunk in deep.

CHAPTER 25 – Townships

I didn't give up. At 22, I auditioned for and won the position of bass player for the already established band "CHESS". Comprised of four white girls and two black girls, Chess claimed to be the first multi-racial-all-girl band in the world. They'd achieved numerous number one hits in South Africa, granting them passage to play at massive stadiums and tour the country several times over…hey, it's not a very big country. Many of the stadiums we played at were inside townships, meaning essentially only black people attended our shows. Being one of four little white girls on stage in a crowd of forty thousand black faces, playing these stadiums was considerably daunting. Especially during the 80's when unrest was rampant and hatred for "whitey" was running disturbingly high.

Townships came into existence in the 1950's, after the state ruled that blacks were allowed to work in white areas, but definitely weren't allowed to live anywhere near the wonderful white populace. This new law evicted 60,000 black people from the city, forcing them to leave their homes and move into the newly formed township of Soweto (strategically placed an hour outside of Johannesburg to avoid blemishing the white suburbs). Townships weren't aimed solely at black people. The government allocated specific areas to different racial groups, thereby enforcing political and social separation for Indians, Blacks and Colored people. These peoples were forced to live separately and, like I said earlier, marriage between the different races was prohibited, as were sexual relations. In fact, sex with a person of a different race constituted a criminal offence. Okay so, Heidi and Seal, Tiger and Elin, Halle and Gabriel – *Luister hierso! Julle ouens moet tronk toe gaan.* (Listen here! You guys have to go to prison.)

How crazily wrong is that? And lastly, neither Africans, nor Indians, nor Coloreds were allowed to acquire land in a white area, and were further banned from using the same restaurants, bars, restrooms, public swimming pools, buses, trains, hospitals, ambulances and beaches as the fabulous white man.

Here endeth your Townships lesson.

I'd visited a township long before Chess. Little, white girl me had crossed the safety-boundary and snuck into Soweto. I'd befriended an African guy named Mavuso. A sweet, gentle character, who invited me to come to his home in Soweto to: "see with my own eyes how it is to live there".

At this point (1986) it was fully inadvisable for white people to enter Soweto. The only whites in Soweto were members of riot squads, SWAT teams and the armed forces.

I liked Mavuso. He was decent. I trusted him.

"I would be very interested to see Soweto," I told him.

A few days later, in we went, Mavuso driving his beat up Sedan, me hiding under blankets in the back seat. I peaked out every now and then, watching in amazement as civilization stepped backwards in time. Houses turned to hovels, paved roads dwindled to dirt, traffic signals ceased to exist along with stop signs and road markings. Litter claimed the neighborhood with not a trashcan in sight, nor a blade of grass; just dry, dusty dirt. Skinny children dressed in threadbare clothes raced unsupervised through the streets. They darted between honking cars whilst vagabond chickens, cows, goats and dogs wandered about aimlessly.

Soweto was a throng of heaving, chaotic activity. Mavuso calmly steered his way through the madness, waving at people he liked, and cursing out those he didn't. To me it appeared refreshingly carefree, a place with no rules. Drive where you want, run where you choose, let your livestock roam free, man. However the sinister black smoke that hung heavy in the air (and even heavier on the lung) contradicted the happy-go-lucky feel. With zero electricity, the entire populace of Soweto lit fires to cook, creating a constant black smog.

Our first stop was Mavuso's home: a dilapidated, corrugated tin shack wherein his three younger sisters huddled at a wood table, completing their homework by candlelight. They were thrilled to meet me, like I was some kind of celebrity (which I certainly wasn't), or perhaps they were simply grateful for an interlude to their lucubration …whichever, they sat giggling, staring at me, clutching each other, and then giggling some more. I smiled back, feeling slightly uncomfortable, faking a bathroom visit in order to escape the attention. Mavuso's mother insisted on digging out a toilet roll.

"For special visitors," she beamed, handing me their precious supply.

Their usual routine: old newspaper.

After spending time with the *fam*, Mavuso and I headed out to the local Shebeen, a place where moonshine/fire water/gut rot…whatever you name your poison, is formulated.

On entering a small jam-packed shack, crammed with party people, the Shebeen Queen, Mama T., greeted us boisterously.

"How lovely that you come," she whooped, enfolding me in rolls of sweaty arm fat. She whisked a green bottle of mystery substance from her apron, and placed it firmly in my hands.

"This is for you, because you come to visit Soweto."

Mavuso smiled knowingly. He knew what that bottle held.

"You must drink or it would be impolite." He winked at me. Hell buddy – no problem there!

Soon I was dancing, singing, and swaying in the teeming room, enjoying the music that blared through the bare-bone speakers:

Reach out and touch someone you love
Make this world a better place

Exuberant singing arose as the room literally "reached out and touched" one another. Hands grasped towards me, people simply wanting to *touch* me. Luckily, the mystery liquid had melted my sober need for obligatory personal space, and before long, I was reaching out and touching them all right back.

A young girl presented me her baby.

"Please, you hold him for good luck." She smiled shyly at me. I rocked her baby for the rest of the song, crooning gently to him. The young mother wedged tightly next to me looked proud enough to pop.

At the end of the festivities, Mavuso drove me home.

"Next week, I'll show you my world," I invited.

I thanked him for a thoroughly enjoyable, eye-opening, evening. The following week, Mavuso joined me at a hangout in downtown Johannesburg, "The King of Clubs". They stopped him at the door.

"No way, man. No blacks allowed in here."

CHAPTER 26 – Chess Pieces

When Chess performed at the stadiums built within the townships, I always felt exceedingly white. In fact, I felt like a bright shining beacon of white, an extremely disliked shining beacon of "possible target-practice" white. Hey, if I'd been out in that crowd, I would have hated the Chess girls myself. Wearing those ridiculous colored coats over spaghetti-strap tops, combined with loud, garish leggings and, forgive me for saying this but, playing our instruments like girls. Chess was definitely no Van Halen.

If anything ran awry at these large concerts, for example, if the sound was of poor quality, or the electricity shut off (which it frequently did), then a fusillade of bottles and cans came hurtling our way as the crowd flung their dissatisfaction at us. Our protection? To squeeze behind the giant speakers whilst shit bombarded the stage.

The Chess girls hadn't exactly reached "major" stardom but they had earned enough success to be the opening act for a sold-out stadium concert for Brenda Fassie, a huge favorite amongst the black people in South Africa. Brenda *had* reached major stardom status with plenty multi-platinum sellers to prove it. Time Magazine bestowed upon her the title, "The Madonna of the Townships". Well, this African Queen of pop, this "Madonna", was also rather bonkers. Batty. Doo-lolly-lolly...lolly.

She once stormed our dressing room and shook a cow's tail over us, telling us we were going to have bad luck...oh such bad, bad luck. It worried me. Had she just cast a spell on us? A curse? A pox? A hex? Had she blighted us with her bad voodoo-hoodoo? Maybe so, because years later, only myself and one other Chess member remain alive. The other four girls are all dead...and Brenda Fassie didn't survive either. She died from a drug overdose after being in and out of rehab more than thirty times. What I'm saying here people is: beware of swishing cows' tails.

At this particular concert, when we opened for Brenda, she was a no show, a stunt she liked to pull occasionally. Her band arrived, but she didn't. We were fast approaching the end of our regular set when the promoter frantically urged us to keep playing.

"Play your hit song again!" he shouted from the wings.

Seriously? It wasn't that good the first time around.

Well, okie-dokie, then, mister panicked-looking promoter.

We played "Down by the River" again, this time drawing the ending out, milking it for all it was worth. It didn't take long for rock confetti to launch our way. Jump, girls. Giant speaker cover time.

Once the irate crowd realized they'd paid an entrance fee only to be jipped out of seeing their "Madonna", the stadium erupted into a full-scale riot.

"Get in your van and leave!" the promoter yelled.

Brilliant idea, except there was about forty thousand people between the exit and us. We piled into our van as bottles, rocks and cans began raining on us. Flat on my stomach, hugging the floor of the van, I listened to the rocks and stones pelt our girly, pink-painted CHESS van. Man, those Brenda Fassie fans were hating on us big time! Maybe Brenda's curse was real? Maybe mob mentality was about to give us a grizzly, limb-from-limb ripping death. By the time the riot squad arrived, I was a quivering mess. Watching the police launch teargas into the angry mob to clear a path for us, I prayed to my "only when I need him God".

Dear Lord God, please don't let me suffer encopresis right now.

For Chess's next tour, our manager, LVW, booked us for a two-week stint at a hotel in an Eastern Cape township. Fabulous! Now we had to live in the township and play at this hotel-club every night for two weeks. Knowing we were all shaken by our previous teargas escape, LVW grinned at us:

"*Moenie* worry. I'm giving Irene my gun, plus I've hired Tulani guards this time."

LVW sure as hell wasn't planning on staying with us…and Irene packing heat, so to speak, was slim comfort. The Tulani guards were a different story, because let me tell you, Tulani guards are serious mofos. They're huge, solid-muscled Troglodytes with a serious violent streak. Armed with sjamboks, they generously beat anyone who dare defy them – a sjambok being a heavy leather whip/baton traditionally fashioned from hippopotamus, or rhinoceros hide, apparently even from the penis skin (now there's a thought). This whip is flexible and extremely tough (as you'd expect a hippo's penis to be), and it's specifically used in South Africa for riot control. I reckon 30 Tulani guards could enforce "peace" in a crowd 40,000 strong. Everyone was scared of them, including me.

Irene, LVW's girlfriend (who eventually became his wife and then his ex-wife), stationed the gun by her bedside in the dank quarters that were to be our home for the next two weeks. Pity for her that she didn't carry the gun with her to the bathroom, or she could have shot at a Tulani Guard who barged in to stare at her naked in the bathtub.

Playing at the club was painful; a nightly melee spent fighting off blind-drunk men who liked to exercise the line, "Is it because I am black that you don't like me?"

Ag Please! Are you trying to guilt trip me? Do you know who my mother is?

Returning to my hotel room one night, I found an Indian man crouched behind my shower curtain.

"Hello there," I said politely, attempting to appear nonchalant, as if men squatted in my shower all day long. "Can I help you?"

My brain, meanwhile, fired at top speed. What could I knock him over the head with? Could I make it to the door before him? How could I placate him long enough to escape?

He stood up. "I want to meet the guitarist," he said, his eyes blinking rapidly. I backed away from him, smiling reassuringly.

"No problem, my friend," I said, picking up the phone to dial Jean's room. "She is very talented, isn't she?"

Jean answered on the first ring.

"Uh...Jean? There's a man here who has been waiting in my room to meet you." I nodded at him, smiling some more.

As I'd hoped, Jean immediately called security and the man was tossed from the hotel like limp spinach.

On recounting the incident to the other girls in the band, Todd (one of the African girls) blurted out angrily: "Why didn't you call me? You should have called me. I would have stabbed him in the head with a pair of scissors."

What is it with South Africans and scissors?

I resigned a few weeks later. No more townships for me.

CHESS – in our fabo clothes. From L-R: Penny, Thelma, Jean, Irene, Me, Todd.

CHAPTER 27 – Outland-ish

Due to my lack of faith in Irene's ability to protect us with her borrowed gun, I left Chess and joined the cover band *Tokyo Rose*. From there, as you know, I joined *Oh Boy!* but had to quit once my belly bulged and Samantha was threatening to shoot out. Following a quick "birthing" break, I teamed up with Myles S., an incredibly talented guitarist whom I'd already worked with in *Oh Boy!* I was proud to work with Myles, seeing that he'd toured with South Africa's biggest bands and was in hot demand as a session guitarist. And more importantly, he had the softest, blonde hair and the hugest, blue, take-me-to-bed eyes. He was the prettiest man I'd ever met.

With my heart all a pitter-patter, I knuckled down to learn copious cover songs and soon Myles and I had a bulky enough repertoire to "play out" at hotels and bars. And I'm sorry to toot my own tooting equipment here, but we were first-rate at what we did. Before long, we signed with a booking agent who secured us a year's worth of hotel gigs. These "hotel gigs" meant we lived in a hotel and performed at the attached club, six nights a week, for a three-month period and then…on to the next hotel. Within a few weeks at our first hotel of six nights a week (plus Saturday afternoons), my throat couldn't handle it. Blisters formed on my vocal chords, making it difficult to talk, never mind sing for long hours, straining to be heard above the drum machine, suffering suffumigation the entire time. Smoking was absolutely allowed, and these clubs were permanently thick with smoke-haze. Three months into playing the hotel club circuit, total discouragement set in. Quartazone injections (that stung like a bitch) needled inadequate aid up my nose, leaving my voice raw and raspy. This was not pop star. This was exhausting and bad for my liver. People bought us drinks all night long, and I needed very little encouragement to partake. At least I wasn't sleeping with anyone, as I had Samantha in my room. She kept me virtuous. She also woke me up at 6 AM when I'd barely collapsed into bed at 3 AM. I became a zombie with a raw throat and enlarged liver.

I told Myles we needed to form an original band. An original band that played our *own* songs, and we simply *had* to land a record deal. I knew I wouldn't manage a year of six nights a week, with no sleep, screaming vocals and constant Jägermeister shots.

I was wholly serious about signing a record deal. Myles thought me idiotic.

"We're not giving up our hotel contract. We're making good money here…and if we ditch, they'll never hire us again."

Myles was right.

"Yes, but my liver…."

Finally I convinced him to bail on our contract and off we went to record three original songs at a friend's studio (thank you Marshall). Armed with our three-song demo cassette, we approached all the main record companies in Johannesburg and…were turned down by every single one of them, Myles hating me more with each rejection. Bummer, man.

Then unexpectedly a jolt of good luck struck. Myles had a friend who worked as an investment banker, and this friend had a lady client who wished to invest in something exciting…a racehorse perhaps? The friend had managed instead to persuade her to invest in a rock band because, come on now, that's excitement to the hilt!

And abracadabra, Myles and I had a lovely little lady backer to the tune of one hundred thousand Rand; and our lady backer, T.A, was amazing. We had won the musician's dream lottery. Oh fortuitous fortune!

We immediately hired the biggest music attorney in South Africa, Derek Rabin (whose famous brother, Trevor Rabin, penned the smash hit "Owner of a Lonely Heart"). Derek trailed our exact same three-song demo back to the exact same record companies, only this time he was fortified with our private backing news broadcast. Within a week, Myles and I signed a substantial record deal with TUSK Music, a subsidiary company of EMI. The head honcho at TUSK beamed at us, telling us that our songs were the best songs he had heard in 15 years.

"Funny," I itched to blurt out. "You didn't like them quite as much when you heard them a few weeks ago."

Welcome to the delightful music industry.

With this "big deal" securely lodged under our belts, Myles and I formed our band *Outland*. We booked into a state-of-the-art studio and busied ourselves recording our first album. T.A supported us 100%. She brought pizza to the studio, allowed us to rehearse in her enormous garage, invited us for lunches and dinners, and arrived at meetings carrying Dom Perignon. It was a thrilling time for all of us.

Like me, T.A was a single mom. Her daughter was the same age as Samantha, which worked out well for me. Samantha could tag along to rehearsals, and she and T.A's daughter would play the entire time. T.A also ran a business, a very successful business, and still managed to be a good mom. I was impressed with her. She was gorgeous, rich, successful, and had never married. Not that there is anything wrong with marrying. I just know first hand how hard it is to juggle a career and a child by oneself, so I was awed she had done it all single handedly, and done it so well.

An important meeting was setup at TUSK with all the big-wigs and muckety-mucks, and I panicked when I couldn't find a baby sitter for Samantha. I couldn't allow Samantha to hamper my big record deal. This was my dream coming true, this was my destiny, this was my pop-star calling – panic, panic, panic!

No problem, the record company said. Bring her along.

Hovering on the edge of an armchair, I tucked Samantha (who was two at the time) behind me. I offered her magazines to look at, or ignore, or destroy, knowing that Samantha was content to busy herself. Paying full attention to the muckety-mucks conversation, I tried not to notice the wriggling at my rear, until someone announced:

"Um, Niki, your daughter is undressing".

And indeed behind me, Samantha had stripped off all her clothes.

"It's bath time," she chirped happily. "I'm ready!"

I lugged Samantha to one more meeting. This time, she urinated on an expensive couch, leaving the velvet covering soaked through and steaming. Obviously, her respect for my pop-star dream was sadly remiss. No more meetings for Samantha.

Myles and I, however, attended meeting upon meeting. There were vital decisions to be made, like: should my hair be cut short? What should the album cover look like? Which song should be our single? How much money should be allocated to the music video budget? Where should the CD launch take place? And of most importance: how should we dress? We were measured, groomed and outfitted. Fluffed and buffed. I modeled leather skirts, leopard print jackets, low cut tight fitting hip-hugging outfits. Gleaming with make up galore, and hair fully poofed, we faced photo shoot after photo shoot, followed by interview after interview. We aired on the radio, on the TV, and splashed the cover of magazines and newspapers.

Even René spotted me on TV at some bar in the middle of a bushy nowhere.

"I saw you on TV the other night," he admitted.

My heart jumped a little. Was he proud of me now? Now that I was a semi-media-darling?

"What the hell ridiculous outfit were you wearing?" he sneered.

Count on René to criticize my efforts. He'd advised me time and again to forge myself a decent livelihood as an accountant.

"You're good with numbers, Nix" was one of the scant few compliments he ever paid me over the years. Funny really, because in all honesty, I suck at numbers - but I'm pretty good at singing. (Plus, accountants can't drink on the job, or drag people home from the office to "make nookie with", or show up at work reeking of stale beer and cigarettes with their hair all haywire. Or can they?)

Global opposition against Apartheid meant South Africa was musically isolated by embargos that blacklisted international stars who dared to perform in the country. Consequently, local music was well supported during the 80s and early 90s. Happily for Myles and me, there was no other choice for South Africans but to rock out with the local bands, and thus, within months, Outland (our now four piece band) had attracted a large and loyal following.

The record company chose my song "White Sugar" as our first single and within weeks it sailed to number one on the local charts…how about that? Revisiting the lyrics from this song, I again think: slightly hoo-haa-ish…but at least this song had balls. It rocked!

Then TUSK paid for a spectacular music video and soon thereafter, Outland was out touring South Africa, playing at stadiums in front of thousands of people, black and white this time.

I was 26 and finally a pop star.

Myles and I – looking very pop star-ish.

CHAPTER 28 - Myles

As you may have surmised by now, Myles and I were an item. A pair. A couple. Double-trouble. We lived together during our (brief) Outland reign, and had done so before while working together at the hotels. You may also have deduced that Myles was the one who suggested Samantha's name. No? Yeah, that was a bit of a long shot...anywho, I was smitten with Myles all right. I couldn't believe it when he took a fancy to me. This good-looking guy who played incredible guitar and sang like a mo-fo to boot, interested in me? Me? What superb luck. I honestly thought I was the luckiest girl on earth. Then we struck the jackpot: a magnanimous investor who helped us solidify a serious record deal. Our songs were playing on the radio, our groomed pop star images were airing on TV, and our fetching faces were spread in magazines. Fantabulous!

But were we happy? Were we tickled pink? Were we perky and peppy, pleased as punch? Thrilled and fulfilled? Nope.

We were arguing. Alas, Myles was also the one who had cheated on me early on in our relationship, and forgiveness was not yet part of my vocabulary.

When Myles woo-wooed me, I was pregnant and vulnerable. I'd recently deserted Leslie to join *Oh Boy!* and my plan was to lay low at the White Horse Inn. With no alcohol, no current boyfriend and a swelling midriff, my defense mechanisms were way down. Perhaps because my nesting instincts were peaking, I toppled head over heels for Myles, something I hadn't been brave enough to do since Mike. Inexplicably, I found myself willing to bend over backwards to please Myles, which is no easy feat when expectant. Sadly, as my stomach grew, so did Myles's embarrassment at being seen with me.

"Walk a few steps behind me," he ordered one day while we roamed through a shopping mall.

And silly, silly me, I did.

To add insult to injury, the night I birthed Samantha, Myles slept with his ex. Then he cheated on me with that hot long-legged blonde whom I happened to meet a few months later at a gig. She was so pretty, that I had to rush to the ladies-room and vomit, sick with jealousy. Oh, don't you worry, I bedded her boyfriend a while later as payback.

Clueless on how to establish a healthy relationship, I guess Myles and I were doomed from day one. I infused love with a whole herd of misplaced emotions and wants, leading to a constant barrage of jealousy and disappointment. Since I'd never received healthy love, I was incapable of giving it. I'd made no effort to fix myself and figured that whoever my partner was should fix everything for me. Myles was supposed to nurture me, love me, protect me, entertain me, pay for me, understand me, support me, placate me and spoil me. And I, in return? Well, I presumed that gracing him with my presence should be payoff enough. Surely I was worth all this effort? Yes sir, I was good at taking. Not so much at giving. Essentially Myles was meant to be my parent, because dammit, I still wanted one. I was, at least, dimly aware of my shortcomings:

Diary entry Nov, 1992

My relationships keep fucking up. I don't think I am a complete person yet, and therefore am not ready to be with someone. I need to be completed...but how? How? How?

How indeed?

Myles had his own baggage to throw around (and a gaggle of gorgeous girls to grope) and pretty soon we did nothing but argue, both of us feeling hurt and let down. The conflict between us veered ugly, turning us vicious and malicious, until we faced a big, fat immobile impasse. We had to call it quits. We separated but, due to Outland, we were forced to work together. And it became increasingly difficult for us to work conjointly. How could we break up when we constantly had to see each other? We had no time to heal, no chance to disconnect. Myles began having migraines. Intense migraines that had him clinging to the toilet bowl, vomiting and begging me to call him an ambulance, which of course I wouldn't.

Towards the end of our relationship I actually beat Myles up. I phoned him late one night after my woman's intuition suddenly sparked on a red-hot, light bulb (duh!) I asked Myles to come over to the hotel where I'd been staying since we'd separated (the White Horse Inn, naturally), and when he arrived, I immediately locked the door behind him and hid the key, ensuring that he couldn't leave. No escape for you, buddy boy.

Staring into his soft blue lying eyes, my resentment overwhelmed me. I wigged out. I yanked his hair, slapped his face and hit him with angry fists, all the while screaming pure fury at him. Myles didn't retaliate. He simply sat lifelessly, tears streaming down his face until I was spent. He then apologized for Lorraine, saying he was going to tell me about her, he truly was. I unlocked the door, hugged him long and hard for the last time, and thanked him for allowing me to manhandle him.

I had no idea how to deal with my hurt. If my "feelings" overwhelmed me, I simply lashed out and shut down. When Myles later, on bended knee, asked me to marry him, saying that he had sold one of his prized guitars to buy me an engagement ring, I laughed in his face. I wouldn't even look at the ring.

"Sorry Myles, I can't marry you right now, I'm too busy cementing a superstructure around my heart."

There was no way I could allow Myles back into my life, even though I desperately wanted to. I am so sorry, Myles.

While we were getting Outland up and running, to earn us some much needed extra cash, Myles and I toured with Steve Hofmeyr (a well established performer in SA). I sang backing vocals, while Myles thrashed out lead guitar. Together with Steve, we performed live TV shows, played huge concerts, filmed music videos and had masses of fun. There's no stress in being the backing vocalist. If a show flopped, it was Steve that bore the fall out, not I. So I kicked back, relishing my temporary demotion. I should have recognized then that I'm no spotlight hog, how un-pop-star is that? I am quite quiet (drunk is another story) and I display no stage antics to speak of. My approach to performing was a bit bi-polar. A sort of: "Hey, look at me, look at me!...no wait...look away, look away."

On stage, I'd block out the audience by staring out over their heads and singing to the back of the room. Myles, on the other hand, performed twirling, gyrating, shredding guitar solos to entertain the crowd. Back at the hotel, Myles further performed "Flaming-A's" to entertain Steve's band members. A *Flaming-A* consists of wedging a length of toilet paper in your anus, and setting the end alight. Then you race down the hotel hallway, banging on doors as you go, to grant the hotel patrons a chance to view you with your buttocks aflame.

Steve's show incorporated pyrotechnics as well. Prior to a show, smoke machines and strategically placed explosives were set about the stage. These mini explosions unnerved me. One incorrectly positioned explosive, pretty much unnerved someone's face, nearly blasting the screaming fan's visage right off.

Steve's mainly Afrikaans fans adored him. Granted, he *was* seriously hot, and sang both in English and Afrikaans with a voice that emulated Neil Diamond. Fans screamed their devotion throughout his set, and sang along to all his songs, as did Irene (the gun-slinging girl from Chess) and I - we were his backing vocalists after all. One fan, who was obviously not that enamored with Steve, catapulted a bottle at the stage. Perhaps it was the scarred, mini-explosive encountering fan? The bottle struck Irene on the shin, making her shriek in pain. That did it for Steve. He leapt off the stage and charged after the culprit, crashing through four thousand bewildered devotees, screaming at the top of his lungs:

"Kom hierso jou poes gesig!"

(Come here you cunt face.)

No wonder his fans adored him.

The Steve Hofmeyer band - bare it all!

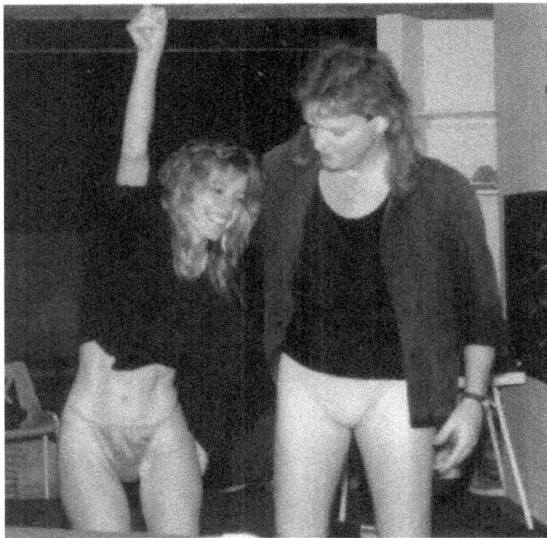

Myles and I also drop our pants!

But mostly we perform with pants on

PART   THREE

The Shit Keeps Mounting

Diary Entry 1993
"I'm sc..sc..sc..scared!"

CHAPTER 29 – WHI again

Two years of semi-serenity with Myles ended in a not-so-serene split up that saw me racing pell-mell back to the White Horse Inn, trailing a now two-year-old Samantha behind me. This upset my mother, seeing as how she'd rented the apartment right next door to Myles and me in order to be closer to Samantha - her new raison d'etre.

"I'll watch Samantha for you while you rest," she'd croon.

"Let me take her off your hands," she'd plead.

"Let me help you, Niksi," became her mantra.

She swooped in on my infant and me while I was too feeble to fend her off.

"I hate my mother!" became my mantra (no, hang on - that had been my mantra for quite some time already).

Anywhere I went, my codependent mother was sure to follow. Like I said, she moved in next door to Myles and me, without asking me first, of course. She picked Samantha up from day school, without asking me first, of course. She whisked Samantha off for haircuts, or to the zoo, or to visit friends, wherever, without asking me first, of course. I couldn't see it in the beginning, but from day one, my mother was planning on taking Samantha away from me, without asking me first, of course.

It was a neighbor of mine who alerted me to my mother's scheming. They'd overheard my mother threatening to lay an "unfit mother" charge against me. This neighbor relayed my mother's rantings about "how useless I was as a parent", how she picked up the slack all the time, and how Samantha suffered because of my instability. Oh yeah! Where on earth did I get that?

The more I brooded over her threat, the more incensed I grew. How was I supposed to emulate a fit mother when I'd never actually seen one in action?

I confronted my mother (in a rather high pitched voice) and made it icy clear that I'd have no problem banishing her from Samantha's life if I heard anymore "unfit mother" shit from her. This tactic seemed to work. My mother immediately typed up a letter, setting to paper the promise that she would never try to take Samantha from me. She then scuttled over to the nearest police station where she asked that a policeman please bear witness to her written proclamation. Begging for my forgiveness, she explained that she was very upset by my upcoming move to the White Horse Inn, that she had threatened only in the heat of the moment, that she hadn't really meant it and that "please my darling", here was a seal of approval, police-stamped, assurance letter to appease me.

I accepted the apology, tucked the letter away, and filed the incident under "CAUTION" in my brain. On a subconscious level I knew this wasn't the end of my mother's clawing at my life, of her needing to somehow immerse herself *in* me. Sadly, I was that accustomed to her invading my space that I didn't pay enough attention to the little, nagging voice warning me to watch out, that my mother's mental state was deteriorating, and that as she sank, my daughter and I were her closest buoyant targets.

Moving back into the White Horse Inn was like a homecoming. There was Basil, shouting in the hallways and Rob, restlessly roaming the restaurants and bars late at night. This time around, Basil granted me the roomiest room in the White Horse Inn. The coveted "L" shaped room. I dragged in a small fridge, a TV, a set of drawers and a cot for Samantha.

Samantha missed "Mylie". I missed Mylie, too, though I would never in a million years have admitted that to anyone, not even myself.

"Don't worry!" I reassured Samantha.

"Fuck him!" I reassured myself.

But "don't worry" doesn't help zilch, and Samantha soon figured that out. She switched from asking for Mylie to asking for daddy.

"Where is my daddy?" she suddenly wanted to know.

I phoned Leslie.

As it happened, Leslie was to be in Johannesburg on a business trip a few days later. We arranged for him to pick up Samantha. Thursday at 4 pm sharp. The plan was: she would fly back to Cape Town with him for a week. I wasn't exactly thrilled at the prospect of letting Samantha out of my sight for a week, but I owed it to Leslie. He was eager for Samantha to meet his mom and dad - her grandparents - and to spend time with the rest of his family!

Over the past two years, Leslie had once more productively sown his virile seed and now had a wife and a son to show for his efforts. Samantha was beyond excited to meet her half brother, Killian, and insisted we buy a doll for him. I managed to convince her that Killian might prefer a teddy. Armed with a little travel bag and the new teddy safely wrapped in shiny paper, Samantha planted herself at the hotel entrance.

"Daddy's coming to get me," she chattily informed any and all passersby.

4 pm Thursday came and went with Samantha stalwartly waiting.

"Let's phone daddy and see what's keeping him," I suggested at 5 pm.

"Daddy's coming to get me," she insisted as I gently pried her away from the front door. "He is!"

I tracked Leslie down through his company.

"I'm sorry ma'am," a secretary informed me "but Mr. P is already on the plane back to Cape Town."

Son-of-a-bitch!

Cradled in my arms, Samantha cried herself to exhaustion. I scanned her blotchy, furrowed, sleeping face and silently vowed to never let that fool hurt her again. All of a sudden the descriptions that the Single Mother's Group used for their "loser-bastard-asshole-cocksucker exes" fit perfectly. Leslie phoned hours later to apologize. He simply forgot, he said.

As before, the people frequenting the White Horse Inn were odd characters. Added to that, Basil had hired a number of extra staff equally as demented as the hotel patrons. A new bartender settled in with her nine month old baby, kindling my curiosity. She was in the same boat as me: a single mom. She kept to herself though, and I didn't see too much of her, but I could hear her baby coughing all night long. It began to freak me out.

"Why doesn't she give her baby something for that cough?" I wondered, listening to its little lungs rattle with phlegm. Eventually I couldn't stand it any more and approached her - cautiously I might add, because she looked frikken hardcore. I timorously asked after the health of her child. Her face was sharp and lined. Her eyes empty. Her humor zero.

"I can't afford a doctor," she snapped, her mouth pinching tight.

Samantha had health insurance from her not completely useless *I simply-forgot* dad, so I offered to bring the bartender's child to the doctor, presenting it as Samantha. The bartender agreed.

The doctor treated the child as Samantha and prescribed antibiotics under Samantha's name, too (which helped us receive the reduced rate at the pharmacy).

"Without medicine, this child could have become deathly ill," the doctor chided me. "Don't wait so long next time."

I suspect that the doctor knew he wasn't treating Samantha, but chose to let us get away with it. I thanked him and apologized for not bringing the baby sooner.

On returning the infant to its hardened, hatchet-faced mother, she briefly thanked me and then assumed us to now be bosom-buddies. I guess for her, gal-pals meant confiding her sordid past to me at length. As she spewed forth her shocking stories, I felt a desire to bolt, fearing her cesspool life would somehow contaminate mine (yeah, 'cos I was living a princess fairy tale), yet I stayed, listening to her increasingly alarming accounts.

The bartender recounted how her ex-husband had beaten her and her two sons repeatedly for years. Social services finally intervened and whisked the boys away, placing them safely with their grandmother. Having a newborn with this pig husband of hers, and nowhere to go, the bartender knuckled under and stayed with him until the night he sliced off her nipples! Yes, you read that correctly. He sheared off her areola. Then he shoved her in a closet and locked her inside for several days, leaving her bleeding and begging him to set her free. What a catch.

Turns out this ex-husband was the bass player from a band called "Hit and Run", a band that had played across the street when I'd been playing with *Tokyo Rose* in Pretoria. Between our music sets, we occasionally crossed the street to watch *Hit and Run* perform. I knew the nipple-less bartender's ex-husband by name: Remo, and I didn't like him.

Neither did a whole slew of other folks, including his band mates. Remo had grown progressively confrontational with his band members, demanding more money; demanding to be the band leader; demanding more attention focused on him; until naturally, *Hit and Run* gave him the old heave ho. Having been with the band for countless years, Remo didn't react well to this ousting. The rejection

162

plain plagued him and when the new bass player arrived to fill his shoes, Remo simply snapped. He found himself a gun, barged into the hotel room where the new bass player and his 6 month pregnant girlfriend were sleeping, and killed them both. Next, he visited the bandleader, Gary V's room, where apparently, Gary and he played chess for a while and chitchatted about the good old days. Gary tried in vain to placate Remo, but a few hours into it, Remo raised his gun and shot Gary point blank in the head. Gary's wife, who'd been at the back of the room trying to sleep, snatched up their toddler and ran for cover in the bathroom. Remo overlooked them in order to chase down the drummer. Thinking ahead, Remo had cut the fuel line on the drummer's car earlier, knowing that the drummer never stayed overnight at the hotel and opted instead to drive home every night. Remo didn't want him escaping. The drummer, however, noticed something amiss with his car and pulled into a nearby gas station to fix the fuel hose himself. He spotted Remo driving by and thought it odd, but remained unaware of the catastrophe unfolding. Unable to track down the drummer, Remo ultimately gave up, lodged the gun in his own mouth and pulled the trigger. Budda-bing, budda-BOOM.
So long *Hit and Run* – more like *Hit and Done*.

The music circuit buzzed briefly with this violent tragedy, but except for a pithy story in the local papers, the massacre of *Hit and Run* disappeared quickly. It was no big deal. Violence was saturating the country, soaking into the very core of South Africa, normalizing incidents like this. I mean, people shot their entire families on a regular basis. One guy took his family out with a crossbow for Chrissakes. The Star Newspaper printed a cartoon of a family with the dad in front and the kids trailing behind him. As they head for the Pearly gates, the youngest calls out from the rear, "Hey Daddy! Tell us again about the time you shot us."

In the early nineties, it seemed that every white South African male carried a gun, typically concealed on their ankles, neatly tucked into their socks. People snoozed with guns under their pillows, drove with guns stashed under their seats, shopped with guns stuck into their socks, belts or jacket pockets.

On entering the club downstairs at the White Horse Inn, you had to surrender your weapon at the front desk, whereupon it was locked in a safe and you were handed a ticket. Come the end of the night, after much partying, you turned in your ticket and reclaimed your weapon. Brilliant idea! This meant that at around 3 AM, drunks wandered the White Horse Inn car park, guns loaded and brains empty. A grim combination. Plus, bear in mind that the legal drinking age in South Africa is 18, and no one gets carded, granting even younger kids access to alcohol. (I myself enjoyed a rip-snorting, thigh-slapping, fine-funky time at all sorts of discos, clubs, and bars from the age of 14 onwards.)

Thank goodness my "L" shaped room faced the side of the building, because the front car park was where all the drama and smack downs occurred. Jealous boyfriends and girlfriends screamed at each other, escalating on occasion to whacking or punching each other; and then, one fatal night, a 19-year-old approached a VW bug loaded with four similar-aged boys. He accused the lad in the passenger seat of eyeing his girlfriend, a crime that probably many were guilty of that night seeing as the girlfriend had a huge set of yayas stuffed in a low cut top. Well, the cocky young gent in the front seat defended himself most fluently.

"Go fuck yourself!" he shouted, and that did it.

BLAM! The 19 year-old fired at point blank range, scorching a bullet into cocky boy's forehead. It exploded out the back of cocky's head, dousing his buddies in the back seat with blood, brains and bits of skull. Johannesburg truly was a modern day Wild West.

Gunshots sounded on a regular basis. I could hear them pop-pop through the night. I'm not a big fan of weapons of any kind, especially guns - they seriously disturb me. I literally can't stay in a room if there is a gun close by. When my friends hauled out their shotguns (or Glocks, or pistols, or whatever stupid weapon they'd chosen to "protect" themselves with) and began cleaning them ever so lovingly, I couldn't stomach it. I'd have to leave the premises.

"But it's not even loaded," they'd guarantee me.

"I don't care," I replied, because I don't trust anyone. They may think it is empty, but what if, just what if, a bullet is still in the chamber? I'm not risking it.

I once broke up with a guy (named Guy) because on arriving at his house to pick him up, I found him asleep with a loaded gun resting on his lap, his finger ready on the trigger. Holy Bananas! If I knocked on the door, he'd be in danger of blowing his own goodies clear off. I didn't knock. I simply left, and that was the end of that guy, Guy, being my guy.

CHAPTER 30 - The Mother Inn-fringement

Samantha settled into the White Horse Inn, swiftly winning over the staff and patrons alike. She possessed a marvelous personality. She was a happy, smiling, content child, and smart as a whip. At six months old, she'd learned to clap her hands, pick her nose, blow kisses and make "aww-waa-waa" sounds by patting a pudgy hand over her mouth. Advancing rapidly, by her first birthday, Samantha was talking, walking, and waddling over with her potty to present me her latest efforts, usually slopping said contents on the floor.

Dresses became her thing. She loved wearing them.

"Pretty Mantha!" she'd compliment her mirrored reflection.

Playgroup started, and I warned Samantha that she'd have to wear shorts and a T-shirt for sandpit play-day. Her dresses were expensive and I didn't want them ruined. On hearing that she'd have to wear shorts and a top, Samantha dug her heels in, refusing any clothing save her party dresses.

"Get dressed, Samantha," I urged her, my impatience mounting. "We're going to be late."

"No!" she howled, fussing on the floor. "I want to wear my dwess."

Grabbing her, I tried to forcefully pull the T-shirt over her head, but she squirmed her way free. Exasperated, I snatched up her dresses and strode to the window (one story up) and dangled out her precious cargo.

"If you don't put on your clothes right now," I threatened her, "I'm going to throw all your dresses out of the window!"

A look of sheer panic hit Samantha. Her little face clenched in desperation. Her whole body stiffened.

"No mommy. Pwease!"

She clumsily plopped down and urgently tugged her shorts on, zipping them on back to front, crying quietly the whole time. And I was the meanest mother in the world.

We had more run-ins. There was a time when she was naughty, I can't remember exactly what it was she'd done, but I lost my cucumber cool completely. Picking Samantha up, I shoved her roughly into her cot. Mad as hell, I raised my arm and was about to smack her bottom when she looked up at me, her eyes big and doleful:

"But I love you mommy," she said softly.

Well, slap-bang me right in the solar plexus. That stopped me in my tracks. Score one for Samantha.

Within a few weeks of Samantha and me moving back into the White Horse Inn, mommy dearest showed up with her suitcases. I watched her lug in her bags with my heart sinking. The White Horse Inn was my sanctuary. However bonkers the place was, it was mine. My mother had never stepped foot in this place before. Not while I was pregnant. Not while I was sick. Not when I had no money. Only now. Now that her granddaughter was living here. *Now* she had a reason to move her stuff right on in. Shit-damn!

Thankfully, the room next to mine was already occupied. A British family with three young girls had moved in a few days prior, and mercifully, my mother was stationed down the hall several rooms away.

Surprisingly, my mother wasn't much of a bother to me, but I can't say the same for poor Samantha. My mother shifted her obsession of feeding me to feeding Samantha.

"Eat!" she begged Samantha. "Just another little spoonful."
Unperturbed, Samantha would cheerfully spit her food out.

"When she's hungry," I reasoned with my mother "she'll eat."

My mother ordered a plate of spaghetti at the restaurant downstairs. The plate arrived and the force-feeding began. Within minutes, Samantha's clothes were a splotchy, tomato-stained mess, and my mother's nerves were taking strain.

"This is expensive food," she cajoled Samantha.

"Don't want it." Samantha pursed her lips tightly together. No spaghetti allowed. Not today. Nope, not one strand.

In due course, my mother lost all patience. She yanked Samantha up by her skinny arms and dragged her upstairs towards my room.

I could hear them coming, my mother *schimpf*-ing away (she is German after all) and Samantha yowling. The din they generated between them prompted people to unbolt their room doors to investigate, the British family included.

Three little Brit heads popped out to stare into the hallway. Their eyes widened as my mother marched the screaming toddler by them. Samantha spiraled back to reach her free arm towards them, pleading: "Help me! Help me!"

I found it hilarious. My mother had met her match. Maybe I was a pushover, but Samantha certainly wasn't. Neither was Basil. When my mother tried to flirt her way out of paying her hotel bill, Basil swiftly kicked her out.

I watched her go, again with sinking heart, not because she was leaving, but because she created such a scene in doing so. Swearing like a (German) trooper, she hurled her belongings into the back of her beat up car and slammed the door shut. In her worked-up state she didn't compute that her back door wasn't shut properly. She fired up her car engine, roared dramatically across the front entrance, then spun sharply to exit. At this precise moment the back door swung open and her suitcases shot out, burst open, and sprayed her clothes, underwear and toiletries across the dirt car park. Crying with rage and frustration, she stumbled about in the dust picking up her possessions. From my window, I observed her, my heart sickeningly heavy. I felt so desperately sorry for her. I wanted to run down there and hug her, help her, shield her, comfort her, pay her bill, apologize for her, fix her life…but I knew it was no use.

As one of my mother's many psychologists had explained to me:

"Your mother's in a whirlpool. If you reach a hand in to help her, she will simply pull you in, too. The only way out of this whirlpool is for your mother to swim out by herself."

I longed for my mother to be well, to function normally, and above all, I wanted her to be happy, to swim beyond her *whirlpool* of vanishing joy. The self-destructive streak I'd possessed before Samantha came along was nothing compared to the one my mother harbored. Her self-destructiveness surpassed mine. Her streak knew no boundaries. Her streak was without end. You don't repeatedly crash your car, get raped, cheat on your violent husband or attempt suicide, if you have a healthy wish to thrive.

Borderline Personality Disorder. Wanna bet?

The British family moved out and a new family moved in: a husband, a wife, and two kids. The boy was about 12, and his sister, Elizabeth, was roughly 10. This family was in for the long haul. I never inquired about their living situation, as to how they had landed up staying at the White Horse Inn. Obviously something had gone askew, or they wouldn't have ended up here. Elizabeth loved Samantha. She carried Samantha all over the hotel, either on her back as a "horsie", or clutched to her chest as "big sister". Samantha loved her right back.

The two became inseparable, and I took full advantage. Given that Elizabeth's family didn't own a television, I'd flick on the TV in my room, adjust the rabbit ears, and lure Samantha, Elizabeth and her brother (whose name I can't for the life of me remember) into my den, thereby freeing myself up to go out and about. Handy for me, these built in babysitters.

I also felt damn sorry for Elizabeth and her brother. Poor kids had nothing. At Christmas time, when I decorated a small tree in my room, Elizabeth stared in wonder at my pitiful attempt.

"We don't really celebrate Christmas," she confided.

"No tree?" I asked.

"No." She smiled glumly.

"What about presents?"

"A few."

Well, that tugged on the old heartstrings. After that, Elizabeth accompanied Samantha and me everywhere we went. We were "The Three Misfit-eers" delighting in shopping trips to the mall, swimming at the pool, playing in the parks. On New Year's Eve, we went to a huge firework display where Samantha hid under her *blankie* terrified while Elizabeth held her hand, giggling with glee. At Easter time, Elizabeth searched the garden for hidden treasures, Samantha hot on her heels. On finding chocolate eggs, their faces shone. They warmed my heart.

Meanwhile Elizabeth's parents were down sliding. I could hear them through the wall arguing loudly. I couldn't make out what they were saying, but it was obvious they were going through hell.

Then Elizabeth reported she'd no longer be attending school.

"Why not?" I wanted to know.

"We don't have a car anymore. I can't get there."

I knocked on their room door. The mom, a mousy blonde with crinkly, weathered skin answered shyly.

"You can use my car to take the kids to school, and to pick them up in the afternoons," I offered.

Her eyes filled with tears.

"Thank you," she said. "Thank you very much."

Things were calm for a spell in our oddball hotel home. I enjoyed my makeshift family, my lazy Sundays at the pool with Rob, my even lazier nights sprawled in front of the telly with Samantha and Elizabeth curled up on the floor. Or the fun outings to flea markets and tea gardens with "my girls", where we'd sing in the car all the way there and all the way home. For someone who hadn't wanted to be a parent, I wasn't doing too badly.

One afternoon, Elizabeth came tearing down the corridor, gushing with excitement.

"Come look," she urged, tugging me downstairs to examine the hall mirrors. "The AWB were here and spat on the mirrors."

AWB stands for "Afrikaaner Weerstands Beweging" or in English "Afrikaner Resistance Movement", or what we mockingly called "Afrikaners Without Brains". With Afrikaans as their sole official language, this bunch of Nazi-like racists were of the mind set that *white is right* and that the *only good kaffir is a dead kaffir*. They were determined to keep South Africa for the whites and blast all blacks to kingdom come. They wore a uniform of khaki shorts and shirts, had a three-legged Swastika-type flag, and held rallies that scared the shit out of sane people.

And spat they had. Globs of mucus snail trailed down the mirrors in the hallway.

"Why?" I wondered aloud, steering clear of the abhorred substance.

Elizabeth shrugged. "Maybe 'cos Basil has black bartenders? Or 'cos he's good to his kaffirs?"

"Don't use that word," I shook my head at her. "It's derogatory."

"What's degoraty mean?"

"It means don't use that word."

"My parents call them kaffirs."

"Well, they shouldn't."

Later that night, while blow-drying my hair, Elizabeth burst into my room.

"They're fighting," she screamed, her pitch so intense it prickled my skin.

I hurried to the room next door, anticipating this was going to be serious. Both mom and dad were naked. Both were yelling and hitting each other. He slapped her hard across the face. She ran at him undaunted, jumped on his back and pummeled him with angry fists.

"Stop it!" I ineffectively attempted to intervene.

They were so deep in it, they didn't even notice me. The boy whimpered against a wall, so I grabbed his arm and ushered him out to the hallway.

"Wait in my room with your sister," I ordered him.

Turning back to the couple, I watched as the dad wound his fingers in the mom's hair and deftly whipped her head around, catapulting her onto the bed. I leapt between them, flapping my arms in an angry goose fashion.

"Stop it. Stop it!" I stared him down, daring him to get past me, my adrenaline soaring.

His eyes blinked, as if it were the first time he'd ever seen me. It was that same weird blank stare that befell René when he was well and truly shnockered.

At least the dad was now registering that I was standing in his room.

"Don't hit her," I rebuked him. "Not in front of your children."

(As if it were okay to hit her when the kids weren't around!)

He grunted and staggered backwards. The mom grabbed the momentary break to dart for the bathroom, where she snatched up a towel, covered herself, and fled the room.

Now it was just the dad and me.

"Don't hit her anymore," I repeated, backing out the room in a hurry.

The next morning, the mom, Elizabeth and her brother were gone. The dad hung about for a day or two, then he, too, disappeared.

Samantha and Elizabeth

CHAPTER 31 – South Africa

Myles announced he was going to marry Lorraine, and I announced a shit-fit. I no longer want to be in Outland. Screw that contract I'd signed. I no longer wanted to be in Johannesburg. Screw that "City of Gold". In fact, I no longer wanted to be in South Africa. Screw that screwed up country. All I could think was: "I have to go to America."

My hurt ego called for a big un-thought-out, totally impractical escape plan. Oops! That resembles my mama's behavior doesn't it? A lot of my behavior seemed to resemble hers. Oh hefty crap! I hate to admit that – ahhhhh!

Having fantasized about living in America throughout my life, I figured the time had come to super-boost my pop star plans and take America by storm. Occasionally, I'd dream that I was already living in the States, only to wake disheartened and find myself still stagnant in South Africa. I longed to live in America; after all, that's where all the pop stars gathered. It was the land of opportunity, the land of fame and fortune, the land of milk and honey, and hopefully some strong booze, too. However, I knew no one in America, making it slightly problematic. I'm doggedly determined, though. Once I decide I want something, I won't let it rest until I get it - *achtung, achtung* - watch out Nicolas Cage!

People told me, "You can't go to America with a toddler."

"Oh yeah?" I replied, eloquent being that I am. Hell, I was a pop star. I was a survivor of incest. I was a semi-competent single mom. I was capable of anything (or so I liked to believe).

Myles's betrothal to Lorraine wasn't the only reason I wished to high tail it out of town. By the early 1990's things were falling apart on the southern tip of Africa. The Rand was plummeting, crime was skyrocketing; and a major, major, major, major shit-storm was steaming a bull's-eye towards the proverbial fan.

Crime swept the country like a turbocharged virus. It spread to every area, and within months, all my friends had horror stories to share. There was Connie who hid in the shower with her baby, waiting for Armed Response to arrive while four men with AK-47s ransacked her house. "Armed Response" responded alright. They shot the four men dead in Connie's yard. Then there was Terry, who found himself hog-tied along with the family he was renting from, all of them lying powerless on the ground as masked men helped themselves to goodies. And Warren, who had his car stolen, only to have it returned to him soon after by the police, with the blood of the thieves splattered across his dashboard.

"Apprehended" was all the police report stated.

Then there was Cheryl, who had a 12 year old African kid smash her car window while she sat at a red traffic light. The kid reached in, snatched her handbag, yanked the necklaces from around her neck, then grabbed her hand to remove a substantial diamond ring from her finger. Only the ring wouldn't budge. Undeterred, the boy stuck Cheryl's finger in his mouth and savagely sunk his teeth into her digit, fully prepared to gnaw her finger off if need be. A passerby fired a shot in the air and the boy ran off, leaving Cheryl's finger intact, but not her nerves.

Kathy was hijacked in her driveway by a group of men. They stole her car and threw her in the boot (trunk), taking her with to ensure that she couldn't phone the police, or follow them. They ditched her later on, in the middle of nowhere. Kathy was thankful to be alive.

Not all my friends were that lucky. Lauren worked at a jewelry store in Sandton City (an elegant shopping plaza in Johannesburg), and when robbers stormed her store, she couldn't stop screaming. To help subdue her, the intruders fired a bullet…into her head.

Daylight robbery dominated the shopping scene, like a new fad, the latest rage. "Shop 'til you drop" took on a whole new meaning. Armed patrols hastily popped up outside all major shopping centers. Similar to an airport check, you now had to pass through serious security in order to gain access to the mall. Then motorcycle gangs invented a drive-by stealing "shoot and loot". They didn't even bother to slow down; they'd simply blast out the store front, lean in, grab whatever they fancied and speed off. Everyone was a potential victim; every area was a possible death field. Nowhere was safe. The atmosphere hung heavy with fear. It was tangible. Anxiety mingled with a growing sense of dread. People erected high electric fences around the perimeter of their properties. Those that hadn't already done so rushed out to purchase guns and other artillery. People peppered their homes with panic buttons. Apparently, I was no longer the only one worrying that black terrorists might come and slit my throat in the middle of the night.

Although this was "black" crime unleashed on "whites", the African people were under a far more severe attack. The black terrorists did show up - they showed up in the form of two political parties, the ANC and the INKATHA Freedom Party – and in the name of peace, these groups proceeded to hack each other to death.

Terror reigned in the shantytowns where homes were savaged in the middle of the night with the "suspect" inhabitants sliced to pieces with machetes. Train killings became a popular show of power in the early 1990s as the ANC denounced all blacks working for the white man, and demonstrated their seriousness by boarding the trains during rush hour, and neatly beheading every fifth person. They simply counted and lopped: one, two, three, four and SWACK - unlucky number five. Terrified passengers sprung to their deaths, squeezing themselves through the windows of the moving trains, many preferring to jump to their death and die by their own hand. The violence was brutal.

Another crowd-pleaser known as "necklacing" emerged. This evil execution entailed forcing a rubber tire filled with gasoline around a victim's chest and arms - then setting it alight. It is not a quick death for the victim. It can take up to 20 minutes to die, a torturous, severely-suffering 20 minutes. While visiting the UK, I happened to see footage of a woman being necklaced on the BBC. With no freedom of speech, press, or media in South Africa, there was no way I would have seen this footage in my own country where it was actually taking place. As the woman fell in the street, her body ablaze, three young boys ran up and kicked her in the head. Children! Nine or ten years of age at the most! I almost threw up. How was it possible for a child to be so completely flooded with hatred?

Endorsed by the ANC, necklacing became the chosen punishment for black folks who were perceived as collaborators with the apartheid regime. Pretty much anyone could be accused, swiftly deemed guilty and maliciously murdered.

A young girl, Maki Skosana, was one of the first victims to be necklaced in July 1985. Not only was her body scorched by fire, but broken pieces of glass were inserted into her vagina as well. Why? Why? WHY? Why be so horrendously cruel? Imagine the last few moments on earth for someone like Maki. Moments filled with utter despair, searing pain and desolate terror. It's no way to leave this earth. No one deserves that.

Although a large portion of South Africa wanted apartheid dismantled and negotiations were in progress, the future did not look bright and rosy. It looked bumpy and lumpy and wobbly, like my thighs. The jingoistic AWB stormed the building where negotiations were taking place, crashing through the glass front in an armored car, threatening an all-out war...brainless buffoons. Then a disgruntled Polish immigrant assassinated Chris Hani, the leader of the ANC, which sparked full scale riots, especially since word on the street was that the government had secretly orchestrated the whole thing. And to top it off, Nelson Mandela, freshly released from prison, was gearing up to be the next president, inciting excitement and upheaval. Everything was coming to a hectic head during the final bloody months of South African apartheid.

Shocking photos appeared as the world turned its focus on the bloodshed in South Africa. The first Photojournalist to capture a Necklacing execution in the mid-1980s was Kevin Carter. He later spoke of the images saying: "I was appalled at what they were doing. I was appalled at what I was doing. But then people started talking about those pictures...then I felt that maybe my actions hadn't been all bad. Being a witness to something this horrible wasn't necessarily such a bad thing to do."

Kevin Carter later gained recognition for his photo of an emaciated toddler stalked by a vulture in Sudan. This photo made the New York Times and won Carter the coveted Pulitzer Prize in 1994. He was awarded a boatload of criticism right along with his prize, for not helping the child. Who snaps a photo of a small helpless child and simply leaves? Who takes photos of people burning alive and thinks it isn't necessarily such a bad thing to do? Apparently *not* Kevin Carter, because only two months after winning his Pulitzer Prize, he drove to a river, taped one end of a hose to his pickup's exhaust pipe and ran the other end through the passenger window. Kevin died of carbon monoxide poisoning at age 33. Portions of his suicide note read:

"I am haunted by the vivid memories of killings and corpses and anger and pain...of starving or wounded children, of trigger-happy madmen, often police, of killer executioners...I have gone to join Ken if I am that lucky."

The Ken that he mentions here is Ken Oosterbroek, and I only mention Ken because he dated a girl up the street from our 9 June Ave, *Hell Camp*. I met Ken several times. He was a quiet and unassuming guy who became the Chief Photographer for The Star newspaper. He and Kevin gained notoriety for their fearless, reckless, photojournalism. If wild shit was going down, Ken and Kevin were there snip-snapping away. Kenny didn't survive either. He died during bloody pre-election fighting, two weeks before South Africa's first historic democratic elections. A month later, Kevin killed himself. (The antics of these journalists are documented in a book and a movie called "The Bang Bang Club.")

These turbulent times saw white people abandoning South Africa in droves. Amongst them were my mother, Samantha and I. I couldn't wait to get out. The country's violent rampage scared the bejesus out of me. The hostility was mounting daily.

On closing my bank account in Johannesburg, the teller confided that roughly thirty people a day were pulling their money out. Take the money and run. The South African government did not permit the removal of vast sums of money from the country, knowing full well that everyone was desperate to get their money out. I'd accumulated R20, 000 in savings, so I padded the bottom of my suitcase with bank notes, smiled sweetly at the custom officials, and carried my boodle onto a plane. Easy Peasy.

CHAPTER 32 - Exit Plan and Bill

Leaving the country that you've grown up is no snap. I was scared shitless, though I refused to admit it. No, I was headstrong, and I required nobody's advice, thank you very much. I'd show them all. Well, let me just say that venturing into the unknown with hardly any money, a toddler, and no marketable skills other than playing guitar and singing, is not recommended. Of course, I naively believed it would be a breeze, and like giving birth, I was once again wrong, wrong, wrong.

Seeing as I held a British passport, I headed for England, in hopes of finding a way to get to America. England seemed a lot closer to America than South Africa did. Plus, I hadn't quite plucked up the courage to fly to a country where I knew no one. At least I had my Boemsie-sister in England.

On arriving in London, I trudged from bank to bank in order to exchange my Rands. Each bank only accepted 200 Rand. Nobody wanted that useless currency. At the end of my trudge I had exactly 2000 British Sterling Pounds. Two thousand pounds with which to start a new life. The exchange rate that had at one point been 1:1 was now 10: 1. Oh pooh!

Mommy dearest followed hot on my heels, and I didn't even argue this time, that's how afraid (and broken-hearted) I was. I was willing to go to England and live together with my mother for a few months... anything to escape the "hack/slash/chop" syndrome that washed over South Africa...anything to avoid Myles and his blushing bride. My plan was to skip from England over to America, and wow those Yankies with my musical genius. Meanwhile, I rented an apartment in North London, and within weeks, "me mum" moved in. It was gloomy. Not just the weather, but my moods. I couldn't find a job, or make any money, and surprisingly, no one wanted to hear me sing. What a shocker! Even worse, I couldn't keep my toes warm - and I need comfortable feet in order to function. I have plenty of weird feet issues. For example, I can't wear shoes that encase my heels. Don't stifle my feet, man! Clogs and flip-flops work, but winter shoes are problematic. Did you notice how I segued from slaughter in the streets to the comfort level of my tootsies? Makes me sound like a mollycoddled little brat doesn't it! Well, whiny me wrapped my cold feet in plastic bags, squished them into thick socks, and strapped them into boots - with my heels in full protest. And all to no avail. My toes numbed up anyway. They turned purple and eventually darkened to a violet black, forcing me to hobble to the nearest pharmacy, where the chemist recommended chilblain cream. Rubbing that stinky cream on my painful toes, I yearned for the barefoot sunshine of South Africa. I was horribly homesick, and on top of that, I was suffering ego agony at having to revert to living with mi madre. I mean for shits-sake! I'd earned pop star status in South Africa and here I was reduced to a nobody, lolling about in a depressing flat with my needy mother.

And need me she did with her constant: "Niki, can you just do this?" and "Niki, can you just do that?"

It didn't take long before she was driving me up the wall, her neediness increasing by the nano-second. When a friend of mine visited, my mother demanded that he take her to the dentist.

"I need my teeth seen to. Make this young man drive me to the dentist," she insisted.

I wasn't about to force my friend to play chauffeur-chauffeur for her.

"It's not my car. I can't tell this guy where to take you," I pretended to reason with her, when in truth I didn't care to help her in any way, ever. Screw her teeth. I felt nothing for her dental welfare.

No more was said until, for some unknown reason, this issue resurfaced in the middle of a crosswalk in Enfield, London. I guess my mother wanted to visit the dentist pretty badly, because as we crossed the street, she suddenly stopped dead in the middle of the road and came unglued. Her arms flailed towards me like a windmill on steroids. She whacked and slapped and swatted, stinging my face and arms, and I in turn hoisted my jacket up over my head and pulled Samantha underneath to shield her. There we muddled in the middle of the crosswalk, cars honking, people staring, while my mother screeched her dissatisfaction and unleashed happy-slappy on my covered form. Under my jacket, I hammed funny faces for Samantha, demonstrating that this was no biggie. We waited out my mother's fury, then finished crossing the road as if it were the most normal thing in the world.

Thankfully, my mother flew back to South Africa to rejoin her latest conquest, Peter. H. They had one of those on-again/off-again relationships that was on-again…again. I remained in London with Samantha, determined to triumph and thrive; to steam full throttle towards America…and super stardom. Tricky stuff.

Instead I steamed full throttle into Bill F., a rich, rowdy, attention grabbing American, who gladly took to spoiling me, whilst I took gladly to being spoiled! Our first date landed us at the Royal Albert Hall enjoying the band "Genesis" from a private balcony, luxuriating in servings of salmon salad and champagne, with Prince Charles and his entourage a few balconies over. What a stupendous kick it gave me when the entire audience stood up to belt out "God save the Queen", old Charlie singing solemnly along.

I felt like royalty myself, seated on my velvet chair in the Royal Albert Hall, with Bill alongside, bedazzling me with stories about his friend, Billy Joel, and ex-girlfriend, Stevie Nicks. He sealed my entrancement by promising we'd meet Phil Collins after the show and suggested I hand him my CD.

"Your CD is great, Niki. I'll make sure he listens to it."

For the rest of the performance, I sat in the darkened balcony, giddy with excitement. I was about to meet Phil Collins. This was it! My destiny was about to shine. Phil would listen to my CD. Naturally he would love it. Maybe he'd want to record one of my songs for himself? Perhaps we could write songs together? And there was a chance he'd find me cute. Possibly we'd hook up, and in time we'd become *the* most dynamic songwriting couple ever. Hah…in your face, Myles!

The show finished and Bill announced he was starving.

"I know a fine restaurant nearby that Michael Caine owns," he grinned at me. "Let's shoot there for a late night bite to eat. Maybe Michael will be there."

Uh…my CD? I stared at Bill stupidly, my giddy excitement grinding to a halt. He must have read my face.

"Forget Phil," he placated me. "We'll catch him next time."

Forget Phil? But I'm practically married to him!…oh wait, did you say Michael Caine?

Maybe Michael would be charmed by my sheer amazingness. Maybe Michael would fall madly in love with me – maybe, bloody, maybe. Of course we never got to meet Michael Caine either, which is a pity, because I really was hoping for a large dose of sexually transmitted fame from him, or Phil, or anyone who had the celebrity I craved.

Bill invited Samantha and me to join him and his friend, Barry, for a weekend of horse riding and fishing in Wales. And, no big surprise, I accepted. Bill may not have been famous, but he was rich, and his richness booked us into a super fancy hotel in the Welsh countryside.

The hotel was horribly proper, the British kind of proper, where the upper class and their stiff upper lips sit up straight, making no noise and having no fun. Paying no heed to the stodgy guests, Bill and Barry held no qualms about competing as to whom could leave their testicles dangling in an ice bucket the longest. The loser, Barry, had to streak through the car park at night in the freezing cold. They were outrageous - and their truly-unruly teenage behavior was right up my alley. We feasted nightly on roast duck or grilled salmon, while stories from all over the world flowed together with sparkling champagne. After tucking Samantha safely into bed one night, I wandered over to Bill's room. He tempted me (effortlessly, I might add) to a nightcap of sherry. Then he slapped a briefcase onto my lap and popped it open.

"Guess how much money is in there." He was obviously immensely pleased with himself.

I stared at the briefcase chock-full with Bill's bills. I'd never witnessed such a sum of money in my life.

"It's a hundred thousand pounds," he boasted, enjoying the shock on my face.

Later that night, lying in my plush four-poster Victorian bed, cupidity engulfed me (that's cupidity, not stupidity). I tossed and turned, wondering and pondering how to steal that money from Bill. Could I possibly slip into his room while he was soused and nab the briefcase? Man, I sure could use that money. America would suddenly hop a lot closer. I struggled to fall asleep with that huge sum of money beckoning me from a few rooms away. "Coo-eee, Niki, coo-ee!"

Bill decided to fly out to South Africa for Christmas, and knowing that SA was our previous homeland, he asked if Samantha and I cared to join him. He suggested we fly out a week or so later, and without batting an eye, he handed me six hundred pounds cash for airline tickets. "I look forward to your arrival," he said.

Had he known how much I wanted to steal his money perhaps he wouldn't have been quite so generous.

The day he landed in Johannesburg he called to let me know he was boarding a smaller plane bound for Kimberly, and then... silence. I heard no more from Bill. Nada. Nichts. Not a peep.

I held onto the six hundred pounds, waiting.

A few weeks into the silence, one of his henchmen rang up to invite me for dinner. During our meal (not roast duck this time), the henchman confided that Bill was a wanted criminal; wanted for embezzlement in various parts of the world. I was honestly shocked, which was stupid, because the more I thought about the whole Bill experience, the more I realized it was obvious. Of course he had lied about everything, and I think on some level I'd always known. I was simply loath to relinquish my fantasy of easy money, easy fame, easy living. My harsh reality of loneliness, poverty, no prospects, a child to rear, my broken heart and my broken spirit, had definitely gotten the better of me. The police arrested Bill at the airport the very afternoon I'd spoken with him. And Bill, not his real name, had been deported to Fort Lauderdale to complete a ten-year sentence. Apparently at his sentencing he'd cried out: "Ten years Judge! Why don't you just fucking throw away the key?"

So that was the end of Bill, or whatever his name was. I bedded his henchman several nights later...moving right along!

I wish I had swiped his briefcase of cold hard cash, because Bill, who said he'd earned the money for being the promoter of the Genesis concert, had in reality swindled the money from people's retirement funds. Some poor unsuspecting chump had foot the bill for all the roast duck and champagne. Nasty, naughty Bill.

Had I stolen his stolen money, would I have given it back to the victims? I like to think I would have, but you can bet your bippy, I hung onto that six hundred pounds. Nasty, naughty Niki.

I was done with London. I packed my bags, strapped Samantha into her car seat and drove off to stay with my sister. With no more wild Bill to distract me, my plan sucked back into focus – my plan of shifting my ass all the way to the US of A, plus, now I had the funds for a plane ticket!

Linda lived about twenty miles out of Oxford, in the Cotswolds, in a quaint village called Burford: grand population = 1,340. Now you might expect that with the average age of, oh I don't know, say 90, the teensy village of Burford would be dull. Not so. With only one main street, "High Street", and five pubs to speak of, Burford absolutely managed to rage. The locals visited all five pubs (practically every night), designating different hours to different venues: The Golden Pheasant at 8 pm, The Cotswold Arms at 9 pm, the Mermaid at 10 pm and so on.

I quickly picked up the schedule and befriended the yokels. Not only did they drink like their very lives depended on it, but they ingested a host of other recreational drugs, too. Since pubs closed at 11 pm, after-parties in people's homes were commonplace. One night I joined the local crew at the home of a midget. He proclaimed that, since I was from South Africa, I must be familiar with Durban Poison. I must be down with the Gold Ganja. He marched into his bedroom and reappeared dragging what looked like two trees behind him. I've never seen so much pot. There was enough cannabis to fell a strapping, broad-shouldered Viking, never mind a pint-sized man. The wee fella proudly told me how he'd traveled to Cape Town, and even more proudly stripped off his shirt to show me large, jagged scars on his back where he'd been stabbed five times while there.

"How horrible," I thought. "Someone stabbed the midget."

"I can't wait to go back there," he enthused. "It's such a beautiful country."

Yeah... fire up another branch, dude.

As much amusement as the batty Burford bunch provided, the green fields and aimlessly meandering sheep of the English countryside just didn't do it for me. I craved warm weather and swimming pools. I hankered after palm trees, sand beaches and the exhilaration of Hollywood. No pop stars populated the Cotswolds. Not one. No, they all leisured in Beverly Hills and I was yet enamored with the idea of mega-stardom, convinced that it was within my reach.

Somewhere around this time, my mother's relationship with Peter H. switched off again, and she flew back to England to join in on the encroachment of my poor sister's now cramped Burford apartment. Rid of Peter, my mother speedily concocted a plan to marry one of the old-timers in Burford. She honed in on an old wrinkly named Ted, who was rich as a lord and drunk as a lumberjack. Ted lounged his days away in the local *Bull Hotel,* drinking, drinking, and then drinking some more. My mother imagined him to be an easy catch, a simple synch. They'd marry, he'd die soon thereafter, and naturally he would leave all of his money to her. It was a solid plan.

On their first date, Ted invited my mother for Chinese food. Seated at their table, he immediately began pounding the rice wine, drinking with great gusto while my mother wilted from hunger. When he finally ordered: for the both of them...he ordered desert. Ted was that smashed that he thought they had already eaten. Days later he was 86-ed from the Bull Hotel for wetting his pants and vomiting on himself. My mother let her marriage plans drop.

Samantha and me on High Street in Burford

CHAPTER 33 – America

Humming and haaing, I dubiously abandoned Samantha to the not so capable hands of my (unmarried) mother. I clear forgot about the incident I'd filed under "caution" in the back of my mind. I consoled myself with the fact that Linda was on hand to supervise my mother, plus I felt I had no other choice than to leave Samantha behind; I couldn't well take a three-year-old to a land where I knew nobody. My plan was to organize myself chop-chop, then hasten back to pick up the Snausage girl - which is what I call her to this day. Snausages.

My mother assured me she would safeguard Samantha, that I could venture forth worry free and seek a new life in America for my daughter and myself, (her words not mine.)

"She is in good hands," she crooned, (uh-huh). "I know you've always dreamed of going to America. Now is your chance. Go follow your dream and don't worry, your daughter is safe."

Cough…choke...splutter.

Well, Snausage girl or not, I deserted my daughter and boarded a plane for America. America! America!

I like to be in America
Okay by me in America
Everything's free in America

On the boats and on the planes
They're coming to America

America, America, God shed his grace on thee

They've all come to look for America
And so on and so on…

Landing in America flooded me with sentiment. Seriously, I emoted big time! Here I was in the land of endless possibility. The place I had dreamt of throughout my childhood. The land where my favorite music had been recorded. The land where my favorite films had been produced. The land where the big stars lived. The land of Bon Jovi, Aerosmith and Mr. Big (hey, I like that band). The land of Nicolas Cage (hubba, hubba!), Matt Dillon, Bruce Willis, John Malkovich. Holy Macaroni! So many men…such little restraint. It made me weepy.

Things moved along screamingly. I landed a job in a cover band, secured a place to live, bought a car and found a school for Samantha. The reason things eased along so magically was Matt H., a warm-hearted soul who became a firm friend and helped me enormously. I doubt I'd have made it through my first months in America had it not been for Matt. By my third night in California, I'd moved in with him. Quick work, huh? Stop it. He was gay, so don't you worry yourself.

Matt tested my knowledge: had I heard of David Letterman or Howard Stern? Jerry Springer? What about Beavis and Butthead? Jay Leno? That I'd never heard of these people was unacceptable and Matt took it upon himself to immerse me into the American culture starting with a 3 hour Beavis and Butthead Moron-athon:

Fire! Fire!…Go on, kick me in the Jimmy. Uh…guacamole?

Following the Beavis and Butthead Moron-athon came Howard Stern's New Years Eve Pageant: an hour of semi-clad contestants strutting before Howard Stern (a somewhat camel-faced man) who crudely tried to goad the contestants into taking off the little they had on, and seemed super keen for them to fondle themselves as well. Nice chap, that Howard.

One topless contestant strummed on a guitar and sang: "Fuck the president, fuck him up the ass. Fuck the President's wife, fuck her up the ass. Fuck the pope, fuck him up the ass" and so on, and so on.

Another topless girl poured maggots down her pants, smooshed them into her bikini bottoms in a gyrating fashion, then ate a handful for good measure. Quality viewing!

And last, but not least, Matt introduced me to Jerry! Jerry! Jerry! This popular American TV show invited all sorts of white trash guests to the stage where they proceeded to scream at one another, beat each other up, and basically *fuck each other up the ass* and then some! These guests tended to expose Neanderthal passions, right along with their breasts, and they'd let loose more emotion on stage than even my mother could muster up. Jerry Springer was drama and über-hysterics galore. I loved it…I hated it.

Ranch dressing was another new entity for me. I slathered my food with this thick, white, creamy poison, adding it to everything: pasta, tuna, chips, salad, potato fries. My diligence was duly rewarded. Extra cellulite formed on my thighs and my cholesterol levels soared. Hey! It's the American way.

Energized by my substantial saturated fat intake, I quickly had my main mallards in a row. I secured a job, bought a car, established a home in a safe area, plus I had the fortification of my new knowledge as to who Jay Leno was, and what enchiladas, burritos and tostadas were. It was time to reclaim Samantha and bring her to live with me in the United States of America. Yeehaa!

During the four months I'd been in America, my mother and I had stayed in touch through the mail. My mother wrote me letters to keep me abreast of Samantha's doings: Samantha had started ballet classes, Samantha had a little friend called Lilly, Samantha was happy and healthy.

Slowly the letters toned more formal, grew more distant. The letters took to lecturing me on how stability and continuity were important for a young child. I balked at this berating:

"That's rich coming from you," I thought.

My mother extended her newfound knowledge on childrearing to claim how hard it would be for Samantha to accustom herself to yet another country, yet another school, yet another household. And how everything my mother did was in Samantha's best interests.

"Samantha has an interview with the headmistress of her new school," she wrote. "I've already bought her the necessary uniforms."

What? Was this my mother marching forward with long-term plans for Samantha's education? It certainly appeared that way. She'd already enrolled Samantha in a school without my agreement or consent. Oh no, no, no. Absolutely not.

The moment I understood that my mother had bought Samantha school uniforms, the incident I'd filed under "caution" in my brain came screeching back. I should never have believed my mother. She was completely unstable. She lied through her teeth. Thing is with my mother, even though she's lying to your face, it comes across as sincere, because in *her* mind, what she's saying *is* actually true. Of course she wanted to help me by looking after Samantha. Of course she wanted me to be able to go to the USA unhindered. Of course she would never try and take Samantha from me…unless that is, of course she suddenly changed her mind. Why should she relinquish Samantha to me after having been her sole provider for 4 months? She probably felt that Samantha was hers now, and I'd wager my good lung that she'd used the past four months to plug my impressionable daughter's mind with phony baloney. How stupid was I?

I dropped everything I was doing, ditched my cover band in Palm Springs (sorry guys) and phoned my mother in Burford to let her know I'd be flying to England to pick up Samantha – immediately.

But my mother one-upped me one last time. Before I could even board the plane, she slapped a restraining order on me. **A restraining order**!

Ach jah, so ein scheiss!

This restraining order stated that I would not be allowed to remove Samantha from the care of my mother without court permission. I flew back to England in a mounting panic. The demented, old bag was planning on taking Samantha away from me…again…only this time she was zooming ahead with her plan.

Jeepers fucking creepers!

CHAPTER 34 – Restraint

And so it came to pass I was gifted a splendidly agonizing two weeks compliments of *meine mutter*. I arrived in Burford (following a plane, train and bus ride) and knocked on my sister's apartment door. My mother opened the door and glared at me with such immeasurable hatred that it twisted her face hard, cold, and unfamiliar. It unsettled me. I'd never seen my mother dole out this look to anyone, least of all me! Her eyes pierced me with such hatred, I almost felt obliged to spontaneously combust right there on the doorstep.

"You're not allowed here," she seethed at me. "I have a restraining order against you."

"Come on, mother. Please, I'm dying to see Samantha...I've missed her enormously."

I simply couldn't believe that my mother wasn't going to allow me to see my own daughter.

"There's a restraining order against you," she repeated through thin, pursed lips. "Go away."

"Yeah, well that's super swell mom, because I just flew five and a half thousand miles, I'm dead tired, and all I want to do is see my daughter whom you promised to never try and take away from me. Remember?"

Judging by her blank hate-face...no, she didn't.

When my mother had descended on the police station to request they sign her "I'll never try to take Samantha away from you" statement, I'd held on to that grand piece of literature...I ain't stupid.

"I want to see Samantha." I stared her down.

"She's not here and I'm not telling you where she is. You need to leave the premises." She stepped back to close the front door.

I stepped forward.

"Where do you expect me to go?" I asked.

"I don't care where you go, just leave."

Ah, excuse me...golden child remember?

"I'm not leaving." I stood my ground and contemplated mimicking Sally Field by yelling: "Not without my daughter!"

"Then I'll leave." She glared daggers at me, yanked the door shut, locked it, and barged past me.

Lucky for me, by this time my brother had joined the encampment at my sister's place. In fact my sister had moved out to due to the entire family moving in. (Sorry Linda, we were a thoughtless bunch.)

Claude granted me access to the apartment, and there I sat, awaiting my mother's return. Except she didn't return, and there was no sign of Samantha. By nightfall, unease gnawed my insides while I wallowed in guilt. Why had I thought my mother could care for Samantha? What was I? A frikken moron? I knew she'd had her sights on the child. I knew it! I just never believed it. Now what? And what was with the hate-face? A few months back, I was her pride and joy. What was I now? Chopped liver with advanced cirrhosis? The fact that my mother was able to hate me so easily, that kind of smarted. I'd read the abhorrence in her face loud and clear. Well, at least now I didn't have to pretend that we still had a civil relationship. We didn't. We were done. Dead and buried, done!

"Golden Child" was pissed beyond pissed...and hurt beyond hurt. I fucking hated my mother with a vengeance and would have had no problem shooting her in the face (except for the gun-touting part). And let me tell you, that unhinged, backstabbing, psycho bitch was **not getting my daughter!**

I telephoned my sister to please come and help me. I had no car, no cell phone, scant money and the area was unfamiliar to me. Linda agreed to lend a hand by driving me about. Together, we navigated the neighborhoods, seeking out various motels and inns, hoping to spot my mother's car. Nothing!

Several hours into it, my sister gave up.

"You might need a lawyer," she advised.

Indeed. The next morning I recruited a likeable, lady lawyer through means of legal aid, because my British passport entitled me to free legal council - thank you kindly, nice British Government. After reading through the restraining order, my lawyer placed a call on my behalf to the legal firm that my mother had hired, asking them to bring her up-to-speed with the situation. Her advice for me was to gather as much paper-proof as possible. Proof that I was employed in America, proof that I had enough money to support Samantha, proof that I had a home to go to and a school to enroll Samantha in, etcetera…and my lawyer further suggested I accumulate letters, postcards, diaries, whatever I could find, to prove that my mother was *not* able to look after Samantha. Oh, you betcha!

I returned to the Burford apartment on a major mission. I telephoned old friends in South Africa and new friends in America, asking them to please send character references and vouch for me. Hey, forget that I shagged your brother; just tell them I'm decent! I sieved through every piece of paper in the apartment, gathering evidence. Day one passed with no word from my mother. Day two passed with no word from my mother. By day three, I could no longer sleep, no longer eat, and spent the bulk of my time pacing the apartment gulping down weak coffee. I was a shaking, palpitating mess; my thoughts racing furiously. I imagined my mother long gone with her vast sum of money. Hell, she could go wherever she wanted with that cash. Oh wait, you didn't know she had a vast sum of money did you? I forgot to mention that. Well, when my grandmother died, she left my mother (her daughter) three hundred thousand Deutsch Mark - a decent caboodle of loot in those days. And although my mother had already mowed through a good portion of her inheritance, more than enough remained for her to do damage with. She had a distinct advantage over me. She had *ganz viel geld!*

With that kind of money she could survive for an extended period in any country. In fact, she may have already left England. She'd had four days to travel God knows where. She could be anywhere. Jesus H Christ and other important deities too! Frantic, I phoned my lawyer.

"I need to see my daughter. I'm freaking out here. I haven't seen Samantha in four months and I'm starting to think I might never see her again. I don't even know that she is still in this country. Please…I need to know. I need to at least talk to my daughter."

My lawyer placed a rush plea to my mother's lawyers, yet no word was heard. After the fifth day of silence, my mother abruptly reappeared at the apartment to collect fresh clothing for herself and Samantha. She barreled past me, making it clear we were *not* going to have a conversation. I was so relieved to see her; to know that she hadn't absconded with Samantha, that I immediately started crying. I could find nothing better to do than follow her silently about the apartment - my heart hammering, my mouth dry, my eyes watering.

She gathered up what she needed, then sat down to rest for a minute at the kitchen table. I sat, too, wondering what on earth to say to her wooden frame. Fresh out of ideas, and overcome with desperation, I suddenly dropped to my knees on the floor beside her and begged: "Please, please don't do this to me. Please don't take Samantha away from me."

I started sobbing, a pitiful shoulder-shuddering-showdown.

My mother stared ahead, stone faced, as if I were some bothersome beggar seeking alms. She'd obviously made her decision and nothing I could say or do was about to change it. Her determined resolve placed her securely beyond my reach.

"Why?" I choked out. "Why are you doing this?"

I wasn't expecting an answer; the question simply fell out of my mouth. Imagine my surprise when my mother squared me up and said,

"Well, you wouldn't come with me to open a restaurant in Spain."

WHAT?

What was she blabbering about? I dimly recalled a night, many moons ago, when a mention of: "Wouldn't it be fun to run a restaurant in Spain" bounced about during dinner, while we were all drinking wine. That was it. Our entire plan of moving to Spain to operate an eatery consisted of one sentence. Besides, my mother habitually had schemes and plans: plans of moving to Rumania to help AIDS orphans, plans to move to France to open a language school, plans to move to Turkey to write children's books, plans to move, and move, and move…and oh damn, look – wherever you go – there you are!

Fear squeezed my heart. My mother was finally crossing the threshold to full-blown gaga. She'd flipped her lid. She'd come unraveled, uncorked, unglued; spooled her line way, way out there…and I had no idea how to reel her back in. All I could do was watch her tail lights disappear as she drove away into the dark.

I sat up all night scouring every piece of correspondence I'd ever received from her. I highlighted each section that struck me as even remotely off kilter. By morning, I had a briefcase full of crazy with which I planned to win back my daughter.

Later that day, my mother phoned to politely inform me that the police were coming to evict me from the property. It was Samantha's home after all, and seeing that the restraining order was against me, I needed to vacate the premises.

Having nowhere to go, no money, and a brain wound so tight I was ready to detonate, I telephoned the police myself.

"My mother has taken my child and I don't know where they are…it's been six days. I understand I have a restraining order against me, but surely I am entitled to see my own child?"

The police advised me to go through legal channels and suggested I charge my mother with kidnapping.

I dialed my lawyer post-haste.

My lawyer contacted my mother's lawyers once again, this time ordering that Samantha be brought to me within 24 hours or my mother would face kidnapping charges. Her lawyers readily agreed, and a plan was set up for my mother and Samantha to meet me at 10 o'clock the next morning at a local teashop.

10 AM, there I was, drinking tea. Fidgety, nervous and super-excited. I was about to see Samantha.

At 10:30 AM, a waiter neared my table to ask if I was Niki.

I nodded.

"There's a phone call for you."

He led me to the back office and handed me a phone. I gripped the receiver.

"Hello?"

I didn't recognize the voice on the other end.

"Hello, my name is Lyn D. You don't know me but my daughter is friends with your daughter and...

"I'm sorry...who is this?"

"Lyn D. Your mother asked me to call you today to tell you she won't be bringing Samantha to see you."

"Will she be late?" I wasn't quite computing.

"She isn't coming today." The lady's voice held calm.

"Can you put my mother on the phone please?"

"She doesn't want to talk to you, which is why I am calling on her behalf."

"Can you please put my mother on the phone, whoever you are?"

My chest constricted as panic mounted.

The lady continued with her irritatingly calm cadence.

"Your mother doesn't think you are ready to see Samantha. She thinks you will upset her. You will not be seeing Samantha today. She will be contacting your lawyer and…"

My vision abruptly narrowed, sucking everything backwards in a bizarre vortex. Inexplicably, the phone receiver weighed 200 pounds and proved too heavy to hold. It crashed to the ground as my hands stiffened and numbed up. My skin surface started tingling. I couldn't figure out who that woman - now talking to the floor - was, but I understood what she was telling me. She was telling me that my mother wasn't bringing Samantha. My mother wasn't coming at all.

The waiter, having heard the phone hit the ground, rushed back to find me slumped on the floor, my hands held stiffly in front of me.

"She's not coming," I choked out. "She won't let me see Samantha." Snot gushed as I broke down in tears. "And I can't feel my hands."

Poor waiter. I wasn't his usual customer.

"Tea's on the house today miss." He said gently.

Crumpled on the floor, struggling to recoup my scattered wits, I knew I would never see Samantha again. Suddenly I realized how I *had* been a bad mother. I'd been short with Samantha. I'd yelled at her. I'd viewed her as a burden. I'd put myself first and left her behind with my unsound mother. Too late I realized how my young daughter meant more to me than any Hollywood nonsense, how I loved Samantha more than life itself, and how I couldn't bear to be without her. I couldn't go back to America, not without Snausages. I would have to spend the rest of my lifetime searching for my daughter. Oh my God. My mother was going to ruin Samantha. I urged to kill my mother. Who was that woman? Lyn? Laura? Why hadn't I paid more attention? I should have got her number. Fuck!

I tried to stand up but the sledgehammer-realization had smashed into my chest and somehow dislodged my core equilibrium. I buckled back down, thinking bitterly how I was the one my mother loved more than life itself. Her golden-fucking-child. How could she do this? My mother had taken my daughter…and I had no idea where.

It hurt like hell.

Once my legs firmed back, I wobbled out of the teashop and headed towards High Street. Standing staring at the oncoming traffic, I had an overwhelming desire to fling myself under the nearest truck. I no longer wished to exist. I wanted to be pulverized. Would my mother feel bad then? Would she wish she had brought me my daughter if I was a mashed up mess in the morgue? Would she miss me? Did she love me at all? I was her child for shit-sake. She should…shouldn't she?

I stared at the traffic my heart pounding. What about Samantha? I couldn't leave her alone on this earth. She needed me. She needed me to find her. She *would* miss me. But what if I never found her? I tore myself away from High Street. Stop it. Stop it!

Half out of my mind, I blurted out to the nearest passerby "My mother has kidnapped my daughter."

The passerby threw me a nervous glance and hurried away.

My lawyer calmed me down. "We'll set up another meeting for tomorrow. Your mother *has* to bring Samantha by order of the court, or we will file kidnapping charges against her."

I drank myself to sleep that night and woke up already crying. A metallic taste permeated my mouth while my heart clanged alarmingly in my chest.

"Jesus. I'm spazzing!"

My body felt crushed, broken…28 years old, yet barely able to move. I shambled to a nearby doctor's office, crying the entire way. I couldn't stop crying. I no longer had control over my tear ducts. I mean, I hate crying in public and avoid it at all costs, but on this day the sluice gates opened and lake misery poured out.

I kept apologizing as I mucus-ed up the front desk.

"May I talk to someone? Please?"

The doc showed me into his office where, in between sobs, I explained what was going on.

"I can't stop crying." Sob.

After clueing him in on the anguish of my last few days he ventured: "Given your circumstances, I don't think it's that unusual that you'd be crying."

"But I don't cry." Sob.

"You do now."

"I want it to stop!"

"It's okay to cry, you know. No one will think any the less of you."

I was not in agreement.

"I find it singularly self indulgent to make such a scene."

"Not if you have a bona fide reason," the doctor assured me. "It's actually quite good for you. It's healthy. Tears release toxins you know."

I didn't know. I sniffed noisily, tears streaming, wads of tissue balled up in my fists.

"What if I see Samantha and I can't stop crying? What will it do to her to have to see me like this?"

"It will show her that you are human. That you've missed her and that you care very much about her."

Now *that* was a novel idea: crying conveying a message of love. I'd certainly never viewed it that way. I'd grown so accustomed to my mother's crying and all that conveyed was: give me. Give me comfort.

Give me love. Give me attention. Give me hugs. Give me. Give me. Give me.

I refused to do that to Samantha. I never wanted her to bear the burden of my well-being, or my moods, or my social life, or my bank account, or my love life, or my lack of love life. I had long decided that I would always carry my own weight, and if I couldn't, I'd bloody well diet.

The lawyers set up another meeting, in yet another teashop. Half an hour early, there I was, my hands all clammy, pacing the pavement outside. Unable to stand still, I skittered about in front of the teashop. Then suddenly I caught sight of my mother and Samantha ambling down the hill. As recognition hit, Samantha broke free from my mother's hand and skipped towards me, her little shining face cocooned by a purple anorak hood. It was one of those moments that imprinted itself deeply into my memory bank. It was a definite "keeper" moment, eidetically engraved.

I scooped Samantha up in my arms and hugged her...and hugged her...and hugged her. Nothing in the world could have made me happier. Not a kajillion record deals. Not a bajillion number one hits. Nothing could compare to having that squeezable little human, with that gigantic smile, firmly in my arms.

Having instigated a full-blown legal process against me, my mother was unable to stop what she had started. The wheels of justice were turning - or rather grinding - towards me and my dream of living in America with Samantha. Like it or not, social services were now involved. A court mandated meeting was set up with an assigned social worker and I anchored down in the interview room, my mouth clamped firmly shut. I feared my motor-mouth might unleash obscenities as my mother aggrandized stories about herself and exaggerated stories about me. Stories to use against me. Stories about

Bill, my "wanted criminal boyfriend". Stories about my anti-social working hours and my propensity to hang out in bars. She presented the welfare worker all her reasons for why I was an unfit parent for Samantha, and all her reasons for why she, herself, would do an oh-so-much spiffier job.

"Are you fucking serious?" I wanted to scream. "You fucked up fantastically the first time around and now think you deserve a second chance. With my child? No fucking way."

Clamp that mouth. Oh, clench those teeth. Don't say a word.

I *was* an unfit mother, hell I was an unfit everything. As a student, I bunked school, then I dropped out of university. As a girlfriend I cheated on every boyfriend I ever had. As an employee, I was fired from numerous positions; **BUT** (big but here), I knew 100 % that I was better equipped to care for Samantha than my mother was.
There would be no *Hell Camp* for the Snausage-girl.

I feared the social worker was veering towards my mother's side. After all, my mother spun a good yarn. She was charming and likable, while I, on the other hand, sat there with my jaw muscles twitching.

Smiling demurely at the social worker, my mother confessed, "I had hoped that Niki would be a little bit famous by now, or that maybe she'd have found a nice, rich man to marry. I would feel much more comfortable letting Samantha go to America if I knew that."

I unclenched my grinding teeth to spit a few words out: "I've only been in America for four months, mother."

It was the turning point. Thankfully, as my mother usually does, she went too far. You know the saying: Give someone enough rope and they'll hang themselves? Oh yahtzee!

Bathing in the social worker's undivided attention, my mother launched into her assorted issues: how she suffers with her health,

how her children have abandoned her, how all men are bastards...
yada, yada, yada...her own loquacious undoing.

The social worker thanked us for coming in, wrote a letter of
recommendation to the judge overseeing the case, and VOILA... no
more restraining order against me. I was free to take my child to
America. Let heavenly choirs of angels sing – **hallelujah!**

Thank you Jebus.

In my absence, my mother dearest had stripped me of "mommy
status" and retrained Samantha to call me Niki. Seated next to me on
the airplane, drawing colorful pictures, Samantha kept lifting her
angelic-blonde head to look my way and say: "I love you Niki."

Be still my swelling, mushy, beating heart.

"I love you too, Samantha."

So much so that it hurts.

PART FOUR

Growing up in America!

"I appreciate my skin holding me together."
    Diary entry 1998

CHAPTER 35 – Samantha

It was a night of a million stars with warm winds whispering, or let's just say that's how I remember it. Samantha had been awake for approximately 18 hours, refusing to sleep on the plane, too engrossed in watching her own little TV and drawing colorful flowers. She was still steaming strong by the time we arrived at Matt's house, there was only one thing for it…Jacuzzi time.

Relaxing in that bubbling joy, I tilted my head back to fully absorb the breathtaking Californian sky, my beautiful child's smiling face beside me. The notion that *my life was finally about to start* drifted down from the twinkling skies to light up my soul. I was in America, with my daughter securely by my side, and nothing could be finer.

Diary entry - April 1994
My relationship with Samantha is brilliant. I'm finally alone with her in my home without Mother. WOW! I get to be with Samantha every day and I love her with every fiber of my being.

Matt mounted a grand effort for Samantha. Assigned the title "Uncle Matt", he exhibited unending patience with the Snausage-girl. One day, finding Samantha upset and crying, Matt dispatched one unsuccessful attempt after another in hopes of plugging her downpour. Finally, he asked in exasperation, "Why are you crying Samantha?" Samantha held up four chubby, little fingers to elucidate for him:

"I am crying for four reasons. Number one, I can't find my blankie. Number two, I am hungry. Number three, I want to watch TV but your music is too loud, and number four, my back is itchy."

Matt was decidedly impressed with the relaying of her problems, and in a systematic order to boot: most important to least important.

"Geez Samantha," he commended her. "You're more astute than most of my adult friends."

Mistaking this for an insult, Samantha quickly defended herself.

"Well, they probably don't need a blankie," she said.

Our first trip to Disneyland found Samantha's face glued to a porthole for the duration of the old submarine ride. Consumed with love for the *Little Mermaid* (right along with a billion other little girls), she was delighted when she glimpsed a life-sized mermaid under the water.

"Oh look, mummy!" (Yay! I'd had my status reinstated.)

"A mermaid! How awfully beautiful."

This was all said in an endearing British accent that Samantha's young sponge brain had soaked up.

Two months later we visited San Diego's SeaWorld. On sighting the shark tank, Samantha enthused:

"Awesome! Check it out mom! That tank is radical!"

Samantha had Americanized overnight.

While Samantha Americanized, I attempted to parentize. I read various books on child rearing, and for the rest, I relied on gut instinct. I wanted to be a good parent for Samantha. No, I wanted to be an exceptional parent for Samantha. I wanted to fill her love tank with pure unconditional love. I wanted her to feel comfortable and confident in her own body, so she wouldn't have to search for years to come for ways to soothe the ache in her chest. The residue of my mother's haphazard dishing out of affection, rules, punishment, and compliments still palpitated my heart to an unhealthy speed. I knew how to *not parent* and that proved a good starting point. I allowed Samantha the space to be her own person. I set clear rules for her, established a routine and stayed 12 years in a neighborhood that I detested in order to afford Samantha the opportunity to attend a decent school. You owe me big time, Samantha!

If a serious matter called for a discussion, I'd shrink to Samantha's height in order to facilitate a face-to-face talk, instead of me talking down to her. I'd strive to be honest with her, which included admitting when I was wrong, or had behaved childishly. Me? Childish? Never.

For some reason this was a tough one - to admit to my child that I'd made a mistake when all I wanted to do was save face and be "right". And I doubt I'm alone here.

Once Samantha was a little older, if she acted out or misbehaved, I'd press her for answers.

"Has someone or something upset you today?" I'd ask.

"I don't know," she'd reply sulkily.

"Well, I bet if you think hard enough, you'll remember something that caused you to feel bad, or angry, or sad, and maybe that will help us figure out what's going on with you right now."

I learned over time that if Samantha lashed out at me, something or someone was bugging her…okay, yes, and sometimes it was purely me. I aimed to seek out the reasons behind her behavior, and before long, Samantha became proficient at analyzing her own actions and situations. This enabled her to choose healthier options for herself, or at least offer up better excuses.

"I didn't clean my room because I'm tired, and I still have a lot of homework."

Now that was a far cry from simply yelling, "You can't make me clean my room!"

Her grasp of taking responsibility for herself, combined with her capacity to express herself eloquently, probably saved us from many a lively showdown.

I further encouraged Samantha to determine her own punishments. Once she understood what it was she had done wrong, she could then select a suitable way to make amends. Here is a list of unacceptable behaviors, and the consequences to follow, that Samantha jotted down for herself when she was five.

(This list now lives in my treasure box)

1. No biting or kicking – or no ice lollies for 4 days
2. No screaming in anger – or no Power Rangers for 1 day
3. Tidy up after yourself – or time-out for 10 minutes
4. You must go to bed when asked – or no bedtime story
5. No drawing on anything except paper – or no crayons for 2 weeks.

She was harder on herself than I would have been. I found her list adorable...and ever so useful.

One child-rearing book suggested not sending a child to their room as a punishment. The bedroom was their little sanctuary, so it shouldn't be used as a place of sentence. I could relate. Better to send them to neutral territory. So the next time Samantha threw a tantrum, I banished her to the bathroom and told her to knock on the door when she was ready to come out and behave. Holding vigil outside, I listened.

Wail! Wail ...wail...wail...wail...silence...more silence...knock-knock.

"I'm ready to be good, Mommy!"

And with that, I'd be reduced to a squishy marshmallow.

If only Samantha could have sent me to the bathroom when I misbehaved. Poor kid had no recourse for my tantrums. If I wished to throw a wobbly, yell, scream and launch things (like cabbage, for example – sorry Manthy – that was a bad day), I bloody well could.

I like to believe that my meltdowns were few and far between, but you'd probably have to ask Samantha for a more accurate analysis.

I was short on patience (still am...could you read a little faster, please) and parenting is one serious test of patience. Since it takes patience to learn patience, I was in for a tough learning period.

Children love to experiment and unfortunately often choose to experiment with your favorite belongings. It could be construed as naughty, but really, how else are they going to learn? Their job is to push the parameters every which way, on every which thing, in order to learn where and what they can or cannot do. It was Samantha's job to drive me batty.

"What happens if I stick a banana in this video machine?"

"What happens if I pour cereal over the dog?"

"What does this caterpillar taste like? (Hmm...it tastes like chicken)."

Ah, the curiosity. You have to watch them 24/7 because they *will* eat the poison under the sink, they *will* draw on the walls, they *will* mess in your car. Unless you are giving birth to a different species, the human element makes children do silly, silly stuff. They're clumsy, they lack logic and they love to touch/taste/spit up on interesting things. And believe you me, your shiny, new, expensive dress/car/carpet/jewelry is of particularly high interest to them. They do this and more as I was to learn over the next several years with Pretty Mantha, the best teacher I've ever had.

CHAPTER 36 - Violence into Therapy

Samantha was my priority. I mean, yeah, yeah, I brought different boyfriends home, a whole slew of them actually, but I never engaged in a long-term relationship. It was too complicated. Samantha would be jealous of the boyfriend, or the boyfriend would be jealous of Samantha.

One potential beau introduced himself to Samantha.

"Hi, I'm Nick. Who are you?"

Samantha didn't even bother looking at him. She kept right on staring at the TV. "I'm George Washington," she answered sarcastically.

"Nice to meet you, George," Nick smiled at her.

Nick lasted three months.

Not that Samantha scared him off. He adored her. It was me. I had slept with *a random* while away on vacation in Lake Tahoe. I hadn't changed my wicked ways...yet. At least I was making progress. I *told* Nick that I had cheated on him. I fessed up. That was a breakthrough for me: being honest. I'd grown up with the idea that you simply bent the truth to suit yourself whenever you needed.

I also grew up with the idea that if you had attempted to verbally solve matters, and you weren't making headway, that you then resorted to physically expressing yourself...you know...with a rock-solid clout, a hefty thwack, a bop 'em, belt 'em, bash 'em, feed them a tasty knuckle sandwich type of approach. I had zero rage control. If you pissed me off enough, I'd happily rip your head off. I physically fought with every guy I ever dated. They must have all pissed me off. I was as abusive as I was abused.

"Please will you stay the night?" I begged the one young lad, "I'm scared of the dark."

"No," he replied, preparing to leave.

"Please. I'm asking you nicely." My heart rate quickened. I really was scared of the dark (as you know), plus I was only nineteen at the time and renting in a rough area of downtown Johannesburg.

"No!" He said decisively.

Okay! Fine!

I walloped that young man on the back of the head with his own motorbike helmet. I made him buckle at the knees. He retaliated with a punch to my face that loosened a tooth and colored the inside of my mouth a sinister purple. I guess I deserved that one.

At fifteen, I crouched in the driveway bushes awaiting my then boyfriend, the beloved Michael. Feeling jealous over something or the other, I figured I'd ambush him…with a fire poker. On seeing him approach, I leapt out and swiped him full swing on the elbow. He doubled in pain as I dropped the poker and ran like Zola Budd. I wasn't quite Zola enough because Mike caught me before I could duck into *Hell Camp*. He hauled me screaming across the yard by the back of my dungarees, and "put the boot in" (kicked me in the face). This left me to nurse two black eyes and a puffy face. I believe I may have deserved that one, too.

Mike and I hit each other frequently and fervidly. I punched him as hard as I could. He dragged me along the street by my hair. I bit him in the face. He smashed my bedroom windows.

It was pure love.

My final physical fight landed me first in a holding cell, and soon thereafter, in a hospital bed. And there I lay for three days, flat on my back, with a lengthy rubber tube speared through my ribcage to help re-inflate my flopping lung and to drain off pretty plasma caused by the pneumothorax.

This particular fight had stormed way out of control and ended up with me making use of my teeth again, savage that I am. This time I bit – let's call him J (seeing as his name is Jeff). I bit J because he foolishly left his naked chest lying on my face. And J had a generous amount of body weight, so when he lay on top of me to stop me from slapping him (which I was), I couldn't breathe. It felt like my shoulders were about to pop out of their sockets. Ah, what to do? I couldn't wriggle free. I couldn't push him off. I couldn't breathe. So I sunk my teeth into his smothering chest and clenched my jaw firmly shut. Now it was J who couldn't wriggle free, or push me off. I clung on like a hardnosed pit-bull terrier. I felt his skin tearing as my teeth sunk in deeper and deeper…hmmm, also tastes like chicken! Poor J! He slammed his knee into my chest in an effort to un-gnash my teeth from his flesh. That worked! My lockjaw slackened, my chest cartilage cracked, and I sucked on empty air with an intelligent "what the…?" expression on my face.

Free of my teeth, J rushed out of the room, and I quickly slammed the bedroom door shut and locked it. When J returned, he kicked the door clear off its hinges. The doorframe splintered as woodchips sprayed the room and J popped his head in to say: "Get dressed. The police are on their way."

And you couldn't have just told me that through the locked door?

With relief, I watched the police arrive, that is, until they arrested me for assault with a deadly weapon. Huh? A deadly weapon? What deadly weapon? Well, apparently my teeth. Damn my sharp incisors; my razor-like canines. The police further handed my 6-foot-two, bulky, 200-pound boyfriend, a pamphlet on domestic violence, loaded with advice on where he could seek shelter from his abusive partner, 5-foot-2, 102 pound me! At that point J admitted to the police that he had started the fight. That he had tipped me out of the bed and slammed my head into the sideboard. That he had smashed the alarm clock and kicked the door clear off its hinges.

"Arrest me instead," he invited, Mr. Gallant all of a sudden.

"You made the call, sir, plus you have blood on your chest. She has no signs of abuse and admits to biting you. We're taking her down to the holding cell."

Oops!

Bail was set at ten thousand dollars. Ten thousand dollars! That's as much as I earned in an entire year. Fortunately, after a few hours locked in the holding cell (in unflattering pajamas), J's dad posted the bail money, and I was released.

I exited the holding cell unable to breathe properly, with a disconcerting sloshing sound emanating from my chest. X-rays revealed two broken ribs and a collapsed lung. So, like I said, three days horizontal in a hospital bed, providing me ample time to think and think. And think I did. Especially when J's parents brought Samantha in for a visit and I shuddered with disgust at myself. How could I have behaved the way I did? I was white trash. I was a frikken Jerry Springer guest. I was the very thing I detested. Was this the kind of behavior I wished to model for my daughter? Being arrested? Handcuffed on my own front lawn? What if both my lungs had collapsed? I could have died. Who would look after Samantha then? My Mother? Noooooooo!

I made myself a vow. I would never-ever touch another person in anger again; in self-defense possibly, but never in anger. If I found myself reaching boiling point, on the verge of lashing out physically, then I'd simply leave the room. I promised myself this at 31 years of age. That's how long it took me to learn that violence is wrong. What an opsimath, but mercifully, I've never raised a hand in anger again.

I may not have been violent anymore, but I was still massively miserable. Feeling mightily disenchanted with my behavior, I reached the point where I couldn't drink myself happy anymore. I couldn't fake my life anymore. In fact, I couldn't really feel anything anymore. Bogged down by my unresolved issues, I made myself another vow. I would bite the psychological bullet (not the psychologist) and enter therapy…and stick with it this time. The out-of-control behavior had to stop. The bacchanalia had to stop. I vowed to start therapy and not to quit until I knew what the hell I was doing. I realized I was a mess: guzzling gallons, changing boyfriends like underwear, and bludgeoning myself with self-hate.

Stupid Niki. Ugly Niki. Undeserving Niki. Slut Niki.

From whence did all this self-loathing arise? What made me believe I was so unworthy? Why did I deserve nothing? And not only did I deserve nothing good, I had to make sure that everyone around me was okay. What driving force impelled me to shoulder responsibility for everyone and everything? Why was it my job, to ensure the entire world was okay? (Any guesses here?)

Diary Entry - 12th February 1997

I feel terrible. I drank and drank and drank and now I can hardly move – nothing new there. I slept at ****'s house and apparently we had sex. I don't remember a thing - I'm still drunk right now – so I don't care. My heart is broken and I don't care about anything anymore. I am sooooooo lonely. I wish I had a mother. I'd call her right now….

It required seven years of couch-chat to undo and reorganize my thinking patterns. Seven years to peel back the layers of faulty logic. Seven years to untangle some serious snafu. Seven years to find a comfortable place where all the vile images in my mind could reside without causing me continuous damage. I made an interminable commitment to *getting* better. Better for me. Better for Samantha.

Better for the world. Better for my therapist, Kathy B., a lovely, warm human being, whom I desperately wanted to please (probably not the healthiest of therapeutic wants).

Week after week, I vented in her office, vomiting up venom, seething with self-loathing, self-pity and self-longing. I dug into my past to build my future, excavating memories for scrupulous examination. Tugging at those memories, poking at them, screaming at them, battering them. Crying. Raging. Hyperventilating. Shaking. Turning numb…whoop-de-woo, fun times!

> Diary entry – March 98
> *I'm not sure what is wrong with me.*
> *Why do I get jealous of people's parents and family?*
> *Why can't I believe anyone will ever be faithful to me?*
> *Why do I get bored with jobs?*
> *Why can't I stick to routine?*
> *Why do I feel bad and undeserving and guilty?*
> *Why do I feel lank (very) sorry for myself sometimes?*
> *Why do I screw around and why does it upset me?*
> *Why does sex mean so little to me, and why do I hate it so much*
> *sometimes.*
> *Why can't I bear to hear, or smell or touch my mother?*
> *Why can't I look after myself?*
> *Why do I often feel sick and seriously tired?*

Kathy proposed she re-parent me, which, over the next several years, she did. I could ask or tell her anything, and she consistently had a sensible observation or response. She steered me through a swamp of ugliness, guiding me safely to the opposite shore. One by one, the answers to the questions above were revealed. It was not quick and it was not easy. Thing is, if you want to get better, really better, you have to commit to it, because when you decide to puncture your protective layer, smoldering lava trickles out that you never knew you had, and by the time you feel the burn, it's too late to turn back. You just have to brave the plunge, leap into the abyss, and hurtle down through your own murky chaos.

And so it is. Once your eyes are open, you can never close them again.

Kathy encouraged me to set boundaries. Sanctioned me to say "NO". Role-played *meine mutter* so I could practice saying no. Hypnotized me for relaxation and regression purposes. Played on the floor with me, simulating childhood. Recorded a tape cassette of her soothing voice for me to listen to at home (which I did, curled in the fetal position, rocking back and forth, howling like a banshee). Kathy analyzed my dreams and my state of mind, and advised me to try kickboxing as a physical vent for the anger boiling blindly inside me.

It took five years of Kathy repeatedly recommending kickboxing before I finally succumbed and enrolled myself in a women's class that trained you to kick and punch a solid, sand filled bag. The bag stood a tad higher than my own 5 ft 2 frame and kindly allowed me to unleash a world of hurt, anger and sadness onto its worn, black leather surface. As the bag dutifully absorbed its beating, I realized it wasn't my mother or René that I was bashing. Strangely enough, the person who showed up to smirk at me, spreading his smarmy face across the sandbag, was my grandfather. Well, I simply tore into him; round house kick to his imaginary face.

"Fuck you, you filthy bastard!"

Uppercut. Elbow. Front kick.

"Die you mother-fucker!"

I whomped on my grandfather. I kicked his lecherous German ass. I destroyed his beastly visage.

"How dare you?"

Karate chop. Jab. Hammer-kick.

"I hate you! I completely hate you!"

I did hate him. I mean, yes, I hated my mother, and René too, but my grandfather, he molested me when I was nine, so he wins the coconut. Molestation is a total mind-fuck. Forcing a child to be sexual before they are near sexual maturation causes wide-ranging damaging effects: depression, anxiety, low self esteem, alcoholism, drug addiction, dysfunctional relationships, dissociative identity disorder, self-mutilation, suicidal thoughts and so on.

Of all these splendid disorders, I owned several:

Depression – check.

Anxiety – check.

Low self esteem – check.

Self-mutilation – check.

Dysfunctional relationships – double check.

Alcoholism – Ooh! Check, check, check.

Kathy recommended a book called "The Courage to heal". And for anyone who has been molested (and by today's statistics, that's one in four of you), I recommend the same. Work your way through that substantial book and please enroll yourself in a kickboxing class. Not the punching, kicking in the air crap, the "beat it out on a leather sand bag and put some stink on it" type.

At my first class, I punched and kicked with such vigor, I could barely see straight. Seriously, I felt slightly delirious with the exertion. Then, inexplicably, I felt euphoric. I must have released a shitload of endorphins, because I was floating on air. It was as if my sweat beads had fastened onto the toxic anger within me and drawn it out through my skin into the open, to be dripped unceremoniously onto the spongy gym floor and hosed away by the janitor.

Kathy was right. Kickboxing was astoundingly refreshing! I attended class five times a week, but that didn't suffice. So insistent was my keenness for kickboxing that I scoured the local paper and found a water-filled bag to buy. I set that baby up in the driveway and punished it whenever the fancy hit. The neighbors must have found me charming. Sweating and swearing like some prize bulldog fighter.

"Fuck you! Take that! I hate you!"

I kicked my way through seven months of total physical release until the urge to be aggressive subsided. Had I gained mastery over my anger, or simply worn that sucker out? Whichever, I traded my sandbag in for a yoga mat and found a whole new world waiting for me…right inside my very own body. Equanimity, here I come. Grant me some Satori glory.

CHAPTER 37 – Rules Schmules!

I'd quaffed down seven beers the night J and I tore into each other. Had I been sober, most probably nothing would have happened. I doubt sober Niki would have taken a bite out of her boyfriend. I reckoned it might be time for me to tee-total, but I never vowed. Are you kidding? I couldn't imagine the rest of my life without another drop of alcohol. However, I was prepared to rest up on the wagon for a stretch. See what results that generated.

My quit-drinking scenario lasted almost two years. At first, I attended AA meetings regularly, but nine months into it, I loathed those meetings. Everyone baring their souls: over and over and over and over and over ad nauseam. Yawn! It felt forced. Unnatural. Their drunk war stories left no lasting impression on me, and it began to sound remarkably like whining.

"When I was drinking this…when I was drinking that…I was such an asshole…I was such a loser…feel sorry for me…waah, waah, waah!"

Surely not everything can be blamed on drink? And quitting booze doesn't necessarily solve deeper underlying issues, nor does reminiscing about the drunk years for the rest of your life. That's just doggone depressing.

Yes, I realize that AA is helpful to a lot of people, but then so is church, and neither of those organizations have proffered me much. I attended a second church service (one that accepted me without a hat), and found myself sitting there wanting to bleat, "baaaaaa". Maybe it's the "Sheppard and his flock" thing - but I am not sheep. I do not want to stand up, sit down, stand up, sit down, when told to do so. I do not want to sing cheesy lyrics about Jesus wanting me for a sunbeam, or clap my hands because I'm happy and I know it. Nor do I want to listen to a droning sermon about God's love when I know that the same church-loving, happy-clappy seated next to me won't sit near a Mexican, or an African, or anyone wearing a turban, or a homosexual, or someone who has had an abortion. The prejudice construed and condoned through religion is absurd. Boy, will those good Christian folks be shocked when they arrive in heaven to be greeted by a black, pregnant, female God donning a sombrero, gaily shouting: "Shalom!"

I recognize that my dislike for AA (waah) and church (baah) stem from my aversion to authority and rules. Hey! I never made them rules, why the hell should I have to play by them? Trust me here, folks, that logic don't fly when you're pulled over for driving solo in the carpool lane. My anti-establishment nature saw me driving not only solo in the carpool lane, but with no driver's license whatsoever. I drove in South Africa with no license, I drove in England with no license, I drove in America with no license. I drove illegally on the roads for 12 years. Traffic cops stopped me on numerous occasions and odd stories would shoot out of my mouth.

"My car was stuck in neutral." That was for speeding on a downhill.

"Of course I have a license. My name is Karen Grobelaar." That was for driving with no license.

"I'm lost!" That was for driving on a one way – the wrong way. I delivered that one along with a flood of tears.

Believe it or not, all of my excuses worked. No fines, just warnings. I still received plenty tickets, though, only they were parking tickets. Somehow I amassed so many parking fines, that at one point in South Africa, I had 3 warrants out for my arrest (before I turned 19). Now, I don't remember my parking habits, but I must have simply left my Mini-Minor wherever I damn well pleased - which does ring true to my nature. The third time the sheriff came to *Hell Camp*, he ordered René to "sort me out".

René persuaded me to gather my various fines and car papers, then he drove me to the downtown Court House himself. Resting my left hand on a bible, I had to swear to tell the truth, the whole truth, and nothing but the truth (ha, ha, ha). Instead I lied and lied, until my fines were reduced from R550 to R60. I doe-eyed the judge, telling him I'd long since sold my car and that whoever had bought my mini, must obviously be parking like a bandit!

My reduced fine had to be paid in cash - in full - immediately. I carried no money on me. Neither did René.

"Leave her here and go find a bank," the head police officer directed René, then piloted me over to a bench and indicated for me to sit. I sat in silence next to the mustached wünder-cop, watching the clock on the wall tick slowly, with René nowhere in sight. I didn't blame René. He was heartily miffed at me and was probably taking his sweet ass time as payback. Maybe he had no intention of coming back at all.

A chain gang shuffled by, handcuffed together. Roughly twelve black men in bright orange jumpsuits, miserable to the core.

"Where are they taking them?" I asked Officer Moustache.

"To be whipped." He eyed me momentarily.

Hmmm...interesting. I'd heard that the South African government punished political prisoners (who surprisingly were 95% black) with a solid whipping. 40,000 people had already undergone said punishment.

"Can I be whipped instead of paying my fine?" I asked tentatively, formulating a plan in case René was a no-show.

"Ja sure, *bokkie*." Officer Moustache smirked at me. "For a R60 fine you get five lashes. On the first lash you'll pass out. Then we'll have to wait for you to come around so we can whip you again. It will take up far too much of our time and there's no way you'll be able to handle it. Just pay the fine, *poppie*."

(*Bokkie* means "young buck" in Afrikaans, and *Poppie* means "little dolly" - both belittling names if you ask me). I longed to let loose in his face with a: "Lash my backside, you smug dip-shit!"
I welcomed their puny whipping. I'd drink it up! I'd stoically endure five lashes, no fucking problem man! But another part of me knew, even with my extra layer of protective cellulite, I'd probably crumble in a pathetic heap.

I suppose I was a *bokkie*. I bucked any and all authority. They could all rot in hell. Where were those authority figures when I had needed them? When I was being beaten, molested and emotionally ruined? Screw them all. I felt no obligation to abide by anyone's rules except my own. Other people's rules didn't apply to me, which is why I held no qualms about driving without a license, or living without papers in America - for 17 years. I lied when necessary. I wangled where needed. I distracted if called for; unapologetically inveigling my way in. Samantha and I lived under the radar for many years, me with full knowledge, Samantha with none.

Poor Samantha. I had to confess when she turned 16 and wished to obtain her driver's license.

"Um Snausage, there's something I need to tell you."

She was outraged.

"What have you done to me?" she sobbed. "I can't get a job, I can't get my license, I can't travel...Oh my God! Oh my God!"

The implications of being an illegal alien were sinking in. I urged her to relax, assuring her that I was a maestro finagler. Indeed, I'd been finagling since I was a kid. I knew how to get what I needed, albeit through somewhat unorthodox methods.

I whisked Samantha and her South African birth certificate to the DMV, where we fell in line. She was pale and silent. I was flushed and sweaty. My heart thumped so fiercely, I feared that my heaving chest might alert the security. Then it was our turn. The DMV lady eagle-eyed Samantha's birth certificate suspiciously and saying nothing, she nudged the woman working alongside her. I momentarily stopped breathing. "Please African-Jewish lady God with happy sombrero on - please don't let us be deported."

The woman working alongside had a fiasco of her own to deal with. A family jostled before her with papers up the ying-yang, clamoring in broken English. Our DMV lady eventually tired of waiting. She stamped the necessary papers before her, handed them to us and said, "That will be $25 please."

Samantha broke into an ear-lifting grin, bounced off to the next line, quickly passed her written test and earned herself a legal learner's permit. Hooray!

CHAPTER 38 – Single Parent

My beer quaffing night of collapsed lung, holding cell and hospital stay sparked another big breakthrough for me. I moved into my *own* place. Up until I turned thirty, I'd never lived by myself. I'd always had a roommate, or more specifically, a boyfriend to bolster me. With no J around, Samantha and I were homeless. Determined to improve myself, determined to look after the Snausage girl, determined not to simply suck onto someone else, I put down $4000 on a mobile home, and six weeks later, Samantha and I moved into our own, 800sqft, hideously carpeted, trailer park home. Y'all come visit now, ya' hear?

I swore off "live in" boyfriends for the next decade. Now I really was a single mom. No boyfriend, no ex-boyfriend, no potential boyfriend. For the first time I was flying solo, or more accurately, hobbling solo. I was a single mother in a thin-walled trailer. It was a hard time financially, emotionally and physically. Down times were rough. If I fell sick, there was no one to pick up the slack. Like the time I had a cyst removed from my eye and Samantha contracted the stomach flu at the same time. While Samantha vomited in the toilet, I held the hair out of her sweating face with one hand, and pressed an ice bag to my swollen eye with the other. My self-pity gage ranked fairly high that day. Then it was my turn to enjoy the stomach flu. Driving Samantha to school racked with nausea, I gripped a plastic bag in hand, ready to drive and heave in unison.

Not only were there times of sickness and exhaustion, but on occupying our new mobile home, I struggled to pay the first month's rent. I'd stretched my money as far as possible to come up with the down payment, and forgotten to factor in the space rent (See René? I suck at numbers).

Lack of money spikes monumental stress in me, and this time it felt like I was spiking into heart attack city. Where on earth could I dig up some extra cash? Then it came to me. I visited the nearest Pawnshop and abandoned my guitar there. I thanked the man for the $250 he counted out, and assured him I'd return within the month to buy my guitar back. And zippity-doo-da-day I did!

I was lonely, I was tired, I was poor. I wasn't heading towards pop-stardom, and the man of my dreams certainly wasn't materializing. Still, I wouldn't trade a second of it. For my hardships and sacrifices, I was given the gift of parenting the most fabulous human being, a marvelous little soul who gave me more than I ever thought possible.

On Valentine's Day, when Samantha was 9 years old, she hopped on her bicycle and rode to the corner 7/11. Bless her heart, she bought me the biggest card in the store, almost as big as she was. So massive in fact, that she had to push her bike home as she couldn't ride her bike and clutch the card at the same time. Samantha shoved her approximately two foot card under her bed and come Valentine's Day, I received an almighty treasure.

"Dear Mommy
I love you with all my heart. Everything in this card is true but no card could show how much I love you. I hope that your day is full of wonderful surprises and that you like the card and presents I give you, yet we both know that we can't show how much we love people through the presents we give them, or how much money we spend on them. It's about how much effort you put into the relationship, how much meaning is in a kiss or a hug, how much you can trust or talk to the person. I'm not saying I don't want to get presents or have people spend money on me though! I want to tell you how much I love you, and I hope that one day we can live in heaven together and watch our great-great grandchildren.

I love you very much and thank you for always being there for me and loving me so much.
Love Samantha
PS. I colored this card. It used to be black and white."

Needless to say, her card had me weeping heartily (in fact it made me shed a few tears again right now as I typed it up.)

Samantha's card style changed over the years. My most recent gem arrived for Mother's day: two kids guiltily holding up chalk after scrawling on the pavement: "Mommy has a big fat ass!"

Samantha had kindly included several slabs of chocolate to encourage the steatopygia of my rump.

At age 10, in 6th grade, Sex Education class brought Samantha home in tears. Since she'd skipped forward a grade, and her birthday fell in June, she was almost two years younger than everybody else in her class. At the time, I thought, "Perfect! She gets a jump-start on life."
But in reality, she was forced to mature too quickly.

"We learned something so disgusting in school today that I can't even say it," she choked out, dismayed by what she'd discovered.

"Could you spell it instead?" I suggested.

She rolled her eyes in disgust.

"S.P.E.R.M," she spelled out, flinching at the very idea.

Hoo-boy! I'm right there with you sister, I thought.

By twelve, indelicate words went from being distressing to providing a source of high entertainment, especially the word "penis". Samantha wrote that one nice and clear in a journal she shared with four friends. Sadly for her, an observant teacher noticed the passing of said book, and confiscated it.

The principle phoned me at home.

"Mrs. Smart?"

"Ms. Smart," I corrected him.

"Yes, your daughter has been writing in a journal with several other pupils and it was brought to my attention today."

"Yes?" I had no idea where this was going.

"There are some disturbing stories in there."

Crap! What had Samantha written about me? Something bad I had done? Narcissist that I am, I immediately imagined it must be all about me.

"There's an entry about Sean going to Amber's place and sticking a tampon in his rectum. He rushed out the bathroom saying he was bleeding and needed help. They were all there at the time and seemed to think it hilarious. I find it very disturbing don't you?" he asked.

I tried not to laugh. At least this Sean guy had some kind of imagination. They were kids. Kids did weird shit like that. It wasn't disturbing to me.

"I'm sure he was just trying to be funny," I ventured.

"Funny, Mrs. Smart? Well they also wrote the word penis all over the journal cover and on the inside pages, too. It's offensive."

His "holier than thou attitude" sailed right up my nose.

"Penis *is* a word, Mr. S. It's the proper term for male genetalia. I don't find the word penis particularly offensive. I'm sure those kids know far worse words than penis."

I used the word "penis" as often as I could, enjoying listening to him suck his breath in slightly with each penis-bomb I dropped.

The line went silent for a moment.

"So will you be dealing with her punishment, or would you like the school to administer one?"

"I will talk to her about it Mr. S. Thank you for letting me know"

Dick. Cock. Shlong. Tool. Baloney-pony. Scrotum-totem. One eyed meat stick. I'm sticking with penis. It's a lot nicer.

Upon Samantha's return home from school, I questioned her about the tampon incident.

"Why did Sean do that?" I asked her.

"He was just trying to be funny."

Hello! Mr. S!

"I also heard about the book with penis written all over it."

Samantha froze. She hated to say "bad" things in front of me as a child...uh...not so much as a teen.

"I'm sorry, mommy," she whispered.

"I know you are, Snausage, and I am too because I still have to punish you."

"What's the punishment going to be?" she asked nervously.

"Well, I have to go to Vons (the grocery store) right now and you'll have to come with me. I'm going to write Penis on your forehead in black marker and you'll have to walk about the store like that."

Samantha went from nervous to mortified.

"What? No, mommy. Please"

I chuckled. I couldn't help it.

"I'm just kidding. I would never make you do that." I smiled at her. "Consider that your punishment right there. And no more writing rude words in school or it is onto the forehead and off to Vons we go."

I didn't care that Samantha had written penis all over the journal. I'd discovered the word *fuck* when I was 10, and promptly wrote a letter to my best friend Diane, using the f-word as many times as possible. My sister helped me. We proudly created sentences like: "Fuck that fucking fuck-upped fuck-face."

Diane's mother found the letter and Linda and I landed in deep, deep doo-doo. The incensed woman demanded we get our patooties over to her house and apologize instantly. I begged my mother to accompany us, but she refused.

"No, you and Linda can go by yourselves," she snapped.

I began to cry. Apologizing to Diane's mother loomed as petrifying. I knew she'd be able to x-ray right through me and somehow discern that Linda and I always referred to her as "the cabbage."

You know how perceptive cruciferous vegetables can be.

Linda led the way, with me sheltering behind her as much as I could. The angry mother marched us into her kitchen where she proceeded to acquaint us with why we were the ugliness that spoiled everything beautiful that God had made in the world. That's right. Us demon spawn stole the gold out of sunsets, smudged rainbows into grey, sullied our sparkling surroundings, and on the whole, pretty much ruined everything. She finished up her severe verbal lashing by letting me know that I could no longer be friends with Diane. I was never to see her again! Harsh, Lady, harsh! Especially since it was her son that had taught us the f-word in the first place. Fuck it, man!

Razor Scooter bikes became the rage, and naturally Samantha wanted one. As always, I couldn't afford it. So I was surprised to find Samantha with a Razor Scooter tucked under her arm when I picked her up from school one afternoon.

"Where did you get that?" I asked.

"Some high school kid came by and said I could have it."

I figured this high school kid must have stolen the razor and then palmed it off on my innocent child.

"That's weird, Samantha. I think you should give it back," I urged her.

She sat quietly as we drove home, and I figured what the heck, she may as well ride it. Once home I said, "Take it for a spin round the park, Manthy, and we'll give it back tomorrow."

Samantha stared at me, her mouth opening and closing.

"What? What you giving me fish face for?" I asked.

Samantha convulsed into howling fits in the passenger seat.

"What's going on, Snausage?" I reached for her, but she shied away from me.

"I stole it," she sobbed. "I stole the razor!"

With her confession out, Samantha barreled inside the house and dove into her bed, to bury herself under shielding blankets.

"We have to take it back," I told her softly, patting her form in the bed.

"Can't we just drop it off at the lost and found?" Her voice muffled up. "Please mommy? Otherwise everyone will know I stole it. The whole school will know I'm a thief if I tell the truth."

"Why did you steal it?" I probed her gently.

"I didn't mean to." She choked between sobs. "The boy who it belongs to went into the library and I thought I'd like to see how it feels to ride one. I hopped on and circled around the quad. Then this man asked me if it was my razor and I lied and said yes. That man was the boy's father, who had come to pick him up and when the boy came out the library he asked me the same thing. I was so ashamed that I lied again. I couldn't tell them I'd stolen his bike."

Samantha was drowning in remorse.

I didn't quite know what to do. I felt so sorry for her. To have the whole school peg you for a thief is a hard one to live down. Samantha was completely repentant and miserable for what she had done, plus she hadn't really meant any harm in the first place. I was tempted to let her return the razor to lost property and claim that she had found it.

I asked Kathy (aka - my guiding light) what to do, not 100% convinced of my own judgment.

"Sorry," Kathy smiled at me, "but Samantha has to return the razor to the boy *and* apologize to the boy and his father for lying. She has to make amends."

We pulled up outside their house, and Samantha, red and swollen from crying, begged one last time to be let off the hook.

"I'll be right beside you," I assured her, remembering my similar apology torture.

I knocked on the front door and the boy opened it.

"Can I help you?" he asked.

Samantha stepped forward, thrust the razor at him and blurted, "I stole your razor! I want to give it back and tell you I'm sorry for taking it."

"Oh!" the boy said, taken aback.

His parents appeared at the door to see what was going on, and fighting back tears, Samantha faced the dad. "I stole your son's razor and I wanted to bring it back and...and I need to apologize to you too sir, for lying to you. I am very sorry."

The father gazed sternly at Samantha: "What's your name?" he asked.

"Samantha," she squeaked out.

Though he appeared grave, his voice was tender when he spoke.

"I forgive you, Samantha," he said.

I'm not sure what Samantha felt at that exact moment, but for me, his words hugged my heart. He forgave her! It was that simple. He forgave Samantha, thus absolving her of her guilt. Lucky Snausages! There'd be no rotting in hell for her!

Samantha couldn't hold her tears back any longer. She bawled big on his doorstep.

"Kids do silly things sometimes," he said, placing a comforting hand on her shoulder. "Just make sure you don't do anything like this again."

Samantha gulped air, nodding her concurrence. I longed to kiss that man for his graciousness, for voicing his forgiveness, for not being like that bitch who never forgave Linda or me.

Samantha's ordeal was over. Back in the car, headed for home, she brightened and was soon smiling, then laughing and chattering; her relief escalating to the point of loopy euphoria.

"Remember this," I told her. "This is how you feel when you do the right thing. It's a good feeling isn't it?"

I don't want to give you the impression that Samantha was a bad kid. Quite the opposite, Samantha was a parent's dream child. She loved going to school, prized learning, and memorized the periodic table of elements for "fun". Her capacity for accountability was far greater than mine. When I'd encourage Samantha to play truant, egging her on to escape a day of school, she would refuse me with a: "I don't *want* to miss school."

"Whose child are you?" I'd ask in complete awe of her.

This is a child, who at age eleven, enrolled herself in summer school to take a daily, five-hour Biology course, and arrived home sparkling out stories of sea anemones, pelicans, ants and spiders.

"Did you know that ants out-number humans 2 million to 1? They could take over the earth if they wanted to."

"No, I did not know."

"Did you know that an elephant weighs less than a killer whale's tongue?"

"Nope, can't say I knew that either."

She thrived on this stuff.

"Did you know that when pelicans dive for fish, they turn their heads to one side and keep their eye wide open, so as not to lose sight of their prey?"

"I didn't know that," I replied, adoring her sweet fervor.

"They use the same eye every time and over time the impact of the water blinds that eye. Then the pelican simply turns its head" (at which point, Samantha turned her head, making her one eye wider than the other) "and uses the opposite eye. Eventually that eye goes blind too …then the pelican starves to death."

Well now. Let that serve as a lesson to those of you who fish with your eyes open.

CHAPTER 39 – The Hood

I instated "Family Night". This meant that every Tuesday evening, Samantha and I had to eat a sit-down meal together and follow up with an activity. We could play a game, or undertake an art project, or go out for a stroll, anything other than watch TV.

Diary entry: Feb 2002

I love coming home. I love being here with Samantha. I get a peaceful feeling and it lasts the whole evening. Before, I could only get that feeling for a few moments, but now it lasts for hours. I love my own safe little world with its few inhabitants.

These focused evenings spent with my daughter infused me with a sense of peace. I'd cook us a semi-healthy dinner then conjure up several activities for the two of us to try. I looked forward to family night and presumed that Samantha did too, until I read her dairy a few years later. She'd written: "Family night?? Who does she think we are? The fucking Brady Bunch?"

I must admit I laughed out loud when I read that. And no, I didn't read her diary on purpose. We were moving and it *fell* open. Honestly. That was the only entry I read. However, I did read her diary later on, when Samantha began to withdraw from me. When full teenage mode struck and she ceased to share anything with me at all. When the rules swung 180 degrees, from hugging and kissing to "don't touch me, don't look at me, and don't breathe on me." I worried that teenage Samantha may be drinking or drugging. I *had* to read her dairy to relieve my fears. Thankfully, she wasn't doing anything too bad. She never did. And according to her, neither did I. She yelled at me one day, fairly enraged that I never set a foot wrong.

"Other parents hit their children. Or at least swear at them," she shouted. "You never do anything I can tell my friends about."

I was somewhat astounded.

"Hang on. Let me get this straight. You're upset with me because I don't hit you?"

"Sean's dad beats him. He always has cool bruises to show us. I have nothing," Samantha moaned and flung herself on the bed. "How can I relate to my friends if you're a good mother?"

Never has a complaint pleased me quite as much.

The conditions that Samantha's "bruised and yelled-at friends" lived in were amazing. I mean, this was Newport Beach. An affluent city populated by the filthy rich, and then again, by the not so rich, and the utterly messed up. There was Kristy, who lived under the stairs in a coat closet. Samantha thought that was the coolest. Kristy's mother said she simply didn't have room for her twelve-year-old daughter.

There was Mindy, whose mother died after a night of Darvocet and vodka, and whose father's drug addiction saw him living in his car. He died a few years later. Without parents, Mindy and her younger brother were shuffled from relative to relative for years to come.

There was Holly, whose step-dad asked her to move out after she ate his leftover bacon in the refrigerator. Seriously!

There was Brittany, whose mom had yet to unpack all their boxes in the living room, although they'd lived in their apartment for three years. The mom slept on the couch while Brittany and her brother shared the one bedroom.

There was John, who lived with his dad in a small office in the industrial part of Costa Mesa with no kitchen or proper bathroom.
There was Nash, who chased down six Valium with a bottle of Jaegermeister and came close to killing himself. When his dad found out, he tossed Nash out on the streets for drinking. Way to go, dad!

And Amy, who cut herself so deeply, she required hospitalization.

Her totally out-to-lunch mother (who was eerily besotted with *Legolas* from the "Lord of the Rings" movie) remarked about the cuttings, saying: "This is going to make me look bad, Amy."

Amy's dad was in prison: drugs again. I believe he held up an ice cream parlor while high as a kite. Amy left school in 10th grade and was married by 19. This is better than some of Samantha's school mates fared. Some never made it past 17. Four of her school friends died from drug overdoses (including Sean the creative tampon chap) and plenty others landed in rehab before reaching 20.

I get why people do drugs in Newport Beach. This plastic-fantastic Mecca has no soul. In Newport two things count: how much money you make, and how good you look. That's the entire criteria by which ye' be judged. This society demands hefty bank accounts and whopping breasts, with little emphasis placed on intellectual, cultural, or spiritual growth. Nothing of real value is encouraged and no deep connections can flourish. It is indeed preferable to be drunk, stoned, or high when mingling with the Barbie and Ken emulators. You have to be fucked up in order to bear the vacuous bullshit, or else you may find yourself wishing to crack Barbie in her makeup perfect, silicone lipped, rhinoplastified, botoxed face...oh Nama-frikken-stay!

But I hit no one. I'd vowed not to, remember? And if my not hitting, beating or mistreating Samantha was a let down for her, then I was happy to disappoint her. I stayed the course. I was tough on Samantha. I wasn't about to consent to the "iffy" things she requested to do. When she asked to catch a bus to Long Beach with her girlfriends (Long Beach being about 40 miles away and not the finest area), I told her: "Over my dead body!"

"That can be arranged," she replied with gusto. "I'm plotting your death as we speak."

Or the time I forbade her to go with Dan, a thirty year old man whom her thirteen-year-old friend, Shaya, had met online.

"He's cool, mom," Samantha pleaded. "He's going to buy us all burgers and soda."

Cool? My dimpled ass!

"Over my extremely dead and mutilated body." I informed her.

I phoned Shaya's parent...her dad (her mom was MIA), but dad seemed completely unperturbed by Dan wanting to buy his daughter lunch.

"Yeah, Shaya told me. Other kids are going too. No big deal."

No big deal? Excuse me? I asked for the names of these *other* kids and phoned all their parents, too. Were they aware that their children had met this guy on the internet? Were they aware that he was 30! Were they aware he was taking them to lunch?

Samantha hated me for doing this.

"You don't even know Dan, mom. He's a good guy. Why can't you give him the benefit of the doubt? You're always so judgmental."

"I don't care if he's Jesus Christ reincarnated. He's 30!"

Teenage girls don't encompass a whole lot of logic.

Samantha vented about that one in her diary as well.

"My mother is a fucking cunt," she wrote.

I didn't laugh when I read that one.

CHAPTER 40 – I have no, NO.

Samantha read my diary too, when she was about 11. I knew something was up when, for three days, Samantha acted weepy and clingy. Finally, on day three, she confessed she had done something really bad.

"Can you tell me what it is?" I asked.

Howling, she shook her head no; wholly riddled with guilt.

"How about if you come and lie in my bed, and I'll be next to you, and you can tell me while I hug you?"

Samantha crawled into my bed, but she still couldn't talk. Her remorse was choking her.

"Okay. How about if you write it down and I'll read what it is that you've done?" I suggested.

Samantha liked that idea. She agreed, gripped the pen I offered her, and scribbled down several words on a piece of paper. I raised the paper to read, but Samantha tugged on my arm to stop.

"Wait! Can I cover my face with your pillow while you read it?" she asked, tears streaming.

"Of course, Snausage." I patted her shoulder. "It won't matter to me what you've done, Samantha. I'll still love you."

Samantha howled louder and covered her face with the pillow.
I scanned the note.

I read your diary it said.

What a relief. By this time, I'd imagined Samantha must have committed some sort of gruesome deed. Then I realized what she had read.

"You read my diary with the cat on the cover?"

Samantha sobbed. "I'm so sorry, mommy."

"You read something you didn't want to know, didn't you?"

Samantha nodded on the verge of exploding with regret.

"You read about my abortion, right?"

Samantha nodded again.

My diary, with the cat on the cover, was my never-ending, enthralling (written) dialog with God. Now you'll probably think that strange, seeing as I pooh-pooh religious folk. Well, I'm not down with religion, but I am down with the idea that there might be an almighty Almighty. I'd written, on this occasion, to ask mister or missus God to forgive me for what I was about to do…have an abortion. I had let myself down badly, and hoped that by writing to God I could somehow ease my plenteous guilt. After 10 months of sobriety, I'd fallen off the wagon, no wait, leapt off the wagon is more accurate; in fact, I'd vaulted off the wagon and flung myself beneath the pounding hooves of the horses, breaking my sobriety with zing. In my drunken state, I'd fallen for Devon D, a sleazy, annelideous life form. He invited me to the movies and I accepted…but we never went to the movies. We never left his apartment. He had me in his bed (which was under a large window, with a door to the left and a bathroom to the right, yup, I have the room layout em-bed-ded in my mind) and even though I was crying and saying "NO!" it made no difference to him. The minute he was done, I quickly escaped to the bathroom, where I frantically tried to wash his S.P.E.R.M from me.

"Come back!" he shouted, "I'm not done with you yet."

Oh we are soooo done, you disgusting scumbag.

I wish I'd punched him, kicked him, anything other than simply slumping there whimpering my feeble "no".

I couldn't keep that child. I couldn't afford it financially or emotionally. I was barely making it with one child. How could I afford another? And the thought of being linked to Devon for the rest of my life by birthing him a child was unbearable.

"I'm so sorry, Samantha." I stroked her hair. "That is not something I ever wanted you to know about. I made a dreadful mistake and I am deeply ashamed. I want to protect you from ugly information like that."

Samantha clung to me, hugging me tightly.

"I'm sorry I read it, mommy," she mumbled into my chest.

"Actually, I read your diary too, Samantha," I admitted. "So I guess we're even now. Let's pinky swear to not read each other's private thoughts again, okay?"

Samantha agreed and we pinkied-firm on it. Of course Samantha stuck to her promise, whereas I read her diary a few years later, like I said, to relieve my fears. Sorry, Snausage.

I hated that I'd let myself down with the Devon incident. Why *had* I felt so powerless to protect myself? Why *couldn't* I safeguard myself? Even worse, there were occasions when I'd failed to protect Samantha as well, due to my inability to say NO.

I'd befriended an elderly man who lived down on the beachfront, Jan, a happy-go-lucky alcoholic, with a big, belly laugh and a cooler persistently full of beer. Non-stop parties dominated his seaside apartment and there was Jan, glugging alcohol like a fish with swollen, purple feet to prove it. You can see why I was drawn to him.

Samantha and I liked to swim in the ocean directly in front of Jan's home, and he'd permit me to park in his driveway (parking being a prime commodity at the beach). Plus, he'd typically invite us in for cold juice and snacks after our dip.

I liked Jan. So did Samantha.

After swimming one afternoon, Jan waved us over. Samantha and I were suited up in matching bikinis (thank you, jilted beau, Nick, for buying us those). Jan offered Samantha candy, which she happily accepted, then he introduced us to his friend from Iceland: a hairy, dirty, oily man who leered at Samantha and me as if we were the candy.

"Do you mind if my friend takes a photo of you and your daughter?" Jan asked. "He's from Iceland and doesn't get to the beach very often."

I wasn't charmed by the idea, but said "sure" anyway.

Samantha and I posed for a shot.

"Do you mind if he joins you in a photo?" Jan pushed his toothless, scabby friend towards us.

"Go on," he grinned. "Get in there with the girls."

The gross Icelandic man placed his massive arms around Samantha and me, his armpits reeking. I noticed Samantha cringe and yet I did nothing. I allowed Jan to take another photo, and then another photo, and another one; the sweaty man posing with just me, the sweaty man posing with just Samantha. Smile - click, smile - click. Vomit!

Once they finished with their impromptu beach photo shoot, Samantha and I escaped back into the waves, mutely trying to wash away the feeling of being soiled. Yet again, it wasn't until afterwards that I wished I'd handled things differently. Why hadn't I said no? No more photos? Why hadn't I said: "I'm not comfortable with this? My daughter and I are not bikini models for Iceland's down and out desperados."

Again, I'm so sorry, Manth. I wish I had known how to say no.

These weren't my sole shortcomings in parenting. Nope - not by a long shot. I was petty. I was mean. I was cheap. I hardly ever did laundry because it cost $3 a pop, and I stole toilet paper to save myself a few bucks. I could be annoyingly childish and pathetically self-pitying, telling Samantha that I hated driving her to school every morning because it was cold and she never thanked me for taking her. That doesn't sound like pure, unconditional love now does it?

Diary Entry - Jan 1998
I feel miserable right now. I'm stressed out of my mind and I'm being a bad parent for Samantha – I'm such a bitch all the time –
I WILL NOT YELL AT HER ANYMORE – it's not her fault my life sucks sooo bad...

I relied heavily on Samantha for companionship (OMG that rings a bell) and spent most of my time with her, utterly enjoying it all – the ocean swims, the picnics, the movies – what's not to enjoy? For me that is....

Needless to say, when Samantha hit her teens, she no longer wanted to hang with mom. No way in hell. Instead she'd vanish for entire weekends to her friends and I'd lash out at her in jealousy. I'd berate her friends, telling Samantha it was unhealthy to stay in a bedroom on a computer all day (as they did), when in all honesty, I was more hurt by the fact that I could no longer join in Samantha's world. I knew it was my job to guide my most favorite human being to a safe destination, and I knew it was Samantha's job as a teenager to hate me. I just wished she wasn't doing it so damn well. I struggled to let her go, while she in turn, struggled to be okay with me letting her go. This child/parent separation phase is a painful, yet necessary passage that all teenagers and parents are forced to navigate at some point. Good luck, fellow travelers.

CHAPTER 41 – The Mother Invasion

My mother pleaded her case, asking for permission to visit Samantha in America.

"Please Niki, I'm still her grandmother…Samantha doesn't have any relatives in America…I won't be a burden to you…I won't interfere...I'll be gone before long…I love Samantha." Bla-di-bla-bla."

She guilt-tripped me until I finally relented. I warned my mother not to expect too much from me. I was still struggling to absorb her betrayal, still struggling to forgive her.

Kathy encouraged me to do just that. Forgive her. Sure, easy to say, not so easy to do. I read every book available on that bloody subject - hell bent on *forgiving* - but it seemed impossible to me. How could I move on? How could I embrace my mom? How could I ever believe her again? Trust her again? How could I bring myself to forgive her for trying to take my child away from me? And no matter how many times she spewed out, "I'm so sorry for hurting you Niki," sorries just didn't crack it.

Arriving with her customary "hard to ignore" flair, my mother toppled onto the baggage carousel while attempting to retrieve her suitcases at John Wayne Airport. Circling the other passengers, she lurched herself sideways and tumbled off the conveyor belt, spraining her ankle on impact with the airport floor. The baggage carousel shut down instantly, causing a delay for everyone, while my mother was whisked away for medical care, sue, sue, sue being on the tip of every employee's tongue. What was I expecting? That she'd pick up her bag and arrive unnoticed like normal people do?

"I rolled off that spinning carousel like Rambo," she proudly reported.

Uh huh…welcome to America, Mother Rambo.

But unlike Rambo, who by all accounts is a fairly resourceful and self-sufficient guy, my mother turned out to be helpless. She had no car, had no idea where she was, had nowhere to stay, had very little money (having burned through the bulk of her inheritance), and to top it off, had a broken ankle! She glommed, totally reliant, onto me…ahhhh…my worst nightmare. Her "I won't be a burden to you" was speed-boxing me in the face.

Kathy moiled and toiled to teach me how to say NO to my mother; how to say NO period, especially after I relayed the Devon and Icelandic man stories to her. Kathy explained how sexually molested children often permit people to do things to them that ordinary people would not allow.

"You're used to being used, Niki. You have to unlearn what has been melded into you."

And so the unlearning began. Kathy role-played my mother, giving me the opportunity to learn how to refuse her demands, and how to build better boundaries that up until this point had escaped my knowledge. I hadn't realized I was permitted to say no.

"May I borrow your car, Niki?" Kathy leveled her eyes at me.

No.

"Please…I'll fill the tank with gas."

No.

"Well, could you please drive me to the hairdresser then?"

No.

"I'm so hungry. Can I have $10 for food…please Niki?"

No.

It wasn't completely successful.

I gave my mother my car; she dented it and returned it fuel gage on empty and knee deep in litter.

I gave my mother money for food; she needed more. I drove my mother to her various appointments; she complained about the awful traffic and critiqued my driving. I listened to her lengthy stories about *her this* and *her that*…with my chest tightening and my knuckles whitening.

"I can't say no to her, Kathy," I lamented in session. "If I say no to her, I feel guilty. If I say yes to her, I feel taken advantage of. It's a total lose-lose situation. I'm trapped by her."

Kathy gently reminded me that I needed to set clear boundaries with my mother.

My mother broke a chair while visiting Matt's house.

"Niki broke that," she fluidly lied to him, while I rushed out to buy him a new chair.

During a bout of gastroenteritis, she sprayed Matt's bathroom with projectile vomit, then left a note saying: "I am too sick. Niki, please clean it up."

And I did.

I hated her. Simply detested her. Loathed her entirely. She stole my air, my voice, my intentions, my being. And what really freaked me out was that she stole my desire to have Samantha. If I didn't have a child, my mother wouldn't be here ruining my life. It's not that I didn't want Samantha, I didn't want my mother.

Let me repeat that…I didn't want my mother.

Help. Help! Get her off me. I'm drowning under her weight. I'm collapsing from the burden of her. I'm suffocating!

My mother stayed for three months.

By the time she left, I'd lost weight and lost faith. I would never have control of my own life.

20th September 1999 - Diary Entry

I lashed out at my mother on the drive to the airport, telling her not to think she can keep coming to the USA – I felt soooo resentful and wanted to remind her of all the shit she's done, because she acts like everything is fine – and it sure ain't. Then I drove home feeling horribly lonely and abandoned. My mother left me again without a tear in her eye. I struggle to find a comfort zone in this relationship, even distance doesn't help. I don't think she loves me and yet I do. I don't think she's sane and yet I do. I don't want her near me and yet I do. It's confusing and exhausting.

I wish I had blessed my mother instead of yelling at her. I wish I had said: "Travel well with love and peace in your heart, and live with courage and honesty." Instead I said "You don't fucking deserve to visit me here in America".

The "travel well" quote comes from the movie "Seven Years in Tibet." The little Dalai Lama says it to Brad Pit. I remember having a crying meltdown on hearing those words in the film. Like a part deep inside of me sat up and said, "Hey! I want that."

I wasn't traveling well myself. Certainly no peace existed in my heart. And honesty? What on earth was that? So there's broken me, wishing I had "blessed" my mother. What a hoot!

CHAPTER 42 - Dreams

This "mother bane" was ruining my life. I understood that I'd never have a healthy relationship with anyone unless I eradicated the tangled-strangled mother mess. There'd be no rest for me while resentment galloped yippie-ki-yay through my veins. I needed to end the mother saga once and for all.

Determined to triumph, I devoured self-help books, embraced inner child work, experimented with out-of-body travels, scheduled ample time with Kathy, and diligently logged my progress in a journal. Regardless of my efforts, thoughts of my mother clogged my brain all day. I was like an old Freudian joke: "you say one thing but mean a mother!"

And as if that weren't enough, thoughts of mumsy began seeping in on me at night too, sullying my REM sleep. What I was unable to grasp consciously during the day visited me in dream-form at night.

Dream One:
My mother is in my house rearranging my furniture. She moves the couches, the chairs and tables to her satisfaction.

"Look Niksi, I'm helping you." She fusses about. "This way works so much better."

"Put it back the way it was!" I yell at her, and wake up shaking.

Dream Two:
My mother has found my photo albums and quietly cuts me out of every picture. She systematically ruins every single childhood photo I own.

"Leave those pictures alone!" I scream at her, and wake up *schwitz*-ing.

Dream Three:

I find myself trapped in a glass coffin and realize that my mother has organized my funeral. I try to tell her that I am still alive, but she simply will not listen.

"I've already paid, Niksi. There's nothing I can do." Her face is expressionless.

"But I'm still alive!" I scream at her.

I wake up palpitating, crying, shaking and sweating.

Heiliger Bimbam!

I relay my dreams to Kathy. I tell her of the most recent one, in which I find myself in a hotel room racked by intense itching. Peering in a mirror, I discover I'm covered in what appears to be little raindrop sacs, filled with blood. These fluid-filled tear-shaped sacs cover my entire body; plus I have a silver rope wrapped about my waist that is constricting me, and making it hard for me to breathe. I understand that I'm in serious trouble here, and even worse, that no one is coming to help me. No one. Not now. Not ever. I cry and cry and cry, feeling hopelessly alone, scared and unloved.

As I described my dream to Kathy, I realized there was something familiar about that silver rope, but I couldn't quite put my finger on it. We finished our session and it wasn't until I was sitting in my car that I identified the restraining rope. It was my version of the umbilical cord...shiny, silver and slender.

And in my dream, this sleek suffocating umbilical cord envelops me, while all the blood is vacuum-sucked out of me into tiny teardrop sacs. Marvelous!

This dream clearly identified for me that my mother (the umbilical chord) had a strangle hold on me, and was sucking the very life force (my blood) out of my body. Well, my vampire-mother revisited America two years later. This time, she stayed for the entire year. She rented a mobile home in my park. My park! This placed her about 20 feet away from me at all times. I upped my visits to Kathy. We added more role-playing.

And suddenly I got it right.

I said NO.

My mother asked to use my car and I said, "No."

I gave her a timetable for the bus service instead. Simple as a pimple. Everything my mother wanted of me, I plainly and clearly said no. No. Nope. Nein. Nicht. Niet. Negative. No way. Uh-uh. Not on your Nelly.

Unbelievably, once my mother realized I was being wholly serious, she adapted in a flash. She quickly befriended a wealthy lady doctor and was soon co-habiting with her new "friend" in a spectacular mansion in Corona Del Mar. Within days of moving in, my mother was driving the doc's spare Mercedes Benz about town, and feasting with her at swanky, upscale restaurants. I discovered that my mother was unendingly resourceful. If I refused to meet her needs, she could dig up someone else who would, pronto.

I had one last *mother* dream: Once again I find myself in a hotel room, but this time I am with my mother. I suddenly feel the urge to urinate. The urge to pee is so strong, that I simply let go and urinate all over the hotel suite. Foul-smelling urine gushes from me in a jet stream. My mother scurries behind me with a towel, attempting to mop up the mess, imploring me to stop. But I don't stop. In fact, I prance about the room spraying whatever I can, ruining as much as possible, galloping about the room soiling everything. It feels fantastic. I'm upsetting my mother, and for a change it is *she* who is cleaning up after me. I keep pissing that ugliness out. Masses and masses of toxic waste comes bucketing out of me.

It is a relief. It is healing. It is superbly therapeutic.

CHAPTER 43 – Turning point

I absolutely needed to "piss out" my anger. Void my emotional bladder. Rid myself of all my regret, my guilt, my severe shame and crushing disappointment. Free my sad soul from this stagnant, noxious sludge. My coping mechanism of "drink it to normal" that had served me so well as a teenager, that had helped me to "laugh off" many insufferable situations, was now leaving me pickled in pointlessness. Having numbed myself to avoid feeling pain, I'd successfully numbed myself to feeling joy as well. All I *could* feel was anger. My survival skill was turning on me. With Kathy's help, I labored my utmost to "get my shit" together. I knew if I didn't, I'd damage Samantha as surely as my mother had damaged me.

It wasn't just my bibulous, frivolous drinking that presented a problem. I recognized my co-dependent habit of constantly merging into my "boyfriend of the month" rather than uncovering myself. I launched a reconnaissance mission to establish what *I* liked, and who *I* was. Operation: Locate Niki.

I discovered I enjoyed running barefoot on the beach, where the sand grains offered up a gentle healing to the tired soles of my tired soul. Come Halloween, I developed a crush on pumpkins. How come I'd never noticed these superb gourds before? I welcomed their wholesome shape and color, and wished nothing more than to surround myself with beautiful, healthy pumpkins that gleamed their orange joy at me. I found that reading in bed was a treat, especially while sipping on green tea with a vanilla-scented candle burning. I soaked in the sound of acoustic guitar and fretless bass, relishing the oscillating of the notes in my bloodstream. I recovered my love of swimming underwater and cheerfully sunk to the bottom of pools to submerge there, sending bubbles to the surface. I began being present in my present, fully appreciating moments such as spreading honey on toast – awesome; sitting in my car at the traffic light feeling the sun on my shoulders – awesome; reclining on the couch listening to my chimes – awesome, baby, awesome.

Then I stumbled upon the most excellent coping skill…yoga! What a wonderful way to experience my body in the here and now. What a wonderful way to gain an appreciation for my chubby thighs, (those cellulite pillars of stoicism that had politely endured every step of the way). What a wonderful way to pay less attention to my exterior and more attention to my interior; a wonderful way to becalm myself; a wonderful way to stay healthy and mindful. Then I added a daily meditation routine to deepen the connection to moi. I started chanting mantras like: Om Ah Hum Vajra Guru Padma Siddhi Hum And may I humbly suggest memorizing that mantra for immediate repetition whenever you feel fearful, upset, or overwhelmed.

As Elizabeth Kubler Ross says:
"There is no need to go to India or anywhere else to find peace. You will find that deep place of silence right in your room, your garden or even your bathtub." (And you know my history with bathtubs - so if I can find peace there, I can find it anywhere)

Armed with my newly re-covered self, I focused on healthy eating, reading volumes on vegetables and vitamins, and ingested spinach, kale and broccoli until they tasted better than any burger ever could. I landed a part-time job at a youth shelter, where I helped council young people, whose problems I felt I could totally identify with. I practiced yoga to the point that I became a teacher, and wound up teaching yoga to the very teens at the youth shelter where I was employed…a most rewarding occupation.

I saluted my additional bad habit of continuously relying on others to get my needs met; of manipulating men to grant me feelings of security. No more of that. I resolved to save myself, protect myself, nurture myself, love myself and behave in ways that made me proud of myself. I performed my first solo gig (sweating like a chocolate teapot) to an audience of roughly fifteen – one of whom was Kathy, my therapist, clapping me on to self-sufficiency. I hauled Samantha off on vacation, driving up the coast by myself (well, with Snausage as navigator), staying in motels that I paid for with money I had earned! A giant step for this woman-kind.

I quickly got the hang of it, and from there you couldn't stop me. I waged a fierce stand of independence. I paid off my mobile home. I took Samantha camping (which wasn't pretty). I enrolled in college. I dove into volunteer work. I changed to fulltime employment at the youth shelter. I registered in a 401K plan. I secured a valid driver's license, and then – hip-hip-hooray – I secured a legitimate green card. I swore off boyfriends as a means to survive, and I swore off sex as a way to manipulate. I even applied for dental insurance.

I finally grew up.

Near the end of my mother's year in USA, it happened. She offered to take Samantha and me out for lunch. Off we zoomed to Fascist Island (Fashion Island), where we ordered soup and salad at the food court in the downstairs section. My mother paid for the lunch, and I don't know why, but it made me happy, her paying for my lunch. Really happy! It wasn't that my mother wasn't generous with money. She was when she had it, but her money had always come glued to an obligation. Most everything my master-manipulator-mother did came loaded up with requirements. She once bought Claude an expensive computer game to lure him to her latest apartment, but when he asked to take the game back to René's house, she erupted in fury and immediately returned the game to the store.

This lunch was different. This lunch rang as a mother purely inviting her daughter and granddaughter to lunch, nothing more. No hidden agenda. My mother wanted nothing in return. She didn't demand a ride; she didn't push for "just a few dollars"; she didn't appeal for another meeting. We simply enjoyed our food and went our separate ways.

I asked her if I could keep the receipt. I still have it.

Wednesday November 28th 2001 - Blueberry Hill - Total = $15.25

It was a turning point in the way I viewed my mother. Up until that day I'd wanted her to be a mother to me. Suddenly I understood - she was trying to be just that. She simply couldn't accomplish it the way I wanted her to. Not because she didn't love me, but because she didn't have the ability. She wasn't able to parent. She wanted to, but was stunted by her own emotional starvation. My outlook shifted and I started viewing my mother as a child - a scared, lonely, vulnerable, desperate, hurt, five-year-old girl. And for a five year old to buy you lunch, that's big.

The more I approached my mother from this new angle, the more things fell into place. She hadn't changed one iota, but my view of her had changed drastically. And then it happened...I suddenly realized that **I'd forgiven my mother.** That was an enormous moment for me.

Driving my mother to the wealthy doctor's house, we stopped en-route to enjoy the sunset in a park overlooking the ocean. She thanked me for driving her, and as we sat side by side silently watching the sun sink, I realized I no longer hated her. I forgave her for everything: the screaming, the crying, the begging, the fainting, the drama, the invasive, pervasive, perverse mothering style, even the Samantha-stealing debacle. As my hatred dissipated, I literally felt a huge weight lift from my shoulders. My body felt lighter.

Alanis Morissette lyrics hummed through my mind:.

"How 'bout how good it feels to finally forgive you."

Indeed, Alanis. How on earth did you know? It felt like shedding a million ton load.

Clearing this mammoth hurdle sparked a domino like effect…toppling and eliminating damaging behaviors one by one: I surfaced through Marlowe's hierarchy of basic needs like a shining, textbook example of human growth. Once I'd secured a roof over my head that a break-up couldn't steal from me, and stocked my pantry with an ongoing food supply that Samantha and I couldn't possibly eat through, the heavy breathers outside my window vanished into thin air. As I branched out into my community, taking on volunteer work and attending city hall meetings, my sense of belonging grew. I began to choose more dependable, considerate friends, and to eat healthier foods, and to engage in safer recreational methods. Keeping steady employment, my bank account boasted savings for the first time. Bolstered by my billowing self-confidence, I could make smarter decisions, I could trust myself,

I could set healthy boundaries. I could rely on myself. I could keep myself safe. I could protect my daughter. I could be proud of my parenting. I could stop drinking. I could stop smoking. I could stop having one night stands. I could stop having meaningless sex. I could stop lying. I could stop hitting. I could stop cheating. I could stop manipulating. I could love myself. I could forgive my mother…and I could *love* my mother without it doing me any further damage.

I was free.

Free at last. Free at last. Thank God Almighty, I was free at last!

So, there's my story, more or less. I survived *Hell Camp*. I had a baby. I moved to America. I didn't become a pop star, but I did come to terms with my past, with myself, and managed to raise a reasonably well-adjusted child.

I evolved, albeit slowly, striving toward overall wellbeing. I fixed my body, fixed my mind and then fixed my innermost me, my spirit. Yes, I am full throttle against religion, but that doesn't mean I am anti God. I thumb my nose at religion because honestly…what a load of hoo-haa!. Gandhi captured my sentiments exactly when he said: "God has no religion."

That's right Mahatma my man, and neither do I. But I do have a spirit, and through my spirit I can love everyone and everything in this universe, good and bad. I can endure, I can forgive, I can empathize, I can love, and best of all, I can experience sheer bliss…I shit you not.

The aim of life is to live, and to live means to be aware, joyously, drunkenly, serenely, divinely aware…Henry Miller

UPDATES:

MY MOTHER: My mother received a small divorce settlement from René and, not surprisingly, burned through it instantaneously. She traveled back and forth to Europe, each time shipping all her furniture with her until those useless fixtures had cost her thousands in handling fees. Unruffled, she abandoned her over-inflated flotsam and jetsam somewhere in Germany. Luckily, she inherited a much larger sum of money from her mother's death, and quickly set about burning through this wealth, too. It required more effort this time and thankfully, before her money dwindled altogether, she managed to purchase a small apartment in Oxford so she could be near my sister and her two daughters. My mother now lives comfortably in Oxford, teaching and learning languages (polyglot that she is) and attending philosophy classes. She has calmed down immensely and has profusely apologized for all her shenanigans. Though she still does crazy on occasion, it does less damage (at least to me). I know I've dragged her over hot coals throughout this book and I hope she can forgive me for that. My mother wasn't a good parent (not surprising given her teachers), but that doesn't make her a bad human. I quite like my mother as a human being. She has remained single, and swears if she could do it over, she would never marry at all. Please know, mother, that I love you regardless of all the crap we have been through. You are fearless (possibly foolishly fearless) and admirably adventurous. I love that you wandered throughout Europe, searching for a new life, sending postcards as you roamed: Turkey, Rumania, Portugal, Spain. I stuck those postcards on my fridge, thinking each time: "Damn, she sure is something."

RENÉ: With my mother finally out of his "rapidly-diminishing" hair, René settled down with a much better choice of a wife - Rita - a genuine sweetheart. Together they operated "The Gallery Inn", their Bed and Breakfast, for many years. When René suffered a stroke, it was understood that he would not recuperate. Those doctors obviously didn't know René very well. He was up and running again in 6 months - *geen problem*. Unfortunately, the fortitude he displayed over his stroke held no weight against those blasted bees.

SAMANTHA: Snausages is astounding me as always with her intellect and dedication. I couldn't be prouder of her. In sixth grade, she won the overall school award for a poem she'd written, and at her graduation ceremony, the principal asked her to read her poem aloud. As Samantha stepped onto a little box strategically placed to enable her 10-year-old frame to reach the microphone, I suddenly understood the saying: "bursting with pride". I literally felt I might platz right there in Samantha's school hall.

Clean up on aisle 14…another proud mother explosion.

Later, Samantha worked 25 hours a week while carrying a 15-unit load at university. On completing university, Samantha landed her dream job (editing movie trailers) and was promoted within 8 months. I'm mightily impressed. I thank the universe daily for gifting me such a fine soul to guide. What a treat. What a joy. What a very lucky me! Snausage girl, you know I love you more than anything – yes, even Marmite - and Merlot.

Samantha has yet to meet Killian, who has over the years been joined by Corbyn, Liam and Sinead. Samantha now has 3 half-brothers and a half- sister…and a father who she finally got to meet at age 21.

LINDA: My sister, The Wise One, earned her PHD in Sanskrit and thus is now Dr. Linda Boemsie (she is too private for me to blab her surname in here). Linda lives contentedly (for the most part) in

Oxford with her husband and two frightfully smart daughters. She has traveled extensively, spending months in India and Thailand, riding elephants, exploring temples and showering herself in different cultures. She is fearless and fabulous. Oh, and she plays violin in a local orchestra and is part of a Bulgarian folk dancing group.

Go Linny baby! You're endless search for self-improvement inspires me beyond. I'm so glad I get to be here on planet mirth at the same time as you.

CLAUDE: As mentioned earlier, Claude grew into a calm, steady, brave and hilarious man. He finally married Janet, a robust ray of sunshine - but sadly, two years into their marriage, doctors detected a tumor in Janet's front temporal lobe. Together, Claude and Janet fought the most courageous battle against stage four cancer. Although the tumor was removed, regrettably it returned within six weeks. Following a second surgery, doctors informed Janet and Claude that the next surgical intrusion would cause brain damage. At this point, Janet was given six months to live. She was 29 years old.

After two surgeries and several rounds of chemo and radiation, Janet was reduced to a mere smattering of her former self. A once cheerful, healthy young woman, Janet was now shaky, weak and semi-lucid, saturated with pain medication. Claude never left her side. Not once. Janet raged against him in anger, strung out on meds and steroids (that cause aggression). She cried on his shoulder, begging him to make the pain stop. She sobbed in the early hours of the morning, calling out that she wasn't ready to die. She leaned on him for constant support as she weakened, and Claude never once faltered. He was her rock, a pillar of strength. With his usual ruse, Claude employed humor to diffuse the toughest of moments, using laughter to gently ease away his wife's tears. As Janet's brother noted: "If laughter is the best medicine, then Claude is a veritable-fucking-pharmacy".

Janet was astoundingly brave as well. She handled her illness with grace and dignity and remained strong, joining in the humor ploy right up until her last day. In the end, attached to a morphine pump, she pressed the gadget in her hand as if it were the *Jeopardy* button.

"I'll take cancer for 200 please, Alex," she'd smile.

Stupid cancer. Even more stupid American Cancer Society that has collected billions of dollars over nine decades and found no cure. I think something wickedly dodgy is afoot in the whole corrupt "find a cure" hoax...*billions of dollars – nine decades* – think about it.

Whether or not a cure for cancer is already out there, on December 13th 2008, Janet succumbed to this disease. The tumor had grown to the size of a lemon for the third time (yes, Wally Lamb is right - tumors do tend to be compared to citrus fruit – the size of a grapefruit, or a lemon, or a lime). Surgery was no longer an option. Chemo had failed. Radiation had failed. The tumor had won, and now swelled Janet's brain to the point that her left eye bulged out. Her headaches raged furiously. She lost her peripheral vision, then lost her vision entirely. At length, she could no longer stand up, no longer sit up, no longer eat, no longer stay lucid. She began bleeding internally, and as Claude stood steadfastly at his wife's side, operating a suction tube to remove blood from her lungs, he tenderly held her hand and whispered her permission to leave this world.

All I can say is: Janet was the finest sister-in-law I could ever have hoped for, and she is sorely missed. Though Claude is yet reeling from the loss of his beloved wife, he has many true friends that rally round him, and I'm confident he'll recover and find love again. He also has a faithful dog to keep him company and he doesn't punch this dog...ever.

Claudie boy. You have kahonies fused from meteorites. I'm humbled by your strength and am extremely proud of you, my brother. You're awesome…like a million hotdogs.

ELIZABETH: The little girl from the White Horse Inn found me 20 years later through Facebook. I was elated to receive a message from her. Elizabeth had become a successful IT lawyer and was doing well, although sadly, her brother died in a shooting accident and her father died from ill health. I am very proud of Elizabeth, knowing what a "hell camp" she has been through. And because she still lives in crazy South Africa, the poor girl has been held at gunpoint three times. Three Times! And each time she survived because she stayed completely calm. This is a girl with guts galore! Elizabeth! Please know that my door is always open to you.

ME, MYSELF, I: My search for stardom bumped along unremarkably, bruising my ego with rejections that pinged my tender skin. Be that as it may, I recorded three CDs chockfull of venti-shmenti. My lyrics dug into child abuse, women's rights, the search for God, broken hearts, environmental responsibility, cheating on lovers and suchlike. A few of my songs managed to find their way into TV commercials, Indy movies and local TV shows…whoopee! I conquered Pro-Tools along the way, a music program which enabled me to enjoy a stint as an audio engineer in an advertising agency. Thank you, JP, for sharing your knowledge, your studio and your friendship with me!

My big claim to fame? I sang an IHOP commercial that aired across the nation on radio and TV…"Anytime's a good time for IHOP". That's the truth, folks – go eat a pancake whenever you want!

I performed at the closing ceremonies for Lance Armstrong's "Tour of Hope" in Washington DC, on the ellipse outside the White

House, my jubilant face projected on a jumbotron – helping to raise money for that ever elusive cancer cure.

I sang at Andre Agassi's New Year's Eve party while he was still married to Brooke Shields. Brooke perched her very beautiful self in front of me and sang along to my songs. She knew *my* lyrics! I hope you are suitably impressed. Thank you, Brooke, for that moment of surreal and incredibly sweet validation.

I opened for The Bangles, Cool and the Gang, Rita Coolidge, Bobby Caldwell, Chris Botti, The Stranglers, and one of my favorites: Joan Armatrading! Through my music I enjoyed a multitude of marvelous moments, from hearing a girl standing next to me at a BBQ singing along to my song as it played on the radio (that gave me a kick), to meeting Tom Jones and grabbing a photo op. with him poolside at Pechanga casino.

Me, in my bikini, and Mr. Jones in his speedo – I love it.

Yes, my music brought me bounteous boogalicious fun, but not the mega fame I sought. However, with age, the desire to be a famous pop star faded into the background and into the foreground stepped yoga! Yoga = to yoke - to tie together - to unite - the union of mind, body and spirit…which I strived for, because I insist on being like "fully unified" dude! Through the practice of yoga, I discovered a tranquil place deep within me, a safe place, a trustworthy place. I went ahead and wrote a song about it entitled "Recover Me". That felt so good, that I took it a step further and wrote a whole book about it.

Oh, lucky you.

And boy do I love you for reading my entire warblings.

THANK YOU!

Dear Kathy
I want you to know, that it took me a while, but I found the swans.
Thank you for all your caring support and guidance.
With whopping amounts of warmth and gratitude
Your impatient patient
Niki

I also wish to publicly acknowledge Mike and Linda Jacobs. Their generosity has been invaluable. Amongst many other things, they paid for Samantha's entire schooling at SFSU.
Thank you M & L from the very bottom of my heart. You certainly impacted Samantha's life in a most profound way.

Names and Places Info:

Help spread awareness to the rape crisis in South Africa
http://rapecrisis.org.za

For teens in trouble
http://www.helpingteens.org/

Help feed the hungry
http://www.foodbank.org.za/

My authoring and musical endeavors can be found at:
www.nikismart.com

Post your own review at:
www.hellcamp.weebly.com

A shameless plug !
My music can be heard and purchased (thanking you) at:
www.Itunes.com/nikismart

My tunes can be heard on Pandora Radio (not in South Africa though)
www.pandora.com

The Gallery Inn – René's B&B bliss – still owned by his much better choice for a wife, Rita.
http://galleryinn.co.za

EXTRA CHAPTER - Rape and AIDS in South Africa.

I'd like to add this EXTRA chapter to hopefully help raise awareness (and action), to the rampant rape calamity that exists in South Africa. By 1994, South Africa had become the rape capital of the world, with a woman raped every 17 seconds. **17 seconds!** You can't drink a cup of tea in that time.

Unfortunately, many African men consider themselves entitled to sex and some even believe that women enjoy being raped. They further judge women responsible for causing sexual violence by "asking for it". A large portion of the African male youth believe that *no* to sex means *yes*, and that forcing sex on someone you know is not sexual violence. Neither is *Jack rolling* ("recreational" gang rape), which is viewed as "just a game".

I, myself, prefer Scrabble.

Then, horror upon horror, somewhere along the line, the notion spread that if you had sex with a virgin, it could cure you of AIDS. Virgin cleansing. This heartbreaking stupidity meant that HIV positive men started raping children and babies. Sexual violence against children increased 400% over a decade and, according to a report by the BBC news, a female born in South Africa has more chance of being raped in her lifetime than learning to read.

And I regret this next paragraph, because it describes actions that are beyond cruel, but this is the world we live in. These are some of the reported cases of child rape in South Africa:

A 9-month-old baby underwent a full hysterectomy and required extensive surgery to repair intestinal damage after being raped by six men, aged between 24 and 66.

A 4-year-old girl died after being raped by her father.

A 14-month-old girl was raped by her two uncles.

An 8-month-old infant was gang raped by four men in Feb 2002. Only one man was charged. This tiny girl also required extensive reconstructive surgery.

In South Africa, some 58 children are raped, or suffer rape attempts, every single day. The insane notion that AIDS could be cured by having sex with a virgin was not helped by the former president of South Africa, Thabo Mbeki, who stated at an international AIDS conference that HIV does not cause AIDS...That's right! All those other millions of people must be mistaken.

Then there was the stunningly inept, Dr. Mantombazana Edmie Tshabalala-Msimang,...wow....try saying that 3 times in a row. Dr. Mantombazana Edmie Tshabalala-Msimang served as Minister of Health from 1999 to 2008 under President Mbeki, and this lady thought it a good idea to treat the AIDS epidemic with vegetables! Her choice? Garlic, lemon and beetroot! Screw those western antiretroviral medicines. The South African Minister of Health further believed that the "Illuminati had conspired with the aliens to bring about AIDS to reduce the African population". Yeah...that must be it! Naughty Aliens.

After the 2006 International AIDS Conference in Toronto, sixty-five of the world's leading HIV/AIDS scientists asked in a letter that Thabo Mbeki dismiss Tshabalala-Msimang. He didn't.

And just in case you don't get how silly this Tshabalala-bla-di-bla-bla woman actually is, here is a transcript of a controversial radio interview in which she refuses to answer talk show host, John Robbie (on South Africa's Radio 702) direct questions about whether or not HIV causes AIDS.

It makes for amusing reading, save the fact that this dialog is all frikken true.

Robbie: You have said that the policy of the ministry is well known. Do you accept that HIV causes Aids?

Tshabalala-Msimang: Why do you ask me that question today? I have answered that question umpteen times.

R: Yes, and the answer is?

T-M: Umpteen times I have answered that question. My whole track record of having worked at the area of HIV and Aids for the last 20 years is testimony. Why should you ask me that question today?

R: You haven't answered the question, Manto.

T-M: Why should you ask me that question?

R: To avoid confusion.

T-M: I have never said anything contrary to what you want me to say today.

R: So, therefore, you accept that HIV causes Aids.

T-M: You are not going to put words into my mouth.

R: I am not putting words into your mouth. I am asking you a question.

T-M: Yes you are.

R: I am asking you a straight - now hold on a second - I am asking you a straight question, the Minister of Health of South Africa, I am asking you a question: does HIV cause Aids?

T-M: I have been party to developing a strategic framework and that strategy testifies what my policy understandings of the HIV epidemic are. If you haven't read that, please go and read it. And then you will understand where I depart from.

R: Manto, Manto. A simple yes or no is the answer I am looking for.

T-M: You will not force me into a corner into saying yes or no.

R: I am not forcing you into a corner, I am asking you a straight question - I find your reaction bizarre.

T-M: I would advise you to read the strategic framework. You have to analyze it. It is important for the media to inform the public about the positions of government...It is time that when you interview people not on yes or no but on the tenets of the framework.

R: Manto, we have gone as far as we can go. I find your reaction to that question absolutely bizarre and that is my final word on it.

T-M: I am not Manto to you. Let me tell you, I am not Manto to you.

R: What are you?

T-M: I am the minister of health and I don't even know you.

R: So, what must I address you as, Miss Minister or Ms Minister or Mrs Minister?

T-M: I don't know whatever you address me, but I am not a friend.

R: How must I address you?

T-M: I don't know - but you have to read the strategic framework.

R: Bizarre.

T-M: And I ...

R: Oh go away!

T-M: And I am ...

R: I cannot take that rubbish any longer.

In 2007 it was estimated that approximately 6.6 million South Africans (of all ages) were infected with HIV and that there were 1.4 million AIDS orphans in South Africa. (And no, Hollywood celebrities can't adopt them all).

A huge effort has been made in South Africa to educate the population on HIV and AIDS, but even so, there's an average of almost 1,000 AIDS related deaths a day in Southern Africa and more than two thousand patients check into the hospital daily as HIV positive.

Unfortunately the new president in South Africa, Jacob Zuma, (who composed himself the theme song "Bring me my machine gun!") staggeringly devolved any AIDS progress when he blithely commented to the newspapers concerning rape charges he was up on in 2006:

"She was wearing a short skirt, and she was sitting in a position that told me she wanted it."

When asked if he was worried since the girl he raped was HIV positive, he pooh-poohed the press.

"I took a long shower afterwards, so I am fine."

Hey Jacob! Bring me *my* machine gun!

Let's hope this arrogant idiot doesn't sit in any compromising positions lest someone come along and do as the Howard Stern's contestant sang:

"Fuck the President. Fuck him up the ass."

Thank you kindly for allowing me to vent my horror.